A PRACTICAL GUIDE TO
THE **ADA** AND
VISUAL IMPAIRMENT

ELGA JOFFEE

AFB

PRESS
NEW YORK

Library of Congress Cataloging-in-Publication Data

A practical guide to the ADA and visual impairment.
    p. cm.
    ISBN 0-89128-318-8
    1. Blind—Legal status, laws, etc.—United States. 2. Visually handicapped—Legal
status, laws, etc.—United States. 3. Blind—Services for. 4. Visually handicapped—Services for
I. American Foundation for the Blind
    KF3739 .B49 1999
    362.4'16—ddc21   98-15740
                                                                    CIP

The mission of the American Foundation for the Blind (AFB) is to enable persons who are blind or visually impaired to achieve equality of access and opportunity that will ensure freedom of choice in their lives.

CONTENTS

Acknowledgments

The author wishes to acknowledge the tireless efforts of those who cherish and protect the civil rights of all our citizens and who have dedicated themselves to the enactment and implementation of the ADA. A personal thank-you to Scott Marshall and Barbara LeMoine of AFB's Governmental Relations Group for their tutelage.

Introduction

Although it is no longer front-page news that the Americans with Disabilities Act (ADA) has been passed into law, a great deal of confusion remains regarding its implementation. The purpose of this book is to help clear up that confusion and to highlight the fact that the ADA is not as complicated as it seems. Despite the perception that the ADA imposes burdens on businesses, local governments, and individuals, the reality is that its requirements enhance accessibility and convenience for everyone. Moreover, complying with the ADA affords businesses and organizations an opportunity to demonstrate their concern for their patrons, customers, and employees. This *Practical Guide to the ADA and Visual Impairment* shows how this law has created a win-win situation for people with disabilities and the business community alike.

Since 1921, the American Foundation for the Blind (AFB) has been a consultant to businesses, boards of directors, and government agencies. AFB's mission is recognized as Helen Keller's legacy— helping people and institutions design and carry out policies that improve the lives of people who are blind or visually impaired and those of their families, as well as the communities in which they live and work. This guide was written as an extension of that mission to clarify the requirements of the ADA that specifically pertain to people who are blind or visually impaired and make this information easily available to the business community and the general public.

We at AFB recognize that there are many companies whose customers, employees, and prospective employees include people who are blind or visually impaired. It is estimated that into the next century, as the so-called baby boom generation continues to age, the number of people aged 55 and over with visual impairments will reach approximately 13 million, double the current number. This group constitutes a significant target market for a large percentage of companies, many of which will want to go beyond minimal legal compliance to actively accommodate and attract this segment of the marketplace and retain current productive relationships. *A Practical Guide to the ADA* contains useful advice on how to do that.

COMMUNICATION BARRIERS

However, understanding the needs of people who are blind or visually impaired first requires understanding the types of barriers that this segment of the population encounters on a daily basis. Constructing a wheelchair ramp or installing an electronic door may be all that is required to accommodate some people with disabilities, but it does not end the need for accommodation for people with other disabilities, including individuals who are blind or visually impaired.

While ramps and special doors remove physical barriers, they do nothing to address the pervasive communication barriers that blind and visually impaired people encounter on a daily basis. These barriers—signs, printed material, computer and video screens—

prevent people with visual impairments from obtaining vital information that our society communicates through the sense of sight—information that is so important for carrying out daily activities. To eliminate communication barriers, business owners and others covered by the ADA must provide timely and effective access to information that is communicated using sight. This goal can be accomplished in a number of practical ways, including the provision of braille and large-print documents and signage, strategically placed wall and overhead signs, adequate lighting, and training programs that help employees to be sensitive to people with visual impairments. This, too, is explained in this guide.

EMPLOYMENT TARGETS

On the eighth anniversary of the passage of the ADA, President Bill Clinton wrote:

> Too many people still are not aware of their rights and responsibilities under the ADA. There is a particular need to educate the small business community, which employs most of the private work force and includes the vast majority of the employers.

At AFB, we are keenly aware that despite the major advances made since the passage of the ADA, a large percentage of blind and visually impaired individuals are still not employed. But we are confident that once potential employers are made aware of the simple strategies that can be used to accommodate people who are blind or visually impaired, the availability of employment opportunities will begin to increase. We also believe that this development will benefit employers as a whole and society at large in addition to people who are blind or visually impaired.

A PRACTICAL COMPANION

A Practical Guide to the ADA is not a restatement of the ADA and its regulations, nor does the information contained in this guide constitute legal advice. Rather, this book is designed to be a practical companion to the law—a clearheaded alternative to much of the confusion and misinformation about how the ADA can be implemented for people who are blind or visually impaired. To this end we invite readers to join us in working toward an ever more productive and harmonious society.

Carl R. Augusto
President
American Foundation for the Blind

SECTION I

The ADA and Visual Impairment

- ADA Basics—An Overview of the Americans with Disabilities Act
- Visual Impairment and Accessibility

ADA Basics—An Overview of the Americans with Disabilities Act

WHAT IS THE ADA?

The Americans with Disabilities Act (ADA) is a landmark piece of civil rights legislation that was signed into law by President George Bush on July 26, 1990. The purpose of the ADA is to *"provide a clear and comprehensive national mandate for the elimination of discrimination against individuals with disabilities."* To accomplish this, the law aims to *"provide clear, strong, consistent, enforceable standards."*

The ADA mandates that individuals with disabilities shall have access to jobs, public accommodations, government services, public transportation, and telecommunications—in short, access to participation in all aspects of society.

THE IMPACT OF THE ADA

The ADA is based, in part, on provisions contained in previously existing law; namely, the Civil Rights Act of 1964 and the Rehabilitation Act of 1973. However, the ADA established, for the first time, that the civil rights of individuals with disabilities is part of the public policy agenda of the federal government. Previous nondiscrimination legislation for people with disabilities has had a far narrower scope. For example, Section 504 of the Rehabilitation Act applied nondiscrimination requirements only to entities that received federal funding, and subsequent court decisions limited these requirements to the department or phase of an organization that was the direct recipient of the federal funds. By contrast, the ADA applies its nondiscrimination requirements to all aspects of how people carry out their affairs in society, including transactions between people with disabilities and employers, state and local governments, places of public accommodations, commercial facilities, and providers of telecommunications. Because of the broad-reaching nature of the ADA, it is possible to make the claim that the ADA has made discrimination on the basis of disability something that society as a whole must address.

The ADA has had a wide-reaching impact since its inception. It has engendered a sense of empowerment for people with disabilities by transforming the removal of barriers to access from a good and fair thing to do to a matter of fundamental rights. The ADA puts the right of people with disabilities on a "level playing field" with the rights of all people in this society. This is felt keenly by people with disabilities who routinely expect their right to access to be respected and recognize any infringement of this right.

For "covered entities" who are required to comply with the ADA—government organizations, private businesses, and all organizations that conduct business with the public—very few aspects of their operations have been untouched by the Act, from building design, planning, and remodeling to the provision of services and information and their employment practices. The effects of the ADA are pervasive in such now commonplace sights as signs displayed in shopping and other public areas advertising the availability of assistance to people with disabilities, assistive listening devices, or volume controls on public telephones, as well as changes in job applications, building department requirements, and restrooms in public facilities.

The ADA has affected people who are blind or visually impaired much as it has all those with disabilities—empowerment, and specific elements and changes in how things are done that address nondiscrimination and access. Braille signs and braille in elevators are becoming a common sight in public places; Internet access has been ruled under the Telecommunications Act of 1996 to be a nondiscrimination requirement under the ADA (Federal Communications Commission, 1998); braille and large-print menus are provided by restaurants to a significantly greater extent; and people with dog guides feel free to say, for example, "Under the ADA you have to let me in with my dog." Businesses and organizations more and more frequently are reaching out to people who are blind or visually impaired when planning services or designing their properties. One area in which the ADA's effect has not been strong is employment. There appears to be no evidence that the ADA resulted in increased employment for people with disabilities in general, and for people who are blind or visually impaired specifically. So many other forces affect employment, however—education, training, and work disincentives, to name just a few—that it is hard to draw any firm conclusions about the ADA in this regard.

THE SCOPE OF THE ADA

As a law, the ADA is "the charging statement," providing a framework for what must be done, the penalties for not doing it, and the mechanisms for enforcement. Regulations are then issued by the appropriate federal agency or agencies to give step-by-step guidelines for implementing the law.

The ADA consists of five titles:

- **Title I:** Employment
- **Title II:** State and local government services, regardless of the receipt of federal funds, including public transportation services
- **Title III:** Public accommodations and commercial facilities, including health care providers, cultural facilities, attorneys' offices, hotels and retail establishments, corporate offices, banks, and transportation services provided by private entities not primarily engaged in the transportation of people
- **Title IV:** Telecommunications for people who are hearing impaired
- **Title V:** Miscellaneous provisions

This publication addresses Titles I, II, and III, focusing in particular on the elimination of barriers to communication that affect people whose disability involves blindness or visual impairment. The sections of Title II on public mass transit and Title III on private transportation services are not covered here, nor are Title II access provisions for outdoor public rights of way (sidewalks, streets, intersections, and traffic controls), because they warrant an entire publication of their own. For more information on these provisions, readers can contact Project ACTION or the Access Board (the U.S. Architectural and Transportation Barriers Compliance Board) (see the Resources section).

The implementation of the ADA relies heavily on more than 700 pages of regulations issued by four agencies of the federal government: the Department of Justice, the Department of Transportation, the Equal Employment Opportunity Commission (EEOC), and the Federal Commerce Commission (FCC). For a quick reference to these and other agencies that provide information and assistance on various aspects of the ADA, see the table "A Quick Guide to Getting Help on the ADA" at the end of this section.

In addition, the U.S. Department of Justice and the EEOC have published technical assistance manuals and issued policy statements that further explain the regulations and provide guidance about how the ADA will be interpreted by these enforcement agencies. (See the Resources section for information about how to obtain these publications, as well as a bibliography of other books on the ADA.)

The ADA does not supersede state and local laws that address discrimination on the basis of disability if these laws provide greater protection or broader coverage. Therefore, it is important for businesses and local governments to become familiar with state laws relating to disability rights as well as with the ADA. For example, some individual states have passed discrimination laws that apply to employers having fewer than 15 employees. Since the ADA does not cover these small employers, the state laws would apply. In addition, since the federal government and religious organizations are exempt from the ADA, the Rehabilitation Act continues to apply to the activities of federal agencies and federally assisted programs.

The ADA is very broad in its wording and allows considerable discretion in the implementation of its provisions. It is designed to be flexible in the way in which state and local governments and businesses can comply with ADA requirements, and recognizes that certain accommodations may be too costly or burdensome for a particular business or government agency to provide. It has taken some time, therefore, to work out in practice the specifics of the accommodations required by the law. This publication is designed to clarify how businesses, local governments, and individuals can comply with the ADA as it pertains to people with visual impairments and to provide simple guidelines and definitions for putting its provisions into practice. It is not designed as a substitute for appropriate legal advice.

The remainder of Section I will clarify the basic requirements of the ADA and the pertinent titles. Section II reviews more specifically provisions of these titles that relate to visual impairment and blindness and explains how they have been interpreted in situations that apply to nearly all businesses. This includes environmental design for accessibility and the ADA Accessibility Guidelines for Buildings and Facilities (ADAAG). Finally, Section III provides guidelines for accommodating people who are blind or visually impaired in employment situations and in a variety of specific business settings.

PROVISIONS OF THE ADA

Who Is Protected by the ADA?

An individual with a disability is defined by the Act as someone who has a physical or mental impairment that substantially limits one or more major life activities. Major life activities include such functions as seeing, walking, hearing, speaking, and breathing. The ADA not only covers individuals who are traditionally thought of as disabled, such as people who are blind or deaf, but also may cover individuals who have a record of such an impairment (such as someone who has recovered from cancer) or those who are disfigured, if they are perceived as having a substantially limiting condition.

What Entities Are Covered by the ADA?

The following entities are obligated to comply with the law:

- businesses with 15 or more employees

- state and local government services

- public transportation services

- public accommodations (e.g., retail establishments, hotels, health care providers)

- commercial facilities (e.g., corporate offices, commercial banks and headquarters)

Key Points in Title I—Employment

Title I of the ADA pertains to employers with 15 or more employees. It stipulates that no employer covered by this title

> shall discriminate against a qualified individual on the basis of disability in regard to job application procedures, the hiring, advancement, or discharge of employees, employee compensation, job training, and other terms, conditions, and privileges of employment.

Title I is administered by the EEOC. A person having a complaint under Title I must file a charge with the EEOC and receive a right-to-sue notice. The individual then has the option to file a private suit in federal court. Remedies include an injunction, reinstatement, back pay, and, in cases of intentional discrimination, up to $300,000 in compensatory and punitive damages depending on the size of the employer. Reimbursement of attorneys' reasonable fees is also available.

Following are important definitions and concepts in Title I of the ADA. (For more information about implementing Title I in your business, see "Employment" in Section III.)

1. **A qualified individual with a disability** is a person who can perform the essential functions of the job with or without reasonable accommodation. The employee with a disability must be qualified in terms of education and experience to do the job, and the employer is free to set production standards, so long as all employees of the same class are expected to meet the same standard.

2. **Reasonable accommodations** are changes in the work environment or in the way things are usually done that result in an equal employment opportunity for the employee or job applicant. Not making reasonable accommodations to the limitations of an otherwise qualified applicant or employee with a disability constitutes discrimination under Title I. Reasonable accommodations for people who are blind or visually impaired include, but are not limited to, such things as audiotaped texts, qualified readers and interpreters, braille and large-print materials, modification or acquisition of equipment and assistive computer technology (such as hardware or software to magnify the image on the screen or provide voice output of the text), reassignment, and adjustment of work schedules.

   Reasonable accommodations are determined on a case-by-case basis and must be effective to afford the applicant or employee an equal employment opportunity. Thus, providing materials in braille or the use of interpreters may be effective accommodations for an employee who is deaf-blind. Audio-taped texts or readers would be effective accommodations for an employee performing the same job who is blind but does not have hearing loss. The employer can choose among several accommodations and may choose the least expensive accommodation, as long as it is effective.

3. Making an accommodation may be considered to impose an **undue hardship** on an employer if it imposes a heavy financial or other burden. Establishing undue hardship as a defense to a charge of discrimination involves analysis of several factors including the size of the employer, number of employees, number of work sites, and costs related to accommodation. (Specific information about a defense of undue hardship or other defenses against charges of discrimination is best obtained from legal counsel.)

4. A person who poses a **direct threat** to his or her health or safety or the safety of others in the workplace is not considered a "qualified individual with a disability" under the ADA and thus is not protected by the law. The determination as to whether an individual poses a direct threat must be based on accurate and objective information; must be decided on a case-by-case basis, using the best available medical or other scientific evidence; and may not be based on stereotype, fear, or ignorance. In the majority of cases, an employer or manager of a place of public accommodation or a government facility is not qualified to make such a determination without information from those who are qualified. For example, a dog guide school would be qualified to determine whether a person using a dog guide poses a danger to others in the workplace. The *AFB Directory of Services for Blind and Visually Impaired Persons in the United States and Canada* (1997) is a source of local or national organizations that can provide such information.

5. An entity covered by the ADA is not required to provide reasonable accommodations to job applicants or employees if doing so results in a **fundamental alteration** in the manner in which it conducts its business. For example, an employer whose cleaning service firm provides night cleaning services only would not be required to hire an applicant with a visual impairment who requests the accommodation of working during daylight hours in order to use public transportation to travel to and from work that runs only between 5:00 A.M. and 7:00 P.M.

For more information on Title I, see "Employment" in Section III.

Key Points in Title II—State and Local Government Services and Public Transportation

Title II of the ADA extends nondiscrimination requirements of the Act to all services, programs, and activities of state and local government entities, whether or not they receive federal funds. It states:

> No qualified individual with a disability shall . . . be excluded from participation in or denied the benefits of the services, programs, or activities of a public entity, or be subjected to discrimination by any such entity.

Section 504 of the Rehabilitation Act continues to apply to institutions receiving federal funds and to agencies of the federal government. Obligations and remedies for violation of Title II are patterned after the obligations and remedies under Sec. 504 of the Rehabilitation Act. Remedies may include damages for intentional discrimination and injunctive relief. The employment provisions of Title I also apply to the state and local government entities covered under Title II, as do the provisions of either the Americans with Disabilities Act Accessibility Guidelines for Buildings and Facilities: State and Local Government Facilities issued by the Access Board as a final rule in January 1998 (36 CFR Part 1191) or the Uniform Federal Accessibility Standards. Public transportation facilities operated by state and local governments are covered by the ADAAG for transportation facilities issued by the Access Board and adopted by the Department of Transportation. (All these regulations are available from the Access Board, the Department of Justice, or the Department of Transportation; see the Resources section.) Because government is to be a model of nondiscrimination and accessibility practices, the defenses for noncompliance under Title II are limited as compared to defenses for noncompliance under Titles I and III. A **defense** is a justification, such as undue burden, that a covered entity may provide as the reason for its failure to comply with the law.

Title II also applies to providers of public transportation—both intracity and intercity bus and rail transportation (Joffe, 1992). Airlines are not covered by the ADA; however, airport terminals are covered under the Title II regulations issued by the U.S. Department of Transportation for transit facilities.

Title II is administered by the U.S. Department of Justice and the U.S. Department of Transportation. Persons having a complaint may file directly with the Departments of Justice or Transportation (see the Resources section and "A Quick Guide to Getting Help on the ADA" in this section) or in federal court.

Key Points in Title III—Public Accommodations

Title III of the ADA stipulates that

> no individual shall be discriminated against on the basis of disability in the full and equal enjoyment of the goods, services, facilities, privileges, advantages, accommodations of any place of public accommodation by any person who owns, leases, or operates a place of public accommodation.

Public accommodations are broadly defined to include almost any entity with which one does business or pays a visit (including retail stores, banks, insurance offices, stadiums, theaters, hospitals, and offices of attorneys or health care providers). In contrast, **commercial facilities** are defined as mercantile establishments (such as office buildings, warehouses, and factories) that affect commerce. The fundamental difference between public accommodations and commercial facilities lies in the fact that one is not required to enter a commercial facility to do business. Examples of commercial facilities would be the headquarters of an insurance underwriting business or a catalog sales company that has no retail outlet store for shoppers.

The building and facility design requirements of Title III apply to commercial facilities only in cases of new construction or alteration of existing facilities. However, an existing commercial facility, such as an office building, may be subject to additional Title III requirements if it is the landlord of a place of public accommodation that rents space in the building.

Following are some important definitions and concepts that appear in Title III of the ADA.

1. Under Title III, **auxiliary aids and services** must be provided for people who are blind or visually impaired. These are accommodations made to provide access to printed or displayed information and to the physical surroundings. Like the concept of reasonable accommodation in the employment context under Title I, auxiliary aids and services must effectively remove communications barriers and are judged on a case-by-case basis. Examples of auxiliary aids and services include, but are not limited to, qualified readers or interpreters, braille, large-print and recorded materials, amplified handsets, and large-print, braille, and audio displays. The provision of auxiliary aids and services can also include modifying procedures for people who are blind or visually impaired and training staff to be aware of how to accommodate people with visual impairments. The defenses of undue burden, direct threat,

and fundamental alteration apply to Title III and involve undertaking the same kind of analysis required under Title I of the ADA.

2. **The ADA Accessibility Guidelines (ADAAG),** an appendix to the Department of Justice's Title III regulations, outline minimum standards for accessible design of buildings and adjacent spaces. (Although the ADAAG is contained in an appendix, it has regulatory impact; that is, it carries the legal full force of the regulations themselves.) As noted earlier, the ADAAG has been adopted by the Departments of Justice and Transportation for Title II, with additional requirements specific to transit vehicles and facilities, public buildings, and public rights of way.

The ADAAG standards vary from very specific design specifications (such as those defining the requirements for the width of doorways to ensure access by individuals using wheelchairs) to performance standards (such as those requiring automatic teller machines to be accessible to blind or visually impaired persons). In addition, the ADAAG includes scoping provisions—that is, provisions that specify requirements for the number and location of accessible features required in a building or facility. Examples of scoping provisions are the number of telecommunication devices for the deaf that must be provided in a facility or the minimum requirements for how many and which elevators are required to have raised-character and braille panels. (Relevant excerpts from the ADAAG are provided in Section IV of this guide.)

The ADAAG standards address design elements to remove both architectural and structural communication barriers. Of particular relevance for the removal of structural communication barriers are the requirements for braille and raised-character signage in new and existing facilities (such as signs designating exit doors, room numbers, and restrooms) and for tactile warnings in certain situations (such as those required at the edges of transit boarding platforms). Compliance with the ADAAG is required in all *new* construction unless doing so is structurally impractical. The ADAAG must also be followed in most *existing* facilities if their requirements are "readily achievable," and compliance may also be required to a greater extent when alterations or renovations affecting the usability of a facility are made. (See the accompanying "Examples of Unlawful Practices under Title III of the ADA." See also "Environmental Design" and "Retrofit" in Section II for more information on the ADAAG and Title III.)

Visual Impairment and Accessibility

BLINDNESS, VISUAL IMPAIRMENT, AND COMMUNICATION BARRIERS

There are approximately 10 million blind or visually impaired people in the United States. Among them are approximately 4.9 million older Americans who experience age-related

Examples of Unlawful Practices Under Title III of the ADA

Unlawful Practice	Example
Using eligibility criteria that screen out individuals with a disability.	Prohibiting blind persons by category from riding a roller coaster unless accompanied by a person serving as a sighted guide (unless the amusement park can prove direct threat of harm or injury in an individual situation).
Failing to provide auxiliary aids or services.	Failing to read price information upon request to a retail store customer who is blind or failing to respond to a customer who is deaf-blind and communicates a request through note cards or other means.
Failing to prevent exclusion, segregation, or different treatment.	Requiring a person who is blind to take a special museum tour when the individual prefers to take the regular tour. Requiring a person who is deaf-blind to sit in a secluded corner of a restaurant because the restaurateur fears the reaction of other customers.
Failing to remove architectural and structural communication barriers when it is "readily achievable" to remove such barriers.	Failing to provide braille and raised-character elevator markings in existing facilities, unless installation of such signage is particularly difficult or expensive.
Failing to modify practices or procedures that result in a denial of services.	Requiring a person who is blind to produce a driver's license as the sole means of identification for cashing a check or for renting a car that will be driven by a licensed driver.
Failing to use readily achievable alternative methods when barriers cannot be removed.	Declining to provide delivery service to a person who uses a wheelchair when it is not readily achievable to make the store's existing premises accessible to a wheelchair.

vision loss resulting from common problems such as macular degeneration, cataracts, glaucoma, and diabetes. The number of people over the age of 65 with visual impairments is expected to double by the year 2030. (See "How Common Is Visual Impairment?")

Although all these people experience some form of uncorrectable visual impairment, the nature of the visual impairment and the range of vision loss experienced vary widely. Approximately 80 percent of those who are considered blind actually have some amount of useful vision. The term **legal blindness** refers to persons who have vision of 20/200 in their better eye even with the best correction using ordinary eyeglasses or contact lenses. It also refers to individuals whose **visual field** (the area of space visible to the eye) is less than 20 degrees.

Many persons do not meet the criteria for legal blindness but still experience vision loss significant enough to interfere with their independent functioning and daily living

How Common Is Visual Impairment?

- 10 million people in the United States, or 4 percent of the adult population, are visually impaired.

- 1.6 million people are *severely* visually impaired.

- Of these, 110,000 are totally blind.

- Of those who are severely visually impaired, about two-thirds are age 65 or older.

- 1 in 6 older Americans is severely visually impaired.

- Every 7 minutes, someone in the United States becomes blind or visually impaired.

- About 46,000 children and youth are legally blind.

- 80 percent of people who are legally blind have some useful vision.

Source: American Foundation for the Blind, Department of Programs and Policy Research, New York, 1997.

activities. These persons are considered **visually impaired**—the preferred generic term to refer to all degrees of vision loss. Persons who are unable to read ordinary newsprint even with correction are considered *severely* visually impaired. The categories of legal blindness and severe visual impairment often overlap.

How do people with severe vision loss live and travel independently? Not everyone who is blind uses a long white cane or dog guide, although many do. Many other visually impaired people rely instead on their available sight and the auditory and tactile cues in their surroundings for carrying out daily activities, such as reading and travel. At one time or another, most people who are blind will rely on a travel technique called the **sighted guide technique,** in which a person with sight serves as a guide to a person who is blind or visually impaired (see "Guidelines for the Sighted Guide Technique" in Section II).

Most people with visual impairments have few problems with the actual act of entering a building or facility. Features such as steps or narrow doorways, which must be modified for persons who use wheelchairs, are usually not barriers for persons who are blind or visually impaired. It is generally once they are inside a building conducting business, interacting with employees, or carrying out their duties as employees that blind or visually impaired persons may require certain accommodations. To ensure that these needs are met, state and local governments, businesses, and others who provide services to the public must go beyond familiar accommodations such as ramps and address the unique needs that result when sight is impaired.

To accommodate people who are blind or visually impaired, the ADA requires the elimination of **communication barriers,** the barriers that prevent persons with visual impairments from gathering and using information. Visible features of the environment become barriers to communication when persons with visual impairments cannot have access to the information these features provide. Elimination of communication barriers is specifically discussed in the regulations governing reasonable accommodations in

Title I, auxiliary aids and services in Titles II and III, and the removal of structural communication barriers in the ADAAG for Titles II and III.

Examples of communication barriers include the following:

- printed signs and notices displayed in buildings or transit stations to convey information and directions

- elevators, stairs, escalators, and other building or facility elements when they cannot be seen, located, or used effectively

- written materials such as office correspondence, job postings, bulletin boards, directories, sales receipts, hotel room guest service guides, patient information materials, consent forms, special event notices in government buildings, and menus in restaurants

Making a facility, its programs, and services accessible for people with visual impairments means ensuring that information is communicated clearly and effectively. This benefits everyone and conveys the message that a business owner provides services that meet the needs of customers. It also makes good business sense, especially considering the large number of people who are severely visually impaired and the growing number of retired Americans who have poor vision. Businesses can attract these persons as valued customers by providing comfortable, convenient, and accessible accommodations.

ELIMINATING COMMUNICATION BARRIERS
Auxiliary Aids and Services

In order to eliminate communication barriers, state and local governments as well as businesses must make visible information accessible in a timely, accurate, and effective manner to ensure that people who are blind or visually impaired benefit from the goods and services available to the general public. Visually delivered materials are to be made accessible through the provision of auxiliary aids and services, which can include the provision of reader services, sighted guide assistance, and information available in large print, on tape, or in braille. (More information can be found under "Auxiliary Aids and Services" in Section II.) Providing auxiliary aids and services can also include modifying procedures for persons who are blind or visually impaired as well as training staff to be sensitive to and accommodate persons with visual impairments (see "Employees' Sensitivity to Blindness and Visual Impairment" in Section II).

Following are some guidelines for providing auxiliary aids and services that comply with ADA requirements:

1. **Communicate effectively** by providing documents in braille and large print or on audiocassette or computer disk, by using multimedia devices with audio output, or by simply reading printed materials to persons who are blind or visually impaired.

2. **Provide accurate, complete, and clear information.**

3. **Provide information in a timely fashion.** This is especially important with time-sensitive documents such as contracts. Producing accessible documents takes organization, resources, and planning and can be time consuming. To address the potential need to provide accessible documents, business owners can conduct an initial review of printed materials and identify resources available for brailling, recording, formatting disks, and creating large print. Sources of information on this topic include the *AFB Directory of Services for Blind and Visually Impaired Persons in the United States and Canada* (1997) and the Resources section of this guide.

4. **Communicate all written business policy.** Make the contents of all posted notices, price tags, sales signs, service bulletins, menus, contracts, public documents, and the like available in accessible forms.

Eliminating Communication Barriers in Employment

Title I of the ADA requires that employers make **reasonable accommodations** to address the communication barriers that people who are blind or visually impaired experience in the employment process, including recruitment and all aspects of employment itself. In addition, many of the communication barriers present in places of public accommodation affect the employer-employee relationship and the opportunities available to blind or visually impaired people. (For more details, see "Employment" in Section III.)

This section has provided an overview of the ADA and its requirements as they affect people who are blind or visually impaired. Section II looks in more depth at solutions for making the accommodations required by the law. It provides a customer service guide to what employees in all types of government organizations and businesses need to know about interacting with customers, clients, or other individuals who are blind or visually impaired. In addition, it explains the kinds of accommodations that will be needed in almost any type of facility, including environmental design and the provision of such amenities as food services that many different types of organizations offer. Section III will look in detail at the needs of several specific types of facilities.

A Quick Guide to Getting Help on the ADA

Agency or Organization	Type of Assistance	Telephone	TDD	Web Site	E-mail Address
Americans with Disabilities Act: Title I Employment					
Equal Employment Opportunity Commission 1801 L Street, N.W. Washington, DC 20507	ADA questions	(800) 669-4000 (202) 663-4900	(800) 669-6820 (202) 663-4494	http://www.eeoc.gov	
	ADA documents and publications	(800) 669-3362	(800) 800-3302		
National Institute on Disability and Rehabilitation Research (NIDRR) 330 C Street, S.W. Washington, DC 20202	Disability and Business Technical Assistance Centers	(202) 205-8134 (800) 949-7234		http://www.ed.gov/ offices/osers/nidrr	
Job Accommodation Network West Virginia University P.O. Box 6080 Morgantown, WV 26506-6080	Information and referrals on job accommodations	(800) 232-9675 (800) 526-4698		http://www.jan. wvu.edu	jan@jan.icdi. wvu.edu
President's Committee on Employment of People with Disabilities 1331 F Street N.W., Suite 300 Washington, DC 20004	ADA information, training, and technical assistance	(202) 376-6200	(202) 376-6205	http://www50. pcepd.gov/pcepd/	info@pcepd.gov
Disability Rights Education and Defense Fund 2212 Sixth Street Berkeley, CA 94710	ADA technical assistance	(800) 466-4232	(510) 644-2555 (510) 644-2626	http://www. dredf.org	dredf@dredf.org
Foundation on Employment and Disability	Information in Spanish, Korean, Cambodian, Vietnamese, Mandarin and Cantonese Chinese, Tagalog, Hindi, Arabic, Armenian, Russian, and Dine	(800) 232-4955	(800) 232-4987		

For additional information and sources of assistance, see the Resources section at the end of this guide.

(continued)

A Quick Guide to Getting Help on the ADA *(continued)*

Americans with Disabilities Act: Title II State and Local Governments; Title III Public Accommodations

Agency or Organization	Type of Assistance	Telephone	TDD	Web Site	E-mail Address
Access Board Architectural and Transportation Barriers Compliance Board 1331 F Street, Suite 1000 Washington, DC 20004	ADAAG documents and questions	(800) 872-2253	(202) 272-5449	http://www.access-board.gov	info@access-board.gov
	Technical assistance hotline	(202) 272-5434			
	To order publications	(800) 872-2253	(800) 993-2822		
Department of Justice Disability Rights Section Civil Rights Division P.O. Box 66738 Washington, DC 20035-6738	ADA documents; technical assistance	(800) 514-0301 (202) 514-030	(800) 514-0383	http://www.usdoj.gov/crt/ada/adahom1/htm	
Department of Transportation Federal Transit Administration Office of Civil Rights 400 Seventh Street, S.W. Washington, DC 20590	ADA documents and general questions on transportation access to public	(888) 446-4511	(800) 877-8339	http://www.fta.dot.gov/office/civil	
Project ACTION National Easter Seal Society 700 Thirteenth Street, N.W., Suite 200 Washington, DC 20005	Information and technical assistance for accessible transportation	(202) 347-3066 (800) 659-6428	(202) 347-7385	http://www.projectaction.org	project_action @easter-sealsdc.org
National Institute on Disability and Rehabilitation Research (NIDRR) 330 C Street, S.W. Washington, DC 20202	Disability and Business Technical Assistance Centers	(800) 949-4232		http://www.ed.gov/offices/osers/nidrr	
Disability Rights Education and Defense Fund 2212 Sixth Street Berkeley, CA 94710	ADA technical assistance	(800) 466-4232 (510) 644-2555	(510) 644-2555	http://www.dredf.org	dredf@dredf.org

For additional information and sources of assistance, see the Resources section at the end of this guide.

(continued)

A Quick Guide to Getting Help on the ADA *(continued)*

Agency or Organization	Type of Assistance	Telephone	TDD	Web Site	E-mail Address
Americans with Disabilities Act: Title IV Telecommunications—Relay services for hearing impaired and speech impaired individuals and equipment and services access for people with disabilities					
Federal Communications Commission 1919 M Street, N.W. Washington, DC 20554	ADA documents and general questions	(202) 418-0500 (202) 632-7260	202-632-6999	http://www.fcc.gov	
	Legal questions	(202) 634-1808	202-632-0484		
	Complaints and enforcement	(202) 632-7553	202-632-0485		
Other Federal Laws					
Internal Revenue Tax Code Internal Revenue Service 111 Commerce Street, 6620 DAL Dallas, TX 75242-1198	General information on tax deduction or credits for complying with the ADA	(800) 829-1040	(800) 829-4059	http://www.irs.ustreas.gov	
Telecommunications Act of 1996 Federal Communications Commission 445 12th Street, S.W. Washington, DC 20554	General information	(202) 418-0200		http://www.fcc.gov	
Rehabilitation Act (Section 503) Department of Labor Office of Federal Contract Compliance Programs 200 Constitution Avenue, N.W., Rm. C3325 Washington, DC 20210	Information on antidiscrimination protection for qualified individuals with disabilities by federal contractors	(202) 219-9475	(202) 219-0069	http://www.dol.gov	

For additional information and sources of assistance, see the Resources section at the end of this guide.

SECTION II

A Customer Service Guide to Accommodating People Who Are Blind or Visually Impaired

- Employees' Sensitivity to Blindness and Visual Impairment
- Auxiliary Aids and Services
- Cash and Credit Transactions
- Food Services
- Environmental Design
- Retrofit

Employees' Sensitivity to Blindness and Visual Impairment

The checklists and tips presented in Section II were developed to provide clear and easy-to-use guidance for evaluating existing facilities and the services they provide to the public as well as for planning new services and facilities that accommodate the access needs of people who are blind or visually impaired. The principles presented here cut across all settings. These lists are not intended to be prescriptive, nor are they exhaustive. Rather, they are offered to enable business and other organizations to establish and carry out an informed and mutually beneficial relationship with people who are blind or visually impaired. (For copies of these checklists that you can use for training staff and evaluating your business or organization, see Section IV.)

COMMUNICATING WITH PEOPLE WHO ARE BLIND OR VISUALLY IMPAIRED

It is understandable that customer service personnel and others whose job responsibilities require them to communicate directly with the public may feel somewhat awkward the first time they are called upon to transact business with a person who is blind or visually impaired. The principles of good customer service—asking how you can be of help and being responsive in a way that meets the customer's needs—are particularly effective when dealing with customers who are blind or visually impaired.

The points that follow serve as a guide to comfortable and effective interaction with people who are blind or visually impaired, in a variety of situations. (A copy of this checklist for readers to use with their own businesses appears in Section IV.)

CHECKLIST FOR COMMUNICATION WITH PEOPLE WHO ARE BLIND OR VISUALLY IMPAIRED

General Guidelines

- ☑ Introduce yourself using your name and/or position, especially if you are wearing a name badge containing this information.
- ☑ Speak directly to persons who are blind or visually impaired, not through a companion, guide, or other individual.
- ☑ Use a natural conversational tone and speed when speaking. Do not speak loudly and slowly unless the person also has a hearing impairment.
- ☑ Address people who are blind or visually impaired by name when possible. This is especially important in crowded areas.
- ☑ Greet people who are blind immediately when they enter a room or a service area to let them know you are present and ready to assist. Initiating conversation right away also eliminates uncomfortable silences.
- ☑ Indicate the end of a conversation or encounter to avoid the embarrassing situation of leaving a person speaking when no one is actually there.

☑ Feel free to use words that refer to vision during the course of conversation. Vision-oriented words such as "look," "see," and "watching TV" are a part of everyday verbal communication. The words "blind" and "visually impaired" are also acceptable words in conversation.

☑ Be precise and thorough when you describe people, places, or things. Don't leave items out or change a description because you think it is unimportant or unpleasant.

☑ Feel free to use visually descriptive language. Making reference to colors, patterns, designs, and shapes is perfectly acceptable.

☑ When referring to a person who is disabled, refer to the person first and then to the disability. For example, say "people who are blind" rather than "blind people."

Orientation and Mobility

☑ Do not leave a person who is totally blind or visually impaired standing alone in "free space" when you serve as a guide. Always be sure that the person you are guiding has a firm grasp on your arm, or is leaning against a chair or a wall if you have to be separated momentarily.

☑ Be calm and clear about what to do if you see a person who is blind or visually impaired about to encounter a dangerous situation. For example, if a person who is blind is about to bump into a stanchion in a hotel lobby, calmly and firmly call out, "Wait there for a moment. There is a pole in front of you."

☑ Use the sighted guide mobility technique (see "Guidelines for the Sighted Guide Technique") to escort those individuals who request it.

☑ Review business policy regarding dog guides. The ADA regulations require places of public accommodation to permit the use of dog guides or other service animals, unless doing so would fundamentally alter the nature of the services provided or jeopardize the safe operations of the facility.

☑ Designate and orient customers, patients, or guests to dog guide relief areas.

Giving Directions

☑ When giving directions to a person who is blind or visually impaired, refer to right and left as they apply to the other person. What is on your right is on the left of a person facing you.

☑ Indicate the approximate distance to a requested location and provide information about landmarks along the way. For example: "When you hear the escalator, walk several feet down the corridor and look for the next open doorway on your left."

☑ Be specific about the location of people, places, or things. Avoid vague terms such as "over there" when telling a person who is blind how to find a destination.

☑ Avoid pointing unless you are sure the gesture can be seen and understood.

Guidelines for the Sighted Guide Technique

The sighted guide technique allows a person who is blind or severely visually impaired to use another person, often someone with sight, as a guide. The technique follows a specific form. The following are some guidelines for using the sighted guide technique:

- Identify yourself and ask the person if he or she would like assistance. It is not always necessary to provide guided assistance. In some instances it can be disorienting and disruptive. Respect the desires of the person you are with.

- If your assistance is accepted, allow the person you are guiding to reach for your arm. To do so, tap the back of the hand you want the person to take hold of against their opposite hand (for example, if you want the person to take hold of your right arm, tap the back of your right hand against his or her left hand). The person will then grasp your arm directly above the elbow (see Figure 1).

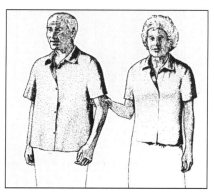

Figure 1. The Sighted Guide Technique. Note that the person who is blind walks slightly behind the guide.
Credit: Yemi

- Never grab a person who is blind or visually impaired by the arm to push him or her forward. Allow the individual to take your arm and follow you.

- Stay relaxed and walk at a comfortable, normal pace. Stay one step ahead of the person you are guiding except at the top and bottom of stairs and when crossing streets.

- Always pause when you change directions. To step up or step down, stop briefly and let the person you are guiding stand alongside you. Then resume travel as before, walking one step ahead of the person you are guiding.

- Tell the person you are guiding about changes in terrain, stairs, narrow spaces, elevators, and escalators.

- When guiding a person who uses a long cane, avoid interfering with the cane's operation.

- Modify the standard form of the sighted guide technique when necessary to accommodate someone who is exceptionally tall or short or has other disabilities than blindness. For example, when assisting a short person it may be helpful for him or her to grasp your arm at the wrist instead of above your elbow. Always be sure to ask the person you are guiding what modifications he or she wishes to use.

- To guide a person to a seat, place the hand of your guiding arm on the back of the chair. The person you are guiding will find the seat by following along your arm. Also indicate verbally that you have arrived at a place where the person can sit.

COMMUNICATING WITH PEOPLE WHO ARE DEAF-BLIND

People who are deaf-blind have a combination of hearing and visual impairments. These individuals may have no sight or hearing at all, or they may have some use of either or both of these two senses. People who are deaf-blind can communicate with others using a wide range of techniques that a business or government organization can accommodate easily when called upon to do so. They use speech or communication aids such as preprinted cards that let others know they are deaf-blind and how to communicate with them simply and effectively. Often, communicating with a person who is deaf-blind is as easy as writing a message clearly using a felt-tipped marker that makes thick bold lines or using a finger to print out words on the person's open palm (see item number 4 in the list that follows).

Some individuals who are deaf-blind speak very clearly; however, they cannot always hear your response. These persons usually learn to indicate when they can hear what is being said and to make concrete suggestions for the best way to speak with them.

Skilled interpreters are available to interpret for persons who are deaf-blind when the situation requires this level of accommodation. A local organization that provides services to persons who are blind, deaf-blind, or deaf, as well as local state schools for children who are blind, deaf, or deaf-blind can provide assistance locating qualified interpreters (see the Resources section and the *AFB Directory of Services for Blind and Visually Impaired Persons in the United States and Canada* [1997]).

What is important to know is that people who are deaf-blind learn how to communicate with people who have no specialized knowledge about deaf-blindness. When you transact business with an individual who is deaf-blind, feel free to ask, "How shall I communicate with you?" as soon as you begin your interaction. Generally, persons who are deaf-blind will identify themselves as such and suggest a manner of communication. Then, using that information, a service provider can verify that he or she has understood correctly, and knows how to recognize if communication is being understood. If the deaf-blind person does not indicate how to communicate, the service provider should reply in the mode of communication the deaf-blind person used initially—for example, using speech if the deaf-blind person spoke or writing with a felt-tipped marker in response to a communication card—to find out how to be of assistance.

Following are some simple guidelines for providing services to people who are deaf-blind.

1. **Ask how you may be of help.** First determine how you can recognize that your message has been understood. Ask the individual who is deaf-blind if the way you are communicating with him or her is effective and, if not, how you can be better understood. Then, using an effective communication method, ask, "How can I be of help?"

2. **Communicate directly.** When communicating with a person who is deaf-blind, interact directly with him or her. Avoid addressing yourself to an interpreter or family member.

3. **Provide interpreters when necessary.** Provide trained interpreters when you must be sure that complex information is being conveyed clearly, accurately,

and in a timely fashion. For example, this service may be required by the ADA for negotiating financial agreements, conveying complex health care information, and at public meetings unless doing so creates an "undue financial burden" for your business.

4. **Learn simple communication skills.** Become familiar with the simple things you can do to communicate with persons who are deaf-blind. For routine communication with a person who has no vision or hearing, printing in the person's palm may be all that is necessary. Use your index finger to form uppercase letters slowly with straight strokes that go from left to right. Pause at the end of each word and sweep your hand across the individual's palm before beginning a new word. Those who have useful vision or hearing may ask you to write notes clearly with a felt-tipped pen or to speak simply and clearly. You should never need to shout to communicate with a person who is deaf-blind.

5. **Be prepared to communicate in an emergency.** Be aware that the universal sign for an emergency situation is the letter X drawn with the fingertips on the back of the person who is deaf-blind. Make your staff aware of this sign, and be sure to reinforce it when a deaf-blind patron visits your business.

Auxiliary Aids and Services

GUIDELINES FOR PROVIDING AUXILIARY AIDS AND SERVICES

Auxiliary aids and services are required under Title III of the ADA to provide access both to physical surroundings and to visually displayed information. The ADA does not prescribe a specific method of providing the auxiliary aids and services that make information accessible. The regulations require all written business policy to be communicated in an effective manner. To do so, the information must be both accurate and timely. The braille or audiotaped version must be correct, for example, and a document such as a lengthy contract transcribed into braille must be received with sufficient time to review it before signing. These general guidelines constitute a valuable approach because they allow businesses and governments to select the most suitable aids or services for specific situations. Thus, there is no hard and fast obligation to have either reading services, braille, large print, or recorded materials available at all times. Businesses and governments should, however, be aware of the kinds of auxiliary aids and services that are used by persons who are blind or visually impaired and be prepared to make them available in a timely manner in accordance with the ADA.

It is acceptable to provide a customer or patron who is totally blind with reader services for a short, simple task, even if the individual uses braille and expresses a preference for braille information, provided that the reader conveys information accurately and effectively. Reader services may not be appropriate, however, if this same individual asks for braille documents in order to review a complex agreement with your business or government agency. (See, for example, "Hotels and Motels" in Section III.)

The following are some examples of providing appropriate auxiliary aids and services:

- furnishing large-print documents at a retirement village (see "Tips for Making Print More Readable")

- producing bank statements in grade 2 braille

- supplying town hall tax guides on audiocassette

- furnishing a digitized tape player with descriptions of paintings at a museum

- providing sighted guide assistance.

Tips for Making Print More Readable

Print Size
Large-print type should be used, preferably 18 point, but at a minimum 16 point. Scalable fonts on the computer make this easy to do.

Font Type and Style
The goal in font selection is to use easily recognizable characters, either standard roman or sans serif fonts.

- Avoid decorative fonts.

- Use bold type because the thickness of the letters make the print more legible.

- Avoid using italics or all capital letters. Both these forms of print make it more difficult to differentiate among letters.

Use of Color
The use of different colored lettering for headings and emphasis creates difficulty in reading for many people with low vision. When color is used, dark blues and greens are most effective. Reds are often difficult to distinguish, as are pastel colors.

Contrast
Contrast is an extremely critical factor in environmental design and in enhancing the visibility of printed materials. Text should be printed with the best possible contrast. For many older people, light lettering—either white or light yellow—on a dark background—usually black—is easier to read than black lettering on a white or yellow background.

Paper Quality
Avoid using paper such as that typically used in magazines. Glossy pages create excess glare, which makes reading more difficult for people who have low vision.

Leading
(Space between Lines of Text)
The recommended spacing between lines of text is 1.5, rather than a single space. Many people who are visually impaired have difficulty finding the beginning of the next line when single spacing is used.

Spacing between Letters
Text with letters very close together makes reading difficult for many people who are visually impaired, particularly for those who have central visual field defects such as macular degeneration. Spacing between letters should be wide, such as that in mono-spaced fonts—fonts which have an equal amount of space allocated for each letter—such as Courier.

Margins
Many low vision devices, such as stand magnifiers and closed-circuit televisions (CCTVs), are easiest to use with a flat surface. An extra-wide binding margin—a minimum of one inch—makes it easier to hold the material flat.

Source: Elga Joffee and Mary Ann Siller, *Reaching Out: A Creative Guide for Designing Cultural Programs and Exhibits for Persons Who Are Blind or Visually Impaired* (New York: AFB Press, 1997).

These types of auxiliary aids and services are discussed in more detail in the sections that follow.

A good rule of thumb in providing auxiliary aids and services is to be guided by your desire to accommodate customers and ensure their patronage. The simplest and most effective way to select an auxiliary aid or service is to ask, "How may I help you?" and then respond, just as you would with any customer. This basic approach is what businesses have always done to market their products and services. It will be especially useful in accommodating visual impairments as the American population ages and more consumers develop vision loss.

BRAILLE

Braille is a system of raised dots that allows people who are blind to read using their fingers (see "What Is Braille?"). Braille is the preferred medium of many individuals who are totally blind, especially those who are congenitally blind (blind since birth) and whose initial instruction in reading was in braille.

Braille allows readers who are blind or visually impaired to review the content of documents easily and in greater detail than can be done with other formats, such as materials recorded on audiocassette. Braille affords easy access to spelling, word formatting, and punctuation that is not typically conveyed in recorded materials. However, it is important to know that documents produced in braille, typically on 11" by 11" pages, can be bulky and awkward to carry. When portability is a factor, other formats, such as recorded materials and computer disk files, may be preferable to braille.

There are a number of different braille codes. Grade 1 braille is a letter-for-letter rendition of print. Grade 2 braille is a more condensed version that uses additional braille signs for certain words and part-word contractions.

In general, documents in braille should be produced by services with experience in preparing accessible materials. However, businesses and governments can also produce their own braille materials on a personal computer using commercially available translation software that converts English and text messages to braille (see the Resources section). You do not have to learn braille to produce simple braille messages in grade 1 braille and documents in grade 2, nor is it necessary to know braille codes and transcription codes to use such software. All that is required is a basic understanding of braille in order to select the proper functions for correct translation. Suppliers of braille translation software provide information about the special features each translation software program offers as well as technical assistance. All braille signs produced using translation software should be checked for accuracy and user-friendliness. (For information on producers of braille materials and sources of translation software, see the Resources section.)

Grade 1 braille for labeling can be created easily using commercially available devices that produce adhesive labels. These labelers have a print alphabet wheel that allows one to select individual letters, which are then produced as braille (see the listing of Selected Sources of Products for Independent Living in the Resources section).

What Is Braille?

What Does Braille Look Like?

- Braille is a series of raised dots that can be read with the fingers by people who are blind or whose eyesight is not sufficient for reading printed material.

- Braille is not a language. Rather, it s a code by which languages such as English or Spanish may be written and read.

- Braille symbols are formed within units of space known as braille cells. A full braille cell consists of six raised dots arranged in two parallel rows, each having three dots, identified by numbers from 1 through 6. Sixty-four combinations are possible using one or more of these six dots. A single cell can be used to represent an alphabet letter, number, punctuation mark, or even a whole word.

Forms of Braille

- When every letter of every word is expressed in braille, it is referred to as grade 1 braille. Very few books or other reading material are transcribed in grade 1 braille.

- The system used for reproducing most textbooks and documents is known as grade 2 braille, which reduces the volume of paper needed and makes the reading process easier. In this system, cells are used individually or in combination with others to form a variety of contractions or whole words. For example, in grade 2 braille, the letters y and l are also used for the whole words you

and like, respectively. Similarly, the word him is formed by combining the letters h and m. There are 189 different letter contractions and 76 short form words used in grade 2 braille.

How Is Braille Produced?

- Just as printed matter can be produced with a paper and pencil, typewriter, or printer, braille can also be written in several ways.

- The braille equivalent of paper and pencil is the **slate and stylus.** This consists of a slate or template with evenly spaced depressions for the dots of braille cells, and a stylus for creating the individual braille dots. With paper placed in the slate, tactile dots are made by pushing the pointed end of the stylus into the paper over the depressions. The paper bulges on the reverse side, forming dots.

- Braille is also produced by a machine known as a **braillewriter.** Unlike a typewriter, which has more than 50 keys, the braillewriter has only six keys and a space bar. These keys are numbered to correspond with the six dots of a braille cell.

- Technological developments in the computer industry continue to expand braille production capabilities. Desktop computers, software and translation programs used with high- and low-speed braille embossers make it possible to produce braille for individual and commercial applications.

Source: American Foundation for the Blind, Information Center, New York.

Grade 1 braille is typically used as an auxiliary aid or service to label items such as the following:

- vending machines
- telephone buttons (other than 12-key)
- machine controls
- price tags
- appliance membrane keypads

- brief product descriptions
- audiocassettes
- shelf edgings identifying merchandise
- computer diskettes
- ownership identification

Grade 2 braille is typically used for documents such as these:

- menus
- newsletters
- business policies
- membership information
- public documents
- price lists
- tax bills
- correspondence
- instructions and directions
- employment documents
- billings
- policy and procedure manuals
- bank and investment statements
- patient information and consent documents

RECORDED MATERIALS

Providing recorded information on audiocassettes is a simple and inexpensive way to provide access to visual information. A well-planned audiocassette can provide access to the wide range of visual information contained in printed documents, offer directions in a guide to wayfinding, and feature information that highlights the unique appeal of a business, such as the ambiance of a restaurant or the personal services at the health club in a hotel or condominium complex.

Recording technology makes it possible to produce documents that contain a wide range of information, such as sales and product information, contractual agreements, health care and patient information, and official policies and procedures. It is also possible to describe the layout of a physical plant or record a sales or service directory. Also, digitized recording devices allow random access to recorded material and have been used effectively, for example, on audio tours for cultural exhibits.

Recorded materials can provide access to almost anyone with visual impairments, regardless of the severity of the visual loss. They are especially useful for people who are totally blind and are not braille readers. Audiocassettes and audiocassette players are compact, inexpensive, and simple to use or fit into devices that can be accessed through a handset. Recorded information is especially helpful to businesses that find a need to convey specific information repeatedly and that wish to be certain that all their customers with visual impairments, including those who are totally blind, receive complete information about the goods and services available. Shopping malls and other large facilities such as sports arenas, museums, and large office buildings can make particularly good use of recorded information by providing a "talking directory" in customer service areas to convey the visual information on maps, signs, and promotional displays. Exciting new interactive multimedia technology now emerging in this area is an appealing way to communicate with the general public as well as with customers with visual impairments. (For information on producers of multimedia information access technology for people who are blind or visually impaired, see the Resources section.)

A business may not charge a patron who is disabled for providing recorded materials as an auxiliary service under the ADA. However, if you offer the temporary use of a personal audiocassette player or other audible output device, you may charge a refundable fee to guarantee return of your equipment. You may not charge a fee to gain access to a talking directory that is provided as an ADA auxiliary aid.

Although you may wish to have your recorded materials produced professionally, it may not be necessary. It is possible to produce effective recorded documents in-house. However, you may need to use a professional recording studio with expertise in producing recordings for persons with visual impairments for complex or technical documents, especially those that contain charts, tables, graphs, or diagrams.

The few simple guidelines that follow for selecting readers and creating recordings will be useful for recording most simple documents. There is no definition of a qualified reader under the ADA; however, the American Foundation for the Blind (AFB) offers these guidelines:

- The reader should be proficient in the language being recorded.

- The reader should be familiar with the subject. An individual from the staff of a mall management company, for example, might be a logical choice to record an audiocassette listing the stores in a shopping mall. This individual would be familiar with the names of the stores and restaurants, the layout of the mall, and other features that the business wishes to communicate to customers.

- The reader should have good diction. Recording should be done in a conversational tone and at a conversational pace.

- The reader should be familiar with the material to minimize stumbling and hesitation.

■ The reader should not editorialize. When recording a document, it should be read in full.

■ Graphic and pictorial information available to sighted readers should be made available in the narrated text. Tables and charts whose contents are not already contained in the text should be converted into text. They should be described fully and included in the recording.

■ The reader should spell difficult or unusual words or names as well as words that are not English.

Information may be recorded on two-track or four-track cassettes. Two-track cassettes are those that are played on a home or personal stereo system. Four-track cassettes are designed to be played only on specialized equipment that is available from the National Library Service for the Blind and Physically Handicapped of the Library of Congress (see the Resources section) to individuals who are blind, visually impaired, or otherwise print impaired. Be sure to specify the kind of recording you want—two-track or four-track—when dealing with commercial recording studios.

ELECTRONIC DOCUMENTS

Electronic documents are those that are produced in electronic formats using a personal computer. These documents, often made available on computer disks, electronic bul-

A refreshable braille display allows people who are blind or deaf-blind to read documents from the computer. This device is a portable electronic braille notetaker with its own braille display.
Credit: Blazie Engineering

Software that allows computers to display text on the screen in large print gives people who are severely visually impaired access to information that is in electronic form. The large-print stickers on the keys shown here also help visually impaired people to use the computer.
Credit: Bradford F. Herzog

letin boards, and web sites, and through electronic transfers such as e-mail, are permanently stored on computer disks.

Personal computer hardware and software is readily available to convert electronically stored information into formats that are usable by persons who are visually impaired, totally blind, or deaf-blind. Electronic information can be made accessible to persons who are blind or visually impaired in a variety of ways, including outputting the text of the document onto the computer screen in **large print**; on paper in large print or braille, as noted earlier (hard copy); in "speech" generated by the computer using a combination of software programs and hardware devices; or on a **refreshable braille display**. (A refreshable braille display is a device made up of plastic pins that pop up to form braille characters corresponding to the text that is generated.) (For sources of these products, see the Resources section.)

People with severe visual impairments can use **large-print screen programs** capable of producing variably sized large-print screen displays. Persons who are totally blind may use computer-generated voice output or refreshable braille displays to access electronic information. Individuals who are deaf-blind can also read documents with the assistance of a refreshable braille output device.

The most acceptable format for producing electronic documents is ASCII—the universal computer format that is usable by a wide range of word-processing programs. Conversion into ASCII creates electronic information that is devoid of all formatting codes except the basic hard return. In ASCII, codes such as tab, center, and flush right are replaced with spaces; soft returns are replaced with hard returns at the end of every line; and codes that produce features such as bold text and underlining are removed. ASCII eliminates columns and converts column text to full-screen-width text.

You can produce an ASCII document by using the appropriate conversion feature of your word-processing program. Some advance preparation of a word-processing document is necessary, however, before it is converted to ASCII. Consult the documentation manual for the word-processing program or contact a local organization or school serving people who are blind or visually impaired for information about preparing documents for use by people who are blind or visually impaired (see *AFB Directory of Services for Blind and Visually Impaired Persons in the United States and Canada* [1997] for listings in each state).

To create a *new* electronic file that will be ready for ASCII conversion, prepare the document using a standard Courier 10 cpi font. Use only hard returns, tabs or indents, and center and flush-right formatting codes. Present all information in linear format, avoiding the use of columns or tables as displays.

To prepare an existing electronic document for ASCII conversion, remove all font codes and insert Courier 10 cpi or another nonproportional font code at the head of the document. This step is important because a proportionally spaced font, such as Times Roman or Helvetica, will cause the text to be unreadable with screen-access technology once you have converted your document to ASCII.

Remove any column formatting and edit the document so that text displayed in columns follows in a logical, linear manner. Do the same for tables. Redesigning tables as continuous text can take time and planning. However, if the content of a table is already fully contained in the text, you may be able to delete the table. Indicate in the document that the table has been removed for the accessible version of the document but that all content is reflected in the text.

Also, remove any graphic lines and graphic boxes that are included in the document. This step is necessary because ASCII will not convert these lines and boxes but will leave a blank space in their place. To preserve meaning, you may need to edit the text of the document to describe the lines or boxes that have been removed. It also may be necessary to describe illustrations or pictures that are part of the document you are converting because there is no way to convert these graphic representations in ASCII.

Finally, remove any extended ASCII codes in the word-processing document. Extended codes are ASCII codes used to produce such characters as bullets (•) or the symbol for the word *section* (§).

Cash and Credit Transactions

Businesses are required under the ADA to provide auxiliary aids and services for cash and credit transactions so that customers will have clear, accurate, and timely information about their financial affairs. Regardless of the specific type of business, if payments change hands, attention must be paid to making all information involved accessible to customers or clients who are blind or visually impaired. Accommodations for cash and credit transactions are an important part of making goods and services accessible to persons who are blind or visually impaired. Following are some tips for handling such transactions:

1. **Provide clear verbal information.** Give clear and accurate verbal information about all the costs and fees appearing on a bill of sale or sales receipt. For complex agreements, you may need to provide information in one of the accessible formats—braille, large print, or audiocassette recording.

2. **Deal directly with customers who are visually impaired.** Personnel must be certain that people who are blind or visually impaired hand their payments directly to authorized sales representatives. Payment with cash or credit cards should not be transacted through an intermediary, such as a friend or another customer. Do not pick out cash, coins, or credit cards from a blind person's hands; instead, allow the individual to offer the payment him or herself. When returning credit cards, cash, and receipts to a person who is blind or visually impaired, place them directly in the individual's hands. Do not place cash or credit cards on counters or tabletops.

3. **Identify currency denominations.** A person who is blind or visually impaired usually stores currency and is able to identify it later by folding it in a specific and systematic manner or by placing different denominations in separate locations in a wallet or purse. Coins are usually easy to identify by their characteristic sizes and milled edges.

   When providing change, tell people who are blind or visually impaired how much money is involved. Group the change by denominations. Then, as you return change, start with bills and finish with coins. Count paper money directly into a blind person's hands. Pause briefly between denominations as you count to provide an opportunity for the person to fold or store the bills. For example, a cashier might say, "Mr. Marshall, your change is $19.49. This is a $10 bill, . . .this is a $5 bill, . . . and here are four $1 bills— one, two, three, four. Here are your coins."

4. **Allow some time and a place to put money away safely and securely.** Invite people who are blind or visually impaired to stand to the side of the cashier after a transaction is completed, just as you might other customers, to give them time to safely put away change and documents without disrupting the smooth flow of other activity.

5. **Make assistance available for completing forms related to a transaction.** Provide assistance in completing sales or other business forms. If a signature is required, offer to guide the person's pen to the correct place. A small high-intensity lamp, felt-tipped pens, and a commercially available signature guide or template may all be useful to have on hand to help with such transactions.

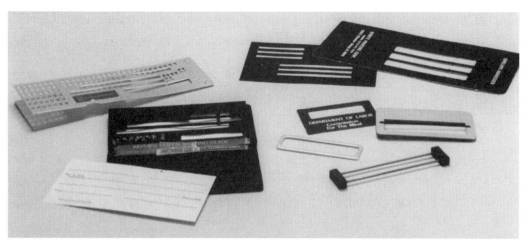

Writing guides that help people who are blind or visually impaired to write checks (left) address envelopes (top right), and write signatures (bottom right) are available commercially.
Credit: Ruth Solomon

To use a signature guide, place the upper edge of the guide on the signature line. To use a signature template that has a cutout opening for a signature, place the opening of the template where a signature is required. (See the Resources section for sources of such products.) Remember to provide assistance in a manner that respects your customer's privacy.

Food Services

Everyone needs to eat outside the home at some time—whether it is a long, leisurely meal on a special night out or a quick bite to eat during a shopping trip—and that includes people who are blind or visually impaired. Many kinds of businesses and places of employment furnish some type of food service. The specific services provided can vary from formal dining service offered in a stand-alone restaurant or hotel to cafeteria service or simple vending machines in a workplace, hospital, or other facility. Regardless of the type or location of the food service, the ADA requires that they be accessible to all patrons.

There are some general guidelines for accessibility for people who are blind or visually impaired that apply to all kinds of food services. Welcome all people who are blind or visually impaired to participate freely in food services. In particular, customers with dog guides must be seated with all other restaurant guests and be allowed to approach buffets and other self-service displays. Avoid seating customers who are deaf-blind in a secluded part of a restaurant because of anticipated or actual reactions from other guests. (Refer also to the section on "Employees' Sensitivity to Blindness and Visual Impairment," earlier in Part II.)

In addition, there are a number of auxiliary aids and services that will help accommodate customers who are blind or visually impaired:

■ Post menus and prices using print that is large, clear, contrasting, and in simple type face.

■ Offer readers and guided assistance when needed.

■ Make braille or large-print menus available.

■ Assist with cash or credit transactions.

Following are some more specific guidelines for providing services to customers who are blind or visually impaired in different food service environments. (A copy of this checklist for you to use with your business appears in Section IV.)

CHECKLIST FOR PROVIDING ACCESSIBLE FOOD SERVICES TO PEOPLE WHO ARE BLIND OR VISUALLY IMPAIRED

Formal Dining Service

☑ Provide priority seating for customers who are blind or visually impaired, if requested to do so, in an area that has adequate lighting or is away from the glare of large picture windows. Note that if dim ambient lighting is an essential part of the dining atmosphere you offer, the ADA does not require you to fundamentally alter the nature of your business by turning up the lights for a person who is visually impaired.

☑ Instruct table service personnel to identify themselves by name and function to customers who are blind or visually impaired. For example, a waiter might say, "Good evening, I'm Walter. I'll be your waiter for the evening. How may I help you?"

☑ Instruct table service personnel to describe the placement of tableware, flowers, ashtrays, candles, or other items on the table.

☑ Offer customers braille or large-print menus if they are available. Be sure to tell guests about any selections that have been added since the menu was prepared. Also, describe daily specials that do not appear on the menu.

☑ Offer to read menus to customers who are totally blind when braille menus are not available or if your customer does not read braille. Likewise, offer to read menus to customers who are visually impaired.

☑ Inform customers when servers are about to place food or items on the dining table. Describe where all food and beverage items are placed as they are served.

☑ Identify the location of food on a plate if requested to do so, using the face of a clock as a reference. For example, say "Your meat is at 12 o'clock, your vegetables are at 3 o'clock, the rice is at 9 o'clock."

☑ Provide assistance in cutting food items or mixing beverages, if requested to do so. Cutting food items in the kitchen prior to serving or returning a plate to the kitchen is a discreet way of handling a request to cut a customer's food.

Buffet Service

- ☑ Identify and briefly describe the food and beverage items available.
- ☑ Assist with locating tableware and utensils.
- ☑ Assist in serving food items from the buffet and escorting customers to a seat.
- ☑ Inform customers about how to obtain assistance for return visits to the buffet.

Food Service Lines and Cafeteria Service

- ☑ Be alert for aging customers or others whose visual impairment may not be readily recognized so you may assist them. These customers may not appear to be blind because they do not carry long white canes or use dog guides, but they may have difficulty reading menus posted above the food service counter or identifying food selections available at steam tables.
- ☑ Provide sighted guide assistance to customers who are totally blind so they can make their way through food service lines, select food, and locate condiments, napkins, and utensils. Guide them to a seat and offer assistance for later disposal of trays and refuse.
- ☑ Provide customers with clear verbal information about visually displayed menus, advertised specials, and promotional services.
- ☑ Have braille or large-print menus available for standard items in a fixed location; for example, at both ends of the service counter. Although braille and large-print menus are not required by the ADA, providing them is a thoughtful service that makes a positive statement about your interest in customers' comfort and convenience.

Vending Machines

- ☑ Install vending machines in areas that are well illuminated and protected from glare or deep shadows.
- ☑ Provide vending machines with raised keypads similar to those on a push-button telephone. Avoid membrane or touch-screen operation controls, which are inaccessible to customers who are severely visually impaired. Characters on keypads should contrast visibly with the background.
- ☑ Provide operation controls (coin and bill slots, change returns, and the like) that contrast clearly with the background of the machine. Label all controls in clear, contrasting large print using a sans serif or a simple serif typeface.
- ☑ Provide braille labels for selection keys and operation controls wherever possible. A commercially available braille label maker and assistance from a local blindness service organization can be very helpful for this (see the Resources section for lists of organizations and sources of products).
- ☑ Consider installing vending machines that "talk" (see the Resources section).

Environmental Design

THE AMERICANS WITH DISABILITIES ACT ACCESSIBILITY GUIDELINES

The environmental design of a business or a space that is not operated by the federal government and that the public enters to carry out business is governed by the Americans with Disabilities Act Accessibility Guidelines (the ADAAG). This includes buildings and facilities operated by state and local governments that have chosen the ADAAG as their accessibility standard as well as public transportation facilities. As noted in Section I, the ADAAG is an appendix to the Department of Justice's regulations for Title III of the ADA, and it has full regulatory impact. The ADAAG were developed and are maintained by the Architectural and Transportation Barriers Compliance Board (commonly known as the Access Board; see the Resources section). They contain the minimum architectural standards and guidelines set up under the ADA to govern the construction of new structures and the renovation of existing structures. These guidelines specify the nature of a variety of elements and architectural features that allow a person with a disability to readily enter and use a building, facility, or public right of way and the conditions under which these features must be present. Excerpts of the relevant sections of the ADAAG and its appendix appear in Section IV.

WHO IS COVERED BY THE ADAAG?

If you are the owner of a public or commercial facility or the operator of a state or local government agency, the ADAAG applies to you. If your property is a place of public accommodation (a facility that is used by the general public) that is being newly constructed, you are required to follow the full ADAAG to ensure that all elements are accessible to persons with disabilities, including persons with physical or sensory (vision or hearing) impairments.

The ADAAG requires owners of already existing properties to do what is **readily achievable** to make their facilities and buildings accessible. This means that they are expected to make renovations (**retrofitting**) that can be accomplished without incurring undue difficulty or expense to make the facilities accessible (see the section on Retrofit later in this Section). The ADA establishes priorities for making readily achievable renovations. These priorities include providing ramps, widening doorways, and providing braille in elevators and on signs that identify permanent rooms and spaces (see the AFB video, *Strategies for Community Access: Braille and Raised Large Print Facility Signs* [1993]).

Buildings and facilities that serve only commercial needs and do not accommodate the general public—such as the corporate headquarters of an insurance company—are not required to comply with the ADAAG. These properties are still required to provide reasonable accommodations for employees who are disabled, however, and these accommodations may involve renovations to buildings and facilities (see "An Overview of the ADA for Employers of Persons Who Are Blind or Visually Impaired" in Section III).

Commercial properties where a portion of the facility is leased or otherwise occupied by attorneys, accountants, or physicians must comply with the ADAAG. The guidelines for new and existing construction for places of public accommodation apply to commercial facilities under these circumstances. The costs for bringing space in commercial properties into compliance with the ADAAG for a tenant in a commercial facility can be negotiated between tenant and landlord and allocated between the parties in lease agreements.

The two entities that are not obligated to comply with the ADAAG are the federal government and religious organizations. Federal government properties must meet the minimum standards of the Uniform Federal Accessibility Standards (UFAS), developed under the Architectural Barriers Act of 1968, which are not the same as the ADAAG. Although it is likely that at some point in the future UFAS will be brought into conformity with the ADAAG, this is not the case at present. (The Access Board enforces UFAS and provides technical assistance.)

Religious organizations do not fall under the ADA and consequently are not covered by the ADAAG, except in certain instances. These instances occur when a building that is owned or leased by a religious organization rents space to a business serving the public. In this situation, the business operating out of the religious organization's facility must comply with the ADAAG standards. As with commercial facilities, costs for bringing property into compliance with the ADAAG may be negotiated and allocated in a lease agreement with a religious facility. However, the final responsibility for compliance rests with the business providing goods or services to the public and not with the religious organization.

The ADAAG's specifications include several requirements that address the removal of structural communication barriers for persons who are blind or visually impaired. What follows is a checklist of specified building elements that allow people who are blind or visually impaired to gather the information they need to navigate their environment. It is also a useful evaluation guide for facility managers to determine how well their facilities meet the needs of people who are blind or visually impaired.

The checklist includes references to the most recent ADAAG specifications as of January 1998, as well as to the appendix to the ADAAG, which provides explanatory and illustrative information about the guidelines and their scope, but is only advisory in nature. Relevant sections from these documents appear in Section IV. In the checklist, specifications from the ADAAG are indicated by a numeric reference to the corresponding section or sections in the ADAAG. References to items from the ADAAG appendix are indicated with the letter *A* ahead of the number. Items from Section 4.1 of the ADAAG refer the reader to the scoping, or technical application requirements, of the specifications. Some items in this checklist are AFB recommendations that are not from the ADAAG and are so indicated.

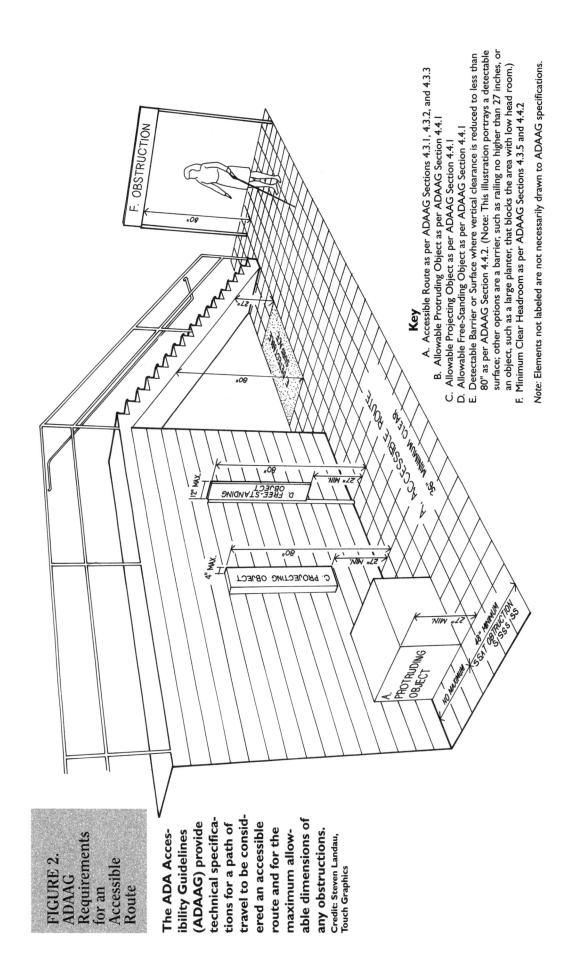

FIGURE 2. ADAAG Requirements for an Accessible Route

The **ADA Accessibility Guidelines (ADAAG)** provide technical specifications for a path of travel to be considered an accessible route and for the maximum allowable dimensions of any obstructions.
Credit: Steven Landau, Touch Graphics

Key

A. Accessible Route as per ADAAG Sections 4.3.1, 4.3.2, and 4.3.3
B. Allowable Protruding Object as per ADAAG Section 4.4.1
C. Allowable Projecting Object as per ADAAG Section 4.4.1
D. Allowable Free-Standing Object as per ADAAG Section 4.4.1
E. Detectable Barrier or Surface where vertical clearance is reduced to less than 80" as per ADAAG Section 4.4.2. (Note: This illustration portrays a detectable surface; other options are a barrier, such as railing no higher than 27 inches, or an object, such as a large planter, that blocks the area with low head room.)
F. Minimum Clear Headroom as per ADAAG Sections 4.3.5 and 4.4.2

Note: Elements not labeled are not necessarily drawn to ADAAG specifications.

CHECKLIST OF REQUIRED ELEMENTS
FOR ACCESSIBILITY UNDER THE ADA RELATING
TO COMMUNICATION BARRIER REMOVAL

Exterior and Interior Accessible Routes (see Figure 2)

☑ At least one accessible route from public transportation stops, accessible parking spaces, passenger loading zones, and public streets and sidewalks to one accessible building entrance.
[4.1.2(1),(2); 4.3.2; A4.3]

☑ Protruding objects protected at ground, mid-, and head level and complying with other ADAAG specifications.
[4.1.2(3); 4.4, A4.4.1]

☑ Detectable warnings complying with the ADAAG at the edge of boarding platforms in transit facilities.
[4.29.2; A4.29.2; 10.3.1(8); 10.3.2(2); 10.3.3]

☑ Surface textures that are firm, stable, and slip resistant.
[4.1.2(4); 4.1.3(3); 4.1.5; 4.1.6(a), (b); 4.5.1; A4.5.1]

☑ Curb cuts, curb ramps, elevators, or platform lifts provided where an accessible route has a vertical change in level greater than ½ inch
[4.1.3; 4.1.5; 4.1.6; 4.3.8]

Stairs

☑ Stairs that have uniform riser heights and tread widths complying with the ADAAG.
[4.1.3(4); 4.1.5; 4.1.6(d); 4.9.2; A4.9.1]

☑ Stairs that do not have open risers.
[4.1.3(4); 4.1.5; 4.1.6(d); 4.9.2; A4.9.1]

☑ Stair treads that are not less than 11 inches wide.
[4.1.3(4); 4.1.5; 4.1.6(d); 4.9.2; A4.9.1]

☑ Stair nosings (the part of the step where the tread and the vertical riser meet) that are curved and not abrupt.
[4.1.3(4); 4.1.5; 4.1.6(d); 4.9.3]

☑ Handrails that are continuous on both sides of all stairs, do not rotate within their fittings, and are mounted according to ADAAG specifications.
[4.1.3(4); 4.1.5; 4.1.6(d); 4.9.4(1), (7); A4.9.1; 4.26; A4.26.1; A4.26.2]

☑ Handrails that extend beyond the top and bottom risers according to ADAAG specifications.
[4.1.3(4); 4.1.5; 4.1.6(d); 4.9.4(2); 4.26; A4.26.1; A4.26.2]

☑ Handrails that have a clear space between the rail and the wall that meets ADAAG specifications.
[4.1.3(4); 4.1.5; 4.1.6(d); 4.9.4(3); A4.9.1; 4.26; A4.26.1]

☑ Handrail gripping surfaces that are uninterrupted by obstructions.
[4.1.3(4); 4.1.5; 4.1.6(d); 4.9.4(4); A4.9.1; 4.26; A4.26.1; A4.26.2]

☑ Handrail endings that are rounded or returned smoothly to the floor, wall, or a post.
[4.1.3(4); 4.1.5; 4.1.6(d); 4.9.4(b); A4.9.1; 4.26; A4.26.1; A4.26.2]

☑ Handrails that contrast visibly with the background to which they are mounted or are clearly visible to persons who are visually impaired. *(Note: This is not required by the ADAAG, but it is recommended by AFB.)*

Elevators

☑ Call buttons in elevator lobbies that meet ADAAG specifications for design and installation.
[4.1.3(5); 4.1.6(1){k}(i); 4.10.3]

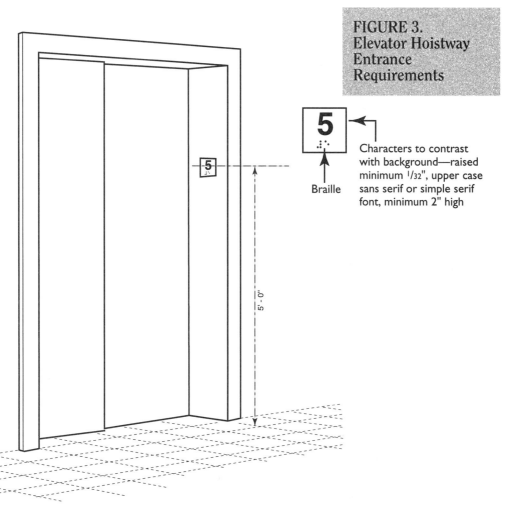

FIGURE 3.
Elevator Hoistway
Entrance
Requirements

Characters to contrast
with background—raised
minimum ¹/₃₂", upper case
sans serif or simple serif
font, minimum 2" high

Braille

5' - 0"

Note: This diagram is provided to illustrate the raised character and braille signage requirements for elevator hoistway entrances only (per ADAAG Section 4.10). Signs are to be on both sides of hoistway entrance.
Credit: Steven Landau, Touch Graphics

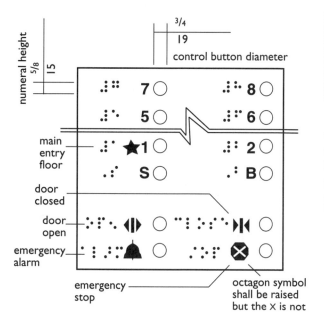

FIGURE 4.
Elevator Control
Panel
Requirements

Elevator control buttons must be designated by raised characters or standard symbols, as well as by braille (see ADAAG section 4.10.12).
Credit: Adapted from *ADA Accessibility Guidelines for Buildings and Facilities*

☑ Visible and audible signals, sounding once for the "up" direction and twice for the "down" direction at each hoistway (elevator shaft) entrance to indicate which elevator car is answering a call.
[4.1.3(5); 4.1.6(1){k}(i); 4.10.4]

☑ Raised and braille floor designations on both elevator door jambs that meet ADAAG specifications (see Figure 3).
[4.1.3(5); 4.1.6(K{i}); 4.10.5]

☑ Illumination at car controls, platforms, and car thresholds that meet ADAAG specifications.
[4.1.3(5); 4.1.6(K{i}); 4.10.11]

☑ Elevator control panels with raised and braille markings that meet ADAAG specifications (see Figure 4).
[4.1.3(5); 4.1.6(K{i}); 4.10.12; A4.10.12]

☑ Visual car position indicators above the car control panel or above the elevator doors with a visible display or one that emits an audible signal.
[4.1.3(5); 4.1.6(K{i}); 4.10.13; A4.10.13]

(For additional information on ADAAG requirements for accessible elevator control panels designations, contact the National Elevator Industry organization listed in the Resources.)

Signage

☑ Signs in raised letters and grade 2 braille that meet ADAAG specifications for design and installation at permanent rooms and spaces.
[4.1.2(7); 4.1.6(1){b}; 4.30.1; 4.30.4; A4.30.4; 4.30.5; 4.30.6]

☑ Informational and directional signs that meet ADAAG specifications for design and installation.
[4.1.2(7); 4.30.1; 4.30.2; 4.30.3; 4.30.5]

☑ Pictogram signs that include a clear verbal description of the pictogram graphic.
[4.1.2(7); 4.30.4; A4.30.4]

☑ Pictogram signs at permanent rooms and spaces (e.g., restrooms) that include raised letters and braille; the pictogram graphic itself need not be raised.
[4.1.2(7); 4.30.4; A4.30.4]

☑ Signs for the International Symbol of Accessibility located at accessible entrances when not all entrances are accessible (see Figure 5).
[4.1; 4.30.7; A4.30.7]

☑ Signs that display the International Symbol of Accessibility at inaccessible entrances that provide information about the location of the closest accessible entrance.
[4.1.2(7){c}; 4.30.7; A4.30.7]

☑ Signs that display the International Symbol of Accessibility at toilet and bathing facilities when all are not accessible.
[4.1.2(7){d}]

☑ Suspended signs that are at least 80 inches above the finished floor or protected with a barrier detectable by people who are blind or visually impaired.
[4.4.2]

Automated Teller Machines

☑ Automated teller machines (ATMs) that provide independent access to all instructions and displayed information in a manner usable by persons with visual impairments. [4.1.3(20); 4.34] Examples of specific accommodations can include voice output devices, refreshable braille displays, electronic voice mail access (using a telephone and keypad to listen to and access the menu choices), tactile marking for operation controls, and braille or speech instructions for ATM use.

ADAAG UPDATE AND THE ANSI ACCESSIBILITY STANDARDS

The U.S. Architectural and Transportation Barriers Compliance Board (known as the Access Board) convened an ADAAG Review Advisory Committee to carry out a fifth-year review of the ADAAG. The committee's final report, *Recommendations for a New ADAAG* (September 1996), will be utilized by the Access Board in any future rulemaking related to the ADAAG, although the recommendations and specifications contained in this report do not themselves have the force of law. A copy of this report as well as any future ADAAG rules or documents can be obtained from the Access Board (see the Resources section).

The International Symbol of Accessibility is displayed at accessible entrances, at accessible bathrooms, and at places where information about accessible facilities is provided.
Credit: *ADA Accessibility Guidelines for Buildings and Facilities*

The American National Standards Institute (ANSI) has recently revised its private-sector accessibility standard, ANSI A117.1, *Accessible and Usable Buildings and Facilities.* ANSI is a private, nonprofit organization that administers and coordinates the development of national standards. It accredits standard-development groups or organizations to do the actual writing in each area in which standards are needed. The revised ANSI A117.1 accessibility standard was developed by the Accredited Standards Committee A117. This group comprised model building code organizations (entities that work to develop national building standards that can be adopted by state or local law) under the umbrella of the Council of American Building Officials (now merged with the International Code Council; see the Resources section), as well as consumers, professionals, and manufacturers with a material interest in the development and implementation of accessibility standards.

The committee worked closely with the ADAAG Review Advisory Committee to harmonize the 1998 edition of ANSI A117.1 with proposed revisions to the ADAAG. The new ANSI standard, which was approved by ANSI's Board of Standards Review in February 1998, does not have the force of law until such time as it is adopted by local jurisdictions, in whole or in part, in local building codes; or, when local jurisdictions adopt **model codes** that reference this standard.

Local building code officials, who can be contacted through local and state building departments, are reliable sources of information about the design requirements for specific jurisdictions. In addition, the Access Board, the International Code Council, and the model building code groups are valuable sources of information about new design requirements based on ANSI A117.1 and future requirements that may be promulgated from the ADAAG Review Advisory Committee Report. The complete 1998 edition of the ANSI A117.1 standard is available for purchase from the following model building code organizations: Building Officials and Code Administrators International, International Code Council, and Southern Building Code Congress International (see the Resources section). Building owners, designers, and architects are advised to seek legal guidance as appropriate in interpreting ADAAG requirements for their properties.

Of particular interest to readers of this guide are the revised sections in the 1998 ANSI A117.1 on signage and automatic teller machines, which especially affect accessibility for people who are blind or visually impaired. These sections, which are reproduced in Section IV of this guide, are expanded from the 1992 edition of ANSI A117.1 and were developed specifically to be harmonized with the ADAAG Review Advisory Committee's report.

ABOVE AND BEYOND THE ADAAG

Although the ADA Accessibility Guidelines are extensive and include requirements that promote accessibility for persons who are blind or visually impaired, there are design elements and strategies that are not included that can enhance accessibility. These modifications do not typically involve major structural changes and can be integrated in a cost-effective manner, especially if they are included during the planning phases of new building design, during the course of property renovations, or as part of routine maintenance. Often, these modifications to facility design result in a clearer presentation of information about a place of business and result in enhanced comfort and usability for *all* customers.

The ideal route to accessibility is to follow principles of **universal design**—that is, design that meets the needs of everyone who uses the environment, so that additional adaptations for people with visual impairments or other disabilities are not necessary. (For more information on universal design, see Joffee & Siller, 1997; Welch, 1995.) Environmental barriers are challenges for everyone, not only people with disabilities. Therefore, making your facility accessible to people of all ages, sizes, and abilities also makes it more attractive to a wide range of people.

There are several rules of thumb to keep in mind when planning designs that accommodate persons with visual impairments:

■ Heightened contrast between figure and ground improves the ease with which building elements and features can be seen.

■ Adequate ambient lighting that is evenly dispersed and does not create glare or deep shadows is important for persons who have visual impairments.

■ Loud ambient noise—such as the kind created by continually humming motors, waterfall displays, or air rushing through heating duct systems—interferes with orientation and travel for persons who are totally blind or have severe visual impairments.

The information that follows illustrates some approaches for going beyond the ADAAG requirements when designing buildings and facilities. Although it focuses specifically on the needs of people who are blind or visually impaired, note how each suggestion will make a facility more attractive and easier to access for *all* users.

1. **Install or adjust lighting to accommodate people who have low vision.** Lighting that is controlled by rheostat (dimmer) switches can be adjusted to increase or decrease illumination during different times of the day. This may also be a useful way for restaurants with low lighting to accommodate a request to raise the lights at a table that is occupied by guests with poor sight. Placing track lighting that evenly disperses light along an otherwise dimly lit corridor may help to define a travel path, similar to the kind of path created by lights located along theater aisles and stairs.

2. **Use contrasting colors or tones to highlight features in the environment.** Highlighting elements in the environment, obstacles, or changes in level with contrasting colors or tones provides excellent information as well as warnings for people who have visual impairments. Providing contrast at strategic locations in the environment can be accomplished in a manner that is consistent with design aesthetics or a corporate image. Examples of effective use of contrast in design include the following:

   - highlighting baseboards, carpet edges, and the nosings of stairs

   - providing handrails that contrast with their surroundings

   - highlighting ramps or other changes in level

   - accenting the edges of protruding elements, such as water coolers and telephone booths

   - creating contrast between doors and walls to aid in recognition and negotiation of long corridors, such as those found in schools, health care facilities, and hotels

   - using contrasting colors, tones, or floor surface treatments at strategic points—such as intersecting hallways—along the path of travel.

3. **Muffle interfering ambient sounds.** Soundproofing insulation and the use of sound-absorbent building materials can help to eliminate ambient noise that masks sound cues used by persons who are blind during travel.

4. **Use audible signage or other innovative information technology.** Audible information displays are being developed as information and guidance systems that can provide easy access to information conveyed by building signage and signage displayed in transit facilities or other large public spaces, such as museums, sports arenas, and shopping malls. Technologies utilize FM signals that can be picked up by a radio receiver, or infrared signals picked up by a handheld receiver or a personal headset. Audible information technology is also used to make building directories accessible through the use of recorded messages that are played through telephone-type voice-mail systems.

(See the Resources section for sources of products.) The audible sign systems being developed as accommodations for persons who are blind or visually impaired have also been used to provide information for persons who do not read English and for the general public in densely crowded areas. Audible information technology has the potential of becoming an element of *universal design,* that is, design whose objective is to meet the needs of everyone who uses the built environment.

5. **Provide information through talking kiosks.** Technology has been developed that uses interactive multimedia software to combine tactile displays, auditory output, and large, contrasting images on a video display screen to provide information about the layout of buildings and facilities and services that are available therein. These talking kiosks, specifically intended for people who are blind or visually impaired, have been shown to be highly appealing to the general public as well as a way of communicating information. (A demonstration video of this exciting new technology showing how it performs at a large transit facility can be obtained from the Computer Center for Visually Impaired People [see Resources].)

Another major innovation for achieving auditory output at information kiosks involves a technology known as Talking Fingertips. This technology provides an interface that can be integrated into video display touch screens, such as those often found in shopping malls or hotels, in which the user touches the menu items to display listings of stores, restaurants, attractions, and the like. It allows a person who is blind or visually impaired to run his or her finger systematically across a video screen and hear the information displayed on the screen spoken aloud. (For more information about this technology, contact the Trace Research and Development Center; see Resources.)

Retrofit

READILY ACHIEVABLE RENOVATIONS

When applied to the ADA, the term *retrofit* refers to the minimum renovations that must be done to bring an existing property into compliance with the ADA and improve access for people with disabilities. As it is applied to the ADA, the term retrofit is more specialized than in the common usage of the real estate industry, in which any repair or replacement work done to improve an existing facility or property is considered a retrofit. Also, ADA retrofit renovations differ distinctly from major path-of-travel renovations, which involve alterations to a facility that affect the usability of the route, or path of travel, that the public uses to access a business's goods and services. The ADA establishes different requirements for retrofitting existing facilities than it does for properties undergoing a major path-of-travel renovation or for new construction. This section addresses retrofit for places of public accommodation and commercial facilities under Title III of the ADA. Title II obligations are not addressed here. Information about Title II retrofit requirements is available from the Access Board or the Department of Transportation for transit facilities (see the Resources section).

Businesses that provide goods and services to the public—places of public accommodation under Title III—are obligated to take certain limited steps to retrofit their existing buildings and facilities to improve access. This mandate includes the obligation to remove architectural barriers in existing facilities, including communication barriers that are structural in nature when it is *readily achievable* to do so; that is, it is easily accomplishable and can be carried out without much difficulty or expense. Retrofit obligations for barrier removal may apply to commercial facilities and to facilities used by religious organizations as well as to any space leased by attorneys, accountants, health care providers, or other businesses that fit the definition of a place of public accommodation under the ADA (see Section I of this guide for definitions and "Who Is Covered by the ADAAG?" under "Environmental Design," earlier in this section).

The removal of barriers for retrofit is covered in Section 36.304 of the regulations for Title III of the ADA issued by the Department of Justice (see "A Quick Guide to Getting Help on the ADA" in Section I for information on obtaining these regulations). This section includes a wide-ranging list of the types of modest measures that may be taken to remove various types of barriers and that are likely to be readily achievable, such as adding raised-letter markings on elevator control buttons and installing flashing alarm lights. This list is not exhaustive, but merely illustrative, and the inclusion of a measure on this list does not mean that it is readily achievable in all cases.

Whether any of the measures included in Section 36.304 is readily achievable has to be determined on a case-by-case basis in light of both the particular circumstances of an individual business and the factors set forth under the definition **readily achievable** in Section 36.104 of the regulations to Title III. These factors are listed in the accompanying box.

The ADA regulations place a heavy emphasis on respecting the discretion of businesses to determine the most effective mix of barrier-removal measures for their particular circumstances in the retrofit of existing buildings and facilities. Consequently, the regulations do not specify either how businesses should go about making decisions for retrofitting their properties or the specific changes they should make in a retrofit. The intent is to enable business to do what business does best—provide products and services that best meet the specific needs of consumers.

Recognizing that retrofitting properties for barrier removal is likely to be relatively new to business and that the process may seem confusing or overwhelming to those whose experience in this area is limited, the ADA regulations suggest steps businesses can take, but are not obligated to, to remove barriers from existing buildings, when these steps make sense for their particular businesses and the customers they serve. It is helpful to note that regulations that include the word *shall* are mandates. Those that

Considerations for Determining What Actions to Improve Access Are Readily Achievable Under Title III of the ADA

- the nature and cost of the action needed to remove an architectural or structural communication barrier

- the overall financial resources of the site or sites involved in the action

- the number of persons employed at the site

- the effect on expenses and resources

- legitimate safety requirements that are necessary for safe operations, including crime prevention measures

- the impact of the action on the operation of the site

- the geographic separateness and administrative or fiscal relationship of the site or sites in question to any parent corporation or entity

- the overall financial resources of any parent corporation or entity; the overall size of the parent corporation or entity with respect to the number of its employees; the number, type, and location of its facilities

- the type of operation or operations of any parent corporation or entity, including the composition, structure, and functions of the workforce of the parent corporation or entity

use the word *should* are advisory. For example, "a public accommodation *shall* eliminate architectural barriers in new construction, including communication barriers that are structural in nature . . ." is a mandate, and "a place of public accommodation *should* take measures to provide access to restrooms in existing facilities" is an example of a statement that is advisory and therefore not mandated.

In this context, the ADA regulations for the removal of barriers in existing construction urge, but do not mandate, businesses that are public accommodations to establish procedures for ongoing assessment of their buildings and facilities to establish their retrofit needs for compliance with the ADA's requirements for barrier removal. The regulations recommend that this process include appropriate consultation with individuals with disabilities or organizations that represent them.

Businesses that establish a serious and ongoing effort at self-assessment and consultation can diminish the threat of litigation and save resources. People who are blind or visually impaired, as well as organizations such as AFB that engage in research and consultation on policy and environmental access, frequently are in a good position to provide informed consultation about cost-effective means for making individual places of public accommodation accessible, allocating scarce resources, and setting priorities. The Resources section of this guide therefore includes contact information for the AFB Information Line as well as for other service organizations for people who are blind or visually impaired.

A business's obligation to engage in readily achievable removal of barriers for retrofit is a continuing one. Over time, barrier removal that initially was not readily achievable may become so. This can be the result of changed circumstances related to newly emerging technology, changes in costs as markets develop, or changes in a business's financial situation or ownership. For example, in the early 1990s, braille and raised-letter signage was new and available mostly by custom order. Less than a decade later, many common braille signs, such as signs for restrooms, are available as inexpensive off-the-shelf items that can be found in large office supply outlets.

The resources available for barrier removal may not be adequate to remove all existing barriers at any given time. Consequently, the ADA regulations suggest priorities for barrier removal that can guide businesses in making decisions about retrofit changes that are both effective in achieving access and are cost-effective. The regulations suggest that businesses place the highest priority on measures that will enable individuals with disabilities to "get through the door," that is, to be able to enter the facility. The next priority suggested is to provide access to where goods and services are made available to the public. The third priority is to provide access to restroom facilities, and the last priority is to put in place any remaining measures required to remove barriers. The barrier removal priorities for retrofit considerations are listed in the accompanying sidebar, along with specific examples.

Businesses that remove architectural and structural communication barriers in retrofit changes are entitled to certain tax benefits to help pay for the cost of compli-

Priorities for Retrofit Changes for Barrier Removal in ADA Title III Regulations

Priority	Example
1. Provide access to a place of public accommodation from public sidewalks, parking, or public transportation.	• Install an entrance ramp. • Widen entrances. • Provide accessible parking spaces.
2. Provide access to areas of a place of public accommodation where goods and services are made available to the public.	• Adjust the layout of display racks. • Rearrange tables. • Provide braille and raised character signs (see the video from AFB [1993], *Strategies for Community Access: Braille and Raised Large Print Facility Signs.*
3. Provide access to restroom facilities.	• Remove obstructing furniture or vending machines. • Widen doors. • Install ramps. • Provide accessible signage in braille and raised characters. • Widen toilet stalls and install grab bars.
4. Take any other measures necessary to provide access to the goods, services, facilities, privileges, advantages, or accommodations of a place of public accommodation.	

ance. As amended in 1990, the Internal Revenue Code allows a deduction of up to $15,000 per year for expenses associated with the removal of qualified architectural and transportation barriers (Section 190). The 1990 amendment also permits eligible small businesses to receive a tax credit (Section 44) for certain costs of compliance with the ADA. An eligible small business is one with gross receipts that do not exceed $1,000,000 or whose work force does not consist of more than 30 full-time workers.

Qualifying businesses may claim a credit of up to 50 percent of eligible access expenditures that exceed $250 but do not exceed $10,250. Examples of eligible access expenditures are the necessary and reasonable costs of removing architectural, physical, communication, and transportation barriers; providing readers, interpreters, and other auxiliary aids (see "Auxiliary Aids and Services" earlier in this section); and acquiring or modifying equipment or devices. (To learn more about tax credits and deductions for barrier removal and providing accessibility, contact the Internal Revenue Service, or call the U.S. Department of Justice ADA Information Line [see the Resources section or "A Quick Guide to Getting Help on the ADA" in Section I].)

The checklists and guidelines that were presented throughout Section II apply to nearly all settings and types of facilities. Some settings, however, require additional special considerations. Section III gives several examples of such settings, and provides detailed information about how to provide accommodations.

Making the ADA Work for Your Business or Organization

SECTION III

Employment

When businesses deal with applicants and employees who are blind or visually impaired, they need to follow the guidelines of ADA Title I (see Section I). This section is addressed specifically to applying the ADA in employment situations.

UNDERSTANDING THE NEEDS OF APPLICANTS AND EMPLOYEES WHO ARE BLIND OR VISUALLY IMPAIRED

When employers first consider hiring a person who is blind or visually impaired, they frequently make three assumptions: (1) that the person is completely blind, (2) that the person uses braille, and (3) that the person travels with a cane or a dog guide. An applicant may fit one or more of these assumptions; however, all three are not likely to be true for most individuals who are visually impaired and seeking employment. It is important for employers to know that many applicants who are severely visually impaired may use braille, whereas others can use print. And, although some may use a cane, others may use a dog guide, or may not need any travel tool for mobility.

People who are blind or visually impaired carry out their activities in various ways, depending on the nature of the eye condition causing their visual impairment. For example, some individuals who are visually impaired can see primarily in the periphery of their visual field, as if the center of their vision is blocked. These people often have difficulty reading small print and require magnification lenses for detailed work. Others can see using only the central portion of their visual field, as if looking through a tunnel. These individuals often do well with written materials but experience difficulty in dimly lit areas and crowded places. Other people with visual impairments may see in all sectors of their visual field, but what they see is distorted in some way.

Many visually impaired people are particularly sensitive to lighting. Direct lighting makes it easier for most people who are visually impaired to perform tasks. However, it is important to realize that too much light may create problems related to glare.

The variability in how visual impairments affect peoples' ability to perform visual tasks means that it is especially important to understand each individual situation when beginning a prospective employer-employee relationship, working with current employees, or dealing with an employee in your organization who becomes visually impaired. Employers can ask an applicant who is visually impaired to provide accurate information about visual functioning, provided that this information is not used to disqualify the applicant prior to a fair job evaluation. In addition, local organizations that provide special education or rehabilitation services involved in job placement are a valuable information resource for employers. (See the *AFB Directory of Services for Blind and Visually Impaired Persons in the United States and Canada* [1997] for a state-by-state listing of relevant organizations and services.)

AN OVERVIEW OF THE ADA FOR EMPLOYERS OF PERSONS WHO ARE BLIND OR VISUALLY IMPAIRED

Title I of the ADA contains specific provisions to ensure that people who are blind or visually impaired have access to all phases and aspects of employment, from job application, hiring, and advancement to training, compensation, and discharge. No employer who employs more than 15 people may discriminate against a **qualified individual** on the basis of his or her disability (see "Key Points in Title I—Employment" in Section I for an overview of Title I and definitions of key terms). Employers must provide reasonable accommodations to qualified employees who are visually impaired to enable them to enjoy equal opportunity and perform the essential functions of a job. What follows is an explanation of relevant concepts for employers of people who are blind or visually impaired.

Reasonable Accommodations

As they pertain to employment, **reasonable accommodations** are changes in the job application process, work environment, or job description that enable a person who is blind or visually impaired to enjoy equal opportunity and perform the essential functions of a job. These accommodations typically take the form of audiotaped texts, qualified readers and interpreters, braille and large print materials, modification or acquisition of adaptive computer equipment, reassignment, and adjustment of work schedules. Making such areas of existing facilities as work areas, lunchrooms, restrooms, and training rooms accessible to employees who are blind or visually impaired are examples of reasonable accommodations.

Reasonable accommodations are determined on a case-by-case basis. However, the accommodations employers provide may not be those specifically requested by an employee who is blind or visually impaired. The employer has the ultimate responsibility to decide whether an accommodation is needed. Once it is decided that accommodation is necessary, an employer may choose from among those available (including the least expensive one), as long as it is effective in allowing an applicant or employee to perform the essential job functions. The employer is also free to set production standards, provided they are administered uniformly and are required of all employees in the same job classification.

There is a wide range of suitable accommodations. Some are as simple as providing a tape recorder for an employee to take notes at a meeting where pads and pens were distributed, but others are more complicated, depending on the specific situation. The following are examples of some common job-related accommodations used by employees who are blind or visually impaired:

- ■ braille or other tactile markings on equipment and documents
- ■ special tools that have been modified for tactile reading, such as a braille micrometer for a carpenter to measure minute distances

- a reader for a time each day to review necessary paperwork

- adjusted work schedules to allow a worker who is blind or visually impaired to use mass transit

- shared job tasks organized so that an employee who is blind or visually impaired performs more of the tasks that do not involve visual inspection or reading

- assistive technology, such as closed-circuit television systems (CCTVs) to magnify printed material; computer hardware and software for braille and speech output and computer software for large-print screen displays; computer systems with the capacity to electronically scan various types of printed material into the system (known as optical character recognition [OCR] systems or scanners) and produce enlarged print, braille, or speech output; and more basic kinds of equipment such as tape recorders, high-intensity lamps, rheostat light switches, and enlarged numbers for telephones. (For information on sources for many of these products and services, see the Resources section.)

An employee who is blind or visually impaired may need none, some, or most of these accommodations to perform a job. However, employers are not required to make non-work-specific accommodations or provide equipment that would help an employee both on and off the job. For example, an employer would not have to provide a dog guide or a long cane for an employee with visual impairments. For the employee who uses a dog guide, however, the reasonable accommodation that is appropriate might be to provide the employee with a work space that has ample room for the dog guide to be comfortable and to arrange work schedules that accommodate the need to relieve the dog guide outdoors. (For detailed explanations of the various accommodations that can be made available to employees, see "Auxiliary Aids and Services" in Section II, since many solutions for auxiliary aids and services can be applied in providing reasonable accommodations.)

AFB maintains a Careers and Technology Information Bank (CTIB) that supplies information about jobs held by people who are blind or visually impaired and the manner in which technology is used to enable these individuals to carry out their responsibilities. A wide range of occupations is represented in the CTIB, which is updated annually. (See the Resources section for more information about the CTIB.)

ESSENTIAL FUNCTIONS OF A JOB

Essential job functions are those components of a job that are fundamental to and define the particular position. For example, a job function is essential when the job exists to perform that function, when the employee holding the job was hired to perform the function, and when only a limited number of employees are available to perform the function. Employers may be expected to reassign nonessential job functions when an employee with a visual impairment cannot perform them.

This concept is illustrated by the following examples: A computer scientist who is totally blind is employed as an information specialist. All professional staff in his department are expected to share in a rotating assignment to read the department's postage meter. This duty is not an essential function of his job as an information specialist and should be reassigned to a colleague on a permanent basis. Similarly, replacing an ink cartridge in a printer may be a nonessential function for an attorney but an essential function for a secretary.

Undue Hardship

Employers are not required to provide reasonable accommodations that would impose **undue hardship** on their business. Several factors must be considered to determine whether such a hardship exists:

■ the type of business operation, including the composition, structure, and functions of the employer's work force; the geographical separateness of the facility; and the administrative or fiscal relationship of the facility to the employer

■ the impact of the accommodation on the operation of the facility, including its impact on the ability of other workers to perform their duties or the facility's ability to carry out business

■ the nature and net cost of the accommodation, taking into account the value of tax credits and deductions, as well as outside funding from organizations such as state or private agencies for people who are blind or visually impaired

■ the overall financial resources of the employer; the size of the business with respect to the number of employees; and the number, type, and location of its facilities

The following checklist will be useful to help employers who may be hiring or may currently employ people who are blind or visually impaired make appropriate and reasonable accommodations. (For a list of general helpful guidelines to interacting with people who are blind and visually impaired, see "Employees' Sensitivity to Blindness and Visual Impairment" in Section II. For a copy of this checklist to use in your own business, see Section IV.)

CHECKLIST FOR EMPLOYERS OF PEOPLE WHO ARE BLIND OR VISUALLY IMPAIRED

Recruitment

☑ Make information about job openings that is posted in print on public bulletin boards in your organization available upon request in an accessible format, such as audiotape, braille, or large print.

☑ State in job notice announcements that applicants who need accommodations for an interview should request them in advance.

- ☑ Place help wanted advertisements in newspapers and publications that are available on the Internet.
- ☑ Carry out recruitment activities in locations that are or have been made accessible.
- ☑ Include information about only the essential functions of a job in position announcements, help wanted advertisements, and other recruitment notices.
- ☑ Provide clear and specific directions to the location where recruitment activities take place.

Preemployment Activities, Interviewing, and Testing

- ☑ Schedule medical examinations for persons who are blind or visually impaired only if these examinations are required for all potential employees.
- ☑ Request medical information or a medical examination only after an applicant has received a conditional job offer.
- ☑ Use medical and eye exams only to determine the applicant's ability to perform the essential functions of the job.
- ☑ Provide forms used for drug screening and medical examinations in accessible format, such as large print, recorded formats, or braille, or through a reader.
- ☑ Accept a nondriver's license as a form of identification.
- ☑ Refrain from asking a job applicant about his or her ability to get to work.
- ☑ Pose interview questions that probe the applicant's ability to perform a job, rather than the nature or extent of the applicant's visual impairment.
- ☑ Ask applicants to describe how specific job functions will be carried out only when it reasonably appears that a visual impairment might interfere with job performance.
- ☑ Provide a suitable location or opportunity for applicants to demonstrate how job functions are performed using adaptive methods or technology.
- ☑ Administer preemployment tests in an effective alternative format, such as in braille, on audiotape, by a reader, or on a computer.
- ☑ Provide sufficient time to complete tests when an applicant requires testing accommodations.
- ☑ When it is not possible to test an individual with a visual impairment in an alternative format, use another means, such as an interview, license or certification, education credentials, prior work experience, or a trial job period, to determine his or her job qualifications.

Management and Supervision

- ☑ Provide job descriptions that are based on job functions and not on individual attributes.

- ☑ Provide the same job orientation and on-the-job training to a new employee who is blind or visually impaired that is provided to all new employees, using effective accommodations as appropriate.
- ☑ Provide employee orientation material, organizational policy and procedures manuals, salary and benefits information, and the like in accessible formats.
- ☑ Provide reasonable accommodations for completing required employment, benefits, and tax documents.
- ☑ Provide orientation to the physical layout of an organization's buildings and facilities.
- ☑ Provide official organizational policy notices, notices of internal job postings, and other essential documents in accessible formats and in a timely manner.
- ☑ Carry out a site survey to eliminate barriers to access in the organization's buildings and facilities.
- ☑ Develop a system for emergency exits with the employee.
- ☑ Work with the employee to establish which equipment and services may be necessary to obtain reasonable accommodations.
- ☑ Provide reader services and document accessibility as appropriate. E-mail transmission of routine office correspondence can be a useful approach for employees who use assistive technology.
- ☑ Create a work space in which adaptive equipment can be installed and operated and that has suitable illumination for the employee's needs. Provide adaptive equipment and work space modifications in a timely manner.
- ☑ Establish work schedules for employees who use dog guides to allow proper toileting for the dog guide.
- ☑ Provide the same nature and quality of supervision or discipline, as well as opportunities for advancement, for employees who are blind or visually impaired that is provided for all employees.
- ☑ Determine that all on-the-job training (on-site or off-site) is carried out with adequate accommodations for information and document accessibility.
- ☑ Identify nonessential functions of a job that a visually impaired person may not be able to perform, and reassign those functions to another employee.

When an employer needs to carry out a site survey of barriers to accessibility, he or she can request the assistance of a trained orientation and mobility (O&M) specialist or a job coach. Sources of such assistance include state vocational rehabilitation agencies, which help obtain job placements for people who are blind or visually impaired, local private agencies for the blind (see the *AFB Directory of Services* [1997]), and the Division IX Environmental Access Committee of the Association for Education and Rehabilitation of the Blind and Visually Impaired [AER] in the Resources section.)

For determining the equipment and services that are necessary to make a reasonable accommodation for an employee who is blind or visually impaired, an employer generally starts by consulting with the individual, who knows best his or her own needs and usually has opinions about the best solutions. For further consultation or alternative views of possible solutions, employers can contact a state or local agency serving people who are blind or visually impaired (see the *AFB Directory of Services* [1997]) the AFB Careers and Technology Information Bank (CTIB), or the Mississippi State Rehabilitation Research and Training Center (see the Resources section).

Health Care Facilities

THE ADA AND HEALTH CARE SERVICES

The requirements of the ADA apply to health care facilities as they do to any other places of public accommodations. However, because of the nature of the services they offer, the accommodations offered by health care facilities related to the needs of patients may be specific to that field.

As with other public facilities and places of business, the ADA requires health care facilities to comply with requirements for structural barrier removal of the ADAAG in accordance with either Title II (for public health care facilities) or Title III (for privately operated health care facilities) and to provide auxiliary aids and services to make visible information available in a timely and effective manner. This obligation begins the moment a person comes under the care of a public or private facility or its services. If these services are provided in the person's home or at another location away from the health care provider's premises, requirements for providing auxiliary aids and services still apply.

Examples of the range of aids and services available to administrators of health care services are described in detail in Section II. In addition, accommodating patients who are blind or visually impaired may include modifying certain procedures and training staff to be sensitive to their needs (see "Employees' Sensitivity to Blindness and Visual Impairment" in Section II). The purpose of these accommodations is to ensure that patients are properly informed about the services they require and receive and that they will benefit from their care.

Privately owned inpatient and ambulatory care facilities are covered under Title III of the ADA, Public Accommodations and Commercial Facilities. Inpatient and ambulatory care facilities operated by state and local governments are covered under ADA Title II, State and Local Government Services. Also, all health care facilities have obligations to their employees under ADA Title I, Employment (for more information, see the preceding section in "Employment").

The ADA prohibits health care providers from discriminating against patients who are blind or visually impaired with respect to treatment decisions. Patients who use dog guides cannot be excluded from health care facilities or asked to leave their dogs outside the facility, unless as part of a competent and well-reasoned policy developed specifically for certain health care functions that is based on objective considerations regarding infection control and sanitation and is applied consistently in evaluating infection control concerns. Health care providers should establish their policy regarding dog guides by gathering factual, unbiased information from reliable sources within their organizations and in the community and communicate this policy clearly to the community they serve. (See the Resources section for information about the Guide Dog Users Association. The *AFB Directory of Services* [1997] also contains listings of dog guide schools and related organizations.)

If a private physician's or health care provider's office occupies leased space in an office building, both the landlord and the medical practice are responsible for ensuring that a person who is blind, deaf-blind, or visually impaired has full access to the services provided. Under the ADA, the tenant and the landlord may allocate the costs and responsibility in their lease agreement. For example, a landlord can assume responsibility for providing accessibility in the lobby, elevators, and other common areas in the office building, and the practice can assume responsibility for access within its individual suite.

The following checklist is a useful guide for evaluating existing facilities and services and for planning health care services that accommodate patients and their families who are blind or visually impaired. Although some of this information is relevant to other areas discussed elsewhere in this guide, it is applied here specifically to the health care industry. (See also Section II, "A Customer Service Guide to Accommodating People Who Are Blind or Visually Impaired," including the section on "Communicating with People Who Are Deaf-Blind" for additional tips on accommodating the needs of people who are blind, deaf-blind, or visually impaired.)

CHECKLIST FOR ACCOMMODATING PATIENTS WHO ARE BLIND OR VISUALLY IMPAIRED

Inpatient Care
Admitting and Financial Services

- ☑ Verbally identify all health care personnel by name and position.
- ☑ Read aloud and assist in completing admission forms and consents.
- ☑ Communicate the contents of important documents, such as patient information brochures, the Patients' Bill of Rights, admission and discharge procedures, health care proxies, and the like.
- ☑ Review bills verbally prior to discharge.
- ☑ Identify and count currency used for all transactions.
- ☑ Ensure that a policy regarding the admittance of dog guides is in place.

Medical Treatment Services and In-Room Patient Care

- ☑ Verbally identify all health care personnel by name and position.
- ☑ Orient patients to the layout of patient rooms, restroom facilities, the nurses' station, patient lounges and waiting areas, and emergency evacuation areas.
- ☑ Orient patients to emergency call buttons located at the bedside and in restrooms, to controls for televisions and radios, and to controls that raise and lower bed positions.

- ☑ Understand and respond to patients' degree of visual functioning. Ask the patient to describe his or her visual impairment and the manner in which it may affect participation in treatment; for example, creating difficulty in measuring fluids to be taken in advance of a medical procedure.
- ☑ Provide treatment consent forms and related patient-care documents in accessible formats.
- ☑ Use basic sighted guide mobility techniques (see "Guidelines for the Sighted Guide Technique" in Section II) to escort patients to and from treatment areas; provide verbal orientation information to patients who are being transported in wheelchairs or on gurneys.
- ☑ Orient patients to treatment or examining rooms and supplies; for example, the location and use of such items as gowns and specimen containers.
- ☑ Explain medical procedures verbally, using language that is precise, or demonstrate them before they are performed.
- ☑ Identify and label medications that are self-administered in a manner patients understand and can use.

Dietary Services

- ☑ Communicate verbally information on written diets or menu plans.
- ☑ Assist patients with filling out forms to indicate menu choices for future meals.
- ☑ Inform patients when food has been delivered.
- ☑ Identify the location of the food tray and where plates, cups, utensils, and other items are placed on the tray.
- ☑ Assist with preparation or cutting of some food items, if requested by patients.
- ☑ Assist with feeding only if it is required by patients' medical conditions and if such assistance is also provided to patients without disabilities.
- ☑ Specify a location for food trays to be left for removal from the room.

Discharge Services

- ☑ Communicate written discharge information (e.g., home care instructions, medication names and dosages, follow-up appointments, etc.) in accessible formats.
- ☑ Provide a signature guide or template for official documents.
- ☑ In cooperation with patients, customize discharge plans to patients' lifestyles as persons who are blind, deaf-blind, or visually impaired.
- ☑ Identify and label medications prescribed at discharge in a manner patients understand and can use.
- ☑ Identify and make referrals when necessary to appropriate community-based programs, such as rehabilitation agencies, local agencies for blind persons, and public school districts. (See *AFB Directory of Services* [1997] for local listings of such resources.)

☑ Provide training in self-care (including the operation of any necessary medical equipment), utilizing strategies and equipment that are effective for patients with visual impairments.

Ambulatory Care
Admitting, Financial, and Discharge Services

☑ Verbally identify all health care personnel by name and position.

☑ Read aloud and assist in completion of admission, discharge, and consent forms.

☑ Communicate contents of important documents, such as patient information brochures, the Patients' Bill of Rights, and follow-up procedures and instructions.

☑ Review bills and charges verbally prior to discharge.

☑ Identify and count currency used for all transactions.

☑ Ensure that a policy regarding the admittance of dog guides is in place.

Medical Treatment Services

☑ Verbally identify all health care personnel by name and position.

☑ Understand and respond to patients' degree of visual functioning.

☑ Provide treatment consent forms and related patient-care documents in accessible formats.

☑ Orient patients to the layout of waiting areas and restroom facilities.

☑ Use basic sighted guide mobility techniques to escort patients to and from treatment areas; provide verbal orientation information to patients who are being transported in wheelchairs or on gurneys.

☑ Orient patients to treatment or examining rooms and supplies; for example, to the location and use of such items as gowns and specimen containers.

☑ Explain medical procedures verbally, using language that is precise, or demonstrate them before they are performed.

☑ Identify and label medications that are self-administered in a manner patients understand and can use.

Cafeteria and Vending Services

☑ Communicate verbally the contents of cafeteria menus or provide braille or large-print menus.

☑ Provide assistance in making menu selections, using self-serve amenities (such as coffee urns and juice bars), carrying food trays, selecting silverware, and locating tables in the cafeteria.

☑ Provide assistance in locating tray disposal areas and in disposing of self-service trays.

☑ Place vending machines in well-lit areas.

☑ Install vending machines with raised key pads, rather than those with membrane pads. Consider installing "talking vending machines" that have voice output for the menu of choices and for confirmation of selection made, cost, amount tendered, and change returned (see the Resources section).

☑ Mark vending machines and microwave ovens with braille labels.

Professional Care in the Private Office of a Health Care Provider

General Office Procedures

☑ Verbally identify all health care personnel by name and position.

☑ Assist with sign-in procedures.

☑ Assist with reading and completing insurance and consent forms.

☑ Assist in completing initial history and intake forms.

☑ Use basic sighted guide mobility techniques to escort patients, when necessary.

☑ Provide clear and specific directions to patients about the location of waiting rooms, examination and treatment rooms, restrooms, and offices.

☑ Orient patients to examination or treatment rooms and supplies; for example, to the location and use of such items as gowns and specimen containers.

☑ Identify medication bottles, containers, or specimen cups in a manner that is useful to patients.

☑ Communicate clearly information about home care instructions, medication names and dosages, and follow-up appointments.

☑ Review billing information and procedures for making follow-up appointments.

☑ Communicate other pertinent information; for example, that a telephone-access system is located at the entry to the building, that a taxi stand is located right outside the door, or that there is an ongoing construction project in a common area of the building or parking lot.

☑ Ensure that a policy regarding the admittance of dog guides is in place.

Medical Treatment Services

☑ Verbally identify all health care personnel by name and position.

☑ Understand and respond to patients' degree of visual functioning.

☑ Provide treatment consent forms and related patient-care documents in accessible formats.

☑ Orient patients to the layout of waiting areas and restroom facilities.

☑ Use basic sighted guide mobility techniques to escort patients to and from treatment areas; provide verbal orientation information to patients who are being transported in wheelchairs or on gurneys.

☑ Orient patients to treatment or examination rooms and supplies; for example, to the location and use of such items as gowns and specimen cups.

☑ Explain medical procedures verbally, using language that is precise, or demonstrate them before they are performed.

☑ Identify and label medications that are self-administered in a manner patients understand and can use.

Retail Establishments

RETAIL ESTABLISHMENTS AND CUSTOMER SERVICE

It is common for individuals in our society today to look forward to a shopping outing, complete with a quick snack in a department store coffee shop or mall food court or dining in a formal restaurant located in a shopping mall. People with visual impairments, like most everyone else, take advantage of retail shopping establishments to fulfill their personal needs to purchase goods and services. They also enjoy participating in the contemporary American pastime of shopping and browsing. Providing auxiliary aids and services as required by Title III of the ADA ensures retail establishments that their customers will enjoy the full benefits of retail services and be satisfied customers.

The auxiliary aids and services that retailers can provide for customers who are blind or visually impaired are simple, inexpensive, and easy to put in place. They range from those related to environmental design (see "Environmental Design" and "Retrofit" in Section II) to those related to customer service and food service (see Section II, "A Customer Service Guide to Accommodating People Who Are Blind or Visually Impaired," including the section on "Food Services"). In many instances, these aids and services enhance the retail atmosphere and increase comfort and convenience for all customers. Providing good service and meeting accessibility requirements for retail establishments under ADA can be one and the same (see "Auxiliary Aids and Services" in Section II). In addition to the general accommodations that are described throughout Section II, the following are some examples of auxiliary aids and services that retail establishments in particular can provide to accommodate customers who are blind or visually impaired:

■ Post sale notices and prices using print that is large, clear, contrasting, and of a simple typeface.

■ Train staff to offer reader and guided assistance when it is needed.

■ Provide descriptions of merchandise.

■ Offer assistance in dressing rooms.

■ Locate and select merchandise, read price tags, and offer to assist with signing sales or credit card slips.

■ Read menus in food service areas or prices posted on walls and message boards.

Sales and customer services departments of retail establishments can provide the following types of specific assistance:

■ Listen to your customers. Observe customers carefully and try to be sensitive by anticipating and responding to their needs. This approach will help sales and service personnel feel at ease and be themselves.

■ Offer to provide assistance with shopping and sales transactions. Feel comfortable doing so. Asking questions such as "How may I be of help?" "Would you like me to get that for you?" and "What else might I do for you?" gives your customers an easy opening to ask for whatever help they require or to decline help politely if they so choose.

■ Inform customers who cannot read the information displayed in your establishment about sales or other special promotions.

■ A reasonable amount of assistance should be offered. The size of a sales staff, the number of customers being served at the time, and the level of service offered to all customers will help determine what is reasonable.

■ Allow customers to examine merchandise and provide clear, accurate descriptions if asked to do so.

■ If your establishment provides a catalog shopping service, provide a reasonable amount of verbal product descriptions, pricing information, and ordering information for telephone and in-store customers.

■ If you provide web-based shopping services, be sure the web site is accessible for people who use screen reader and large-print assistive technology. (For additional information, contact the AFB National Technology Program; see Resources section.)

■ Modify policies and practices that may cause hardship or embarrassment for customers who are blind or visually impaired. Examples of such practices include requiring a driver's license as the sole means of identification or prohibiting two persons in a dressing room.

The following checklist is an easy and clear way to evaluate existing retail facilities as well to plan innovative customer services to accommodate shoppers who are blind or visually impaired. Although these accommodations help to fulfill a retailer's obligations under the ADA, they also go a long way toward improving the retail experience for all shoppers, not only those with visual impairments. (See also the "Checklist for Communicating with People Who Are Blind or Visually Impaired" and the section on "Communicating with People Who Are Deaf-Blind" in Section II for accommodations that may be needed by customers who are deaf-blind.)

CHECKLIST FOR ACCOMMODATING CUSTOMERS WHO ARE BLIND OR VISUALLY IMPAIRED

Courtesy and Information Services

- ☑ Assist with completion of printed service request forms, order forms, and sales documents.
- ☑ Review or read aloud fee schedules, and credit, loan, or layaway agreements.
- ☑ Use basic sighted guide and mobility techniques to escort customers who request assistance (see "Guidelines for the Sighted Guide Technique" in Section II).
- ☑ Provide clear information and directions when customers ask for assistance locating store facilities or departments.

Retail Sales Areas

- ☑ Inform customers of the location of merchandise.
- ☑ Provide clear information and directions to destinations such as dressing rooms and lounges.
- ☑ Read aloud size, price, and other product information.
- ☑ Assist customers in retrieving items from shelves or displays.
- ☑ Describe the colors, patterns, and other features of clothing and other items.
- ☑ Read aloud a customer's itemized bill, if requested.
- ☑ Count and identify currency during financial transactions.
- ☑ Place all cash, credit cards, and receipts directly in the customer's hand.
- ☑ Hand credit cards back to customers after they are imprinted.
- ☑ Make signature guides or templates, felt-tipped pens, or high-intensity lighting available at sales desks.
- ☑ Use basic sighted guide and mobility techniques to escort customers, if requested.
- ☑ Ensure that a policy allowing the admittance of dog guides is in place, unless doing so would fundamentally alter the nature of the services provided or jeopardize the safe operations of the facility.

Facilities and Environmental Access

- ☑ Provide clear aisle space between displays.
- ☑ Provide display racks, water fountains, ice machines, telephones, signage, and other elements that do not protrude dangerously into the path of travel.
- ☑ Provide braille, large-print, or voice access to customer-operated equipment, such as vending or other point-of-sale machines.
- ☑ Provide posted information regarding sale notices and return policies using large, clear signs printed on nonglare material.
- ☑ Provide price tags that use large, clear lettering and numbers.

☑ Train staff to orient customers to common-use areas and elements, including restrooms, lounges, elevators, stairs, and escalators.

☑ Install raised-character and braille signs that meet ADAAG requirements in elevators, at restrooms, and at exits (see "The Americans with Disabilities Act Accessibility Guidelines" in Section II).

☑ Install or modify stairs, escalators, and elevators to meet ADAAG standards.

☑ Control environmental background noise created by fountains, ventilators, or music that may mask environmental sound clues used for orientation by customers who are blind or visually impaired.

☑ Provide adequate lighting, controlling glare and shadows in public-access areas.

☑ Highlight contrast on stair handrails, stair nosings, door frames, and store aisles.

Hotels and Motels

Hoteliers are required to comply with the requirements of the ADAAG for existing and new construction and can expect to be called upon to provide auxiliary aids and services when people who are blind or visually impaired are their guests. People who are blind or visually impaired are frequent customers at hotels and motels. They particularly enjoy the convenience that hotels offer for dining, socializing, making use of health club and exercise facilities, and conducting business within the buildings and grounds of a single facility. In addition, many older persons who enjoy traveling and who may be experiencing age-related vision changes visit hotels and motels for leisure-time and recreational activities. Hotel facilities will find that commonsense attention to providing auxiliary aids and services, such as adequate lighting and easy-to-read documents in clear, large type, will enhance the services they provide to their customers and attract older persons.

It is acceptable to provide a guest who is totally blind with reader services at check-in, even if the guest uses braille and expresses a preference for braille information, provided that the reader conveys information about check-in documents accurately and effectively. Reader services may not be appropriate, however, if this same guest asks for braille or recorded documents in order to review a complex purchase agreement, registration, or consent form (see "Auxiliary Aids and Services" in Section II).

The following checklist provides hotel personnel with a simple and clear way to evaluate their existing hotel facilities and services. It is also a useful guide for planning innovative services to accommodate guests who are blind or visually impaired. Refer to Section II for guidelines for customer service (including giving directions and sighted guide technique), requirements for environmental accommodations, and auxiliary aids and services. The Resources section provides listings of sources for specific products and for services that help businesses make the required accommodations.

CHECKLIST FOR ACCOMMODATING HOTEL AND MOTEL GUESTS WHO ARE BLIND OR VISUALLY IMPAIRED

Front Desk or Reception Services

- ☑ Train staff to orient guests to common-use areas, including the lobby, restaurants, meeting rooms, exhibit areas, and business center.
- ☑ Assist with completion of any registration documents.
- ☑ Assist with completion of other required forms.
- ☑ Review or read aloud all consents, service guides, and the final bill.
- ☑ Provide clear information and directions about the layout and any special features of buildings and rooms.
- ☑ Provide clear information and directions about the location of stairs, elevators, and emergency exits.
- ☑ If plastic card keys are used for hotel rooms, mark them for orientation and demonstrate how they are used, provide room numbers and clear descriptions of rooms.

Facilities and Environmental Access

- ☑ Provide guests with essential safety information for evacuation and rescue in accessible formats (braille, large print, or audiocassette).
- ☑ When providing water fountains, ice machines, telephones, and other amenities, make sure that they do not protrude dangerously into the path of travel.
- ☑ Provide access to guest-operated equipment such as laundry, vending, or other point-of-sale machines in braille, large print, or voice output.
- ☑ Install raised-character and braille signs that comply with ADAAG requirements in elevators, at rooms, and at exits (see "The Americans with Disabilities Act Accessibility Guidelines" in Section II and the AFB video, *Strategies for Community Access: Braille and Raised Large Print Facility Signs* [1993]).
- ☑ Install or modify stairs, escalators, and elevators to meet the ADAAG standards.
- ☑ Have on hand equipment such as talking or large-print clocks and BrailleTalk alphabet for persons who are deaf-blind (BrailleTalk is a small plastic board with both raised print and braille characters that a deaf-blind person can use to spell out words). (See the Resources section for a list of Selected Sources of Products for Independent Living.)
- ☑ Control environmental background noise, such as that created by fountains, ventilators, or music, that may mask environmental sound clues used for orientation by people who are blind or visually impaired.
- ☑ Provide adequate lighting that controls glare and shadows in common-use areas.
- ☑ Highlight contrast on stair handrails, stair nosings, door frames, and baseboards.

In-Room Services

- ☑ Communicate contents of in-room documents, such as menus and information brochures. Consider having these available in braille, in large print, or on audiotape.
- ☑ Use basic sighted guide mobility techniques and clear, descriptive language to orient guests to their rooms.
- ☑ Orient guests to the location of fire alarms, emergency exits, and other equipment in their rooms and in corridors.
- ☑ Orient guests to the location and operation of heating and air conditioning controls, pay and free TV service, minibars, and the telephone message retrieval system.
- ☑ Provide clear information about the features of the room, including closets, lavatory, shower, dressers, and telephone.
- ☑ Provide bedside alarm clocks and radios that have clear, large print for guests with poor vision.
- ☑ Provide bedside alarm clocks with vibrating displays for guests who are deaf-blind.
- ☑ Provide felt-tipped writing pens and writing pads large enough for a large-print message.
- ☑ Inform guests about where luggage, laundry boxes, food trays, and the like will be placed in the room.

Dining and Food Services
Formal Dining Service

- ☑ Provide priority seating for customers who are blind or visually impaired, if requested to do so, in an area that has adequate lighting or is away from the glare of large picture windows. Note that if dim ambient lighting is an essential part of the dining atmosphere you offer, the ADA does not require you to fundamentally alter the nature of your business by turning up the lights for a person who is visually impaired.
- ☑ Instruct table service personnel to identify themselves by name and function to customers who are blind or visually impaired. For example, a waiter might say, "Good evening, I'm Walter. I'll be your waiter for the evening. How may I help you?"
- ☑ Instruct table service personnel to describe the placement of tableware, flowers, ashtrays, candles, or other items on the table.
- ☑ Offer customers braille or large-print menus if they are available. Be sure to tell guests about any selections that have been added since the menu was prepared. Also, describe daily specials that do not appear on the menu.
- ☑ Offer to read menus to customers who are totally blind when braille menus are not available or if your customer does not read braille. Likewise, offer to read menus to customers who are visually impaired.

☑ Inform customers when servers are about to place food or items on the dining table. Describe where all food and beverage items are placed as they are served.

☑ Identify the location of food on a plate if requested to do so, using the face of a clock as a reference. For example, say "Your meat is at 12 o'clock, your vegetables are at 3 o'clock, the rice is at 9 o'clock."

☑ Provide assistance in cutting food items or mixing beverages, if requested to do so. Cutting food items in the kitchen prior to serving or returning a plate to the kitchen is a discreet way of handling a request to cut a customer's food.

Buffet Service

☑ Identify and briefly describe the food and beverage items available.

☑ Assist with locating tableware and utensils.

☑ Assist in serving food items from the buffet and escorting customers to a seat.

☑ Inform customers about how to obtain assistance for return visits to the buffet.

Food Service Lines and Cafeteria Service

☑ Be alert for aging customers or others whose visual impairment may not be readily recognized so you may assist them. These customers may not appear to be blind because they do not carry long white canes or use dog guides, but they may have difficulty reading menus posted above the food service counter or identifying food selections available at steam tables.

☑ Provide sighted guide assistance to customers who are totally blind so they can make their way through food service lines, select food, and locate condiments, napkins, and utensils. Guide them to a seat and offer assistance for later disposal of trays and refuse.

☑ Provide customers with clear verbal information about visually displayed menus, advertised specials, and promotional services.

☑ Have braille or large-print menus available for standard items in a fixed location; for example, at both ends of the service counter. Although braille and large-print menus are not required by the ADA, providing them is a thoughtful service that makes a positive statement about your interest in customers' comfort and convenience.

Vending Machines

☑ Install vending machines in areas that are well illuminated and protected from glare or deep shadows.

☑ Provide vending machines with raised keypads similar to those on a push-button telephone. Avoid membrane or touch-screen operation controls, which are inaccessible to customers who are severely visually impaired. Characters on keypads should contrast visibly with the background.

☑ Provide operation controls (coin and bill slots, change returns, and the like) that contrast clearly with the background of the machine. Label all controls in clear, contrasting large print using a sans serif or a simple serif typeface.

☑ Provide braille labels for selection keys and operation controls wherever possible. A commercially available braille label maker and assistance from a local blindness service organization can be very helpful for this (see the Resources section for lists of organizations and sources of products).

☑ Consider installing vending machines that "talk" (see the Resources section).

Conclusion

The better part of a decade has elapsed since the passage of the Americans with Disabilities Act. While impressive progress has occurred in many areas for people who are blind or visually impaired, sustaining and accelerating this momentum will require ongoing efforts at education and clarification regarding the ADA's requirements for removal of communication barriers and the advancement of practical cost-effective solutions for ADA compliance. It is especially important that these efforts be tailored to meet present and rapidly changing needs of business and other organizations covered under the ADA.

ADA compliance is not as complicated as it seems. Commonsense information provided by those with practical experience goes a long way to easing the compliance process for everyone. *A Practical Guide to the ADA and Visual Impairment* has cast basic information about blindness and visual impairment and the manner in which people who are blind or visually impaired manage their daily affairs in the context of industry-specific ADA requirements for communication barrier removal. Employers, architects, designers, building managers, health care providers, retail and hospitality establishments, and others who serve the public are now equipped to overcome the communication barriers that have excluded valuable employees and customers. Armed with concrete information, practical solutions, checklists, and resources, businesses covered by the ADA can do what business does best—understand and meet constituents' needs for the benefit of all.

In closing, the idea that ADA compliance causes great financial burdens is not supported by the provisions of the law itself or by practical experience to date in implementing the law. Rather than imposing burdens, the ADA enhances accessibility, convenience, and opportunity for patrons, customers, business, and government alike.

References

Accessible and Usable Buildings and Facilities (ANSI 117.1, rev. ed.). (1998). Falls Church, VA: American National Standards Institute.

ADAAG Review Advisory Committee. (September 1996). *Recommendations for a New ADAAG.* Washington, DC: U.S. Architectural and Transportation Barriers Compliance Board.

AFB ADA Consulting Group. (1992). *Making the ADA work for you: A video training seminar* [videotape]. New York: AFB Press.

AFB ADA Consulting Group. (1993). *Strategies for community access: Braille and raised large print facility signs* [videotape]. New York: American Foundation for the Blind.

AFB Directory of Services for Blind and Visually Impaired Persons in the United States and Canada, 25th ed. (1997, book and CD-ROM). New York: AFB Press.

Federal Communications Commission. (1998, May 22). Notice of proposed rulemaking from the Federal Communications Commission. *Federal Register* (63 FR28456).

Joffee, E. (1992). Transportation. *Accomodation and accessibility: Implementing the ADA on a local level.* New York: American Foundation for the Blind. [Published as a special supplement to *Journal of Visual Impairment & Blindness, 86* (7), September 1992.]

Joffee, E., & Siller, M. A. (1997). *Reaching out: A creative access guide for designing exhibits and cultural programs for persons who are blind or visually impaired.* New York: AFB Press.

Welch, P. (Ed.). (1995). *Strategies for Teaching Universal Design.* Boston: Adaptive Environments Center.

SECTION IV Resources

- Sources of Information, Technical Assistance, Products, and Services

- Recommended Reading

- Americans with Disabilities Act of 1990

- Excerpts from the Americans with Disabilities Act Accessibility Guidelines (ADAAG)

- Excerpts from ICC/ANSI Standards A117.1, *Accessible and Usable Buildings and Facilities*

- Checklists

Sources of Information, Technical Assistance, Products, and Services

The listings that follow are a selection intended to provide readers with comprehensive sources of information and technical assistance for making places that transact business with the public accessible to people who are blind or visually impaired.

The resources are grouped for the reader's convenience in selecting the appropriate combinations of sources and resource materials to individualize access solutions that meet individual business and customer needs. The first section lists the federal government agencies that are charged with enforcing aspects of the ADA, writing regulations, and providing information and assistance to the general public. Next are national organizations in the field of blindness and visual impairment that serve as important sources of information and referral for various products and services. Organizations that provide consultation and technical assistance on ADA-related matters are arranged under categories of general consultation, human resources, braille signage, and model building codes. The final section lists selected sources of products and services, which are categorized into those related to braille materials, recorded materials, multimedia and access technology, assistive technology and computer products, and products for independent living.

These resources are not intended to be exhaustive; however, the organizations included here will be able to provide additional information and sources for further research. The American Foundation for the Blind (AFB) operates a toll-free Information Line. In addition, the *AFB Directory of Services for Blind and Visually Impaired Persons in the United States and Canada* (1997) provides extensive listings of organizations, services, and products that are available for people who are blind or visually impaired.

Readers should note that addresses and telephone numbers provided for the organizations and agencies listed in the guide are current as of the time of publication. However, all such information is subject to frequent change.

FEDERAL AGENCIES

The agencies and organizations listed in this section are those government agencies that are primarily charged with writing regulations for the provisions of the ADA, enforcing them, and providing technical assistance and services to assist in complying with or obtaining rights under the ADA.

Access Board
U.S. Architectural and Transportation
Barriers Compliance Board
1331 F Street, Suite 1000
Washington, DC 20004-1111
Telephone: (202) 272-5434;
(800) 872-2253
TDD: (202) 272-5449, (800) 993-2822

Fax: (202) 272-5447
E-mail: info@access-board.gov
http://www.access-board.gov
As an independent federal agency, develops guidelines and requirements and provides technical assistance for standards issued under the ADA and accessibility guidelines for telecommunications under the Tele-

communications Act, as well as for sections of the Rehabilitation Act, and enforces the Architectural Barriers Act. Promotes accessibility for people with disabilities. Distributes a number of publications and publishes a free newsletter, *Access Currents.*

Equal Employment Opportunity Commission
1801 L Street, N.W.
Washington, DC 20507
Telephone: (202) 663-4900;
(800) 669-4000
TDD: (202) 663-4494; (800) 669-6820
Publications: (800) 669-3362;
(800) 800-3302 (TDD)
http://www.eeoc.gov
As the federal agency charged with enforcing the provisions of Title I of the ADA regarding employment of people with disabilities, works with local civil rights enforcement agencies to investigate and file charges of discrimination based on disability. Offers information and assistance to individuals with disabilities and employers. Provides technical assistance to employers to promote voluntary compliance and assists efforts at mediation of disputes. Publishes a Technical Assistance Manual and distributes other publications and documents relating to employment rights under the ADA.

National Institute on Disability and Rehabilitation Research (NIDRR)
330 C Street, S.W.
Washington, DC 20202
Telephone: (202) 205-8134;
(800) 949-4232
http://www.ed.gov/offices/osers/nidrr
Funds grants to maintain Disability and Business Technical Assistance Centers, whose purpose is to ensure that information and expertise are available on how to make reasonable accommodation for disabled employees in the work setting and comply with the ADA.

National Library Service for the Blind and Physically Handicapped
Library of Congress
1291 Taylor Street, N.W.
Washington, DC 20542
Telephone: (202) 707-5100;
(800) 424-8567
Fax: (202) 707-0712
Conducts a national program to distribute free reading materials on tape or in braille to individuals who are blind or have physical disabilities that prevent them from reading print. Provides talking book machines and cassette machines for disc records and cassette tapes. Provides reference information on all aspects of blindness and other physical disabilities that affect reading.

President's Committee on Employment of People with Disabilities (PCEPD)
1331 F Street, N.W., 3rd Floor
Washington, DC 20004
Telephone: (202) 376-6200
Fax: (202) 376-6219
E-mail: info@pcepd.gov
http://www50.pcepd.gov/pcepd/
As a small federal agency that reports directly to the President, PCEPD facilitates the communication, coordination, and promotion of public and private efforts to enhance the employment of people with disabilities. Provides information, training, and technical assistance to business, labor, rehabilitation and service providers, advocacy organizations, and individuals with disabilities and their families. Distributes publications and fact sheets.

U.S. Department of Justice
Disability Rights Section
Civil Rights Division
P.O. Box 66738
Washington, DC 20035-6738
Telephone: (202) 514-0301;
(800) 514-0301
TDD: (800) 514-0383

http://www.dinf.org/crt/ada/adahom1.htm
Enforces the ADA requirements in Titles I, II, and III, receives complaints, and files lawsuits. Provides technical assistance to businesses, state, and local governments as well as individuals with rights and responsibilities under the law. Supplies a variety of materials and publications for technical assistance, as well as copies of the regulations for these titles. Operates the ADA Mediation Program, which refers appropriate disputes to professional mediators located throughout the country who have been trained in the legal requirements of the ADA.

U.S. Department of Transportation
Federal Transit Administration
Office of Civil Rights
400 Seventh Street, S.W.
Washington, DC 20590
ADA Assistance Line: (888) 446-4511;
(800) 877-8339 (TDD)
http://www.fta.dot.gov/office/civil
Monitors the implementation of and compliance with the ADA in areas of transportation by investigating complaints and conducting compliance reviews. Supplies copies of relevant regulations and publishes an ADA newsletter.

ORGANIZATIONS IN THE FIELD OF BLINDNESS

This section lists key national organizations in the field of blindness and visual impairment. Each one provides general information regarding blindness and visual impairment as well as referrals to sources of auxiliary aids and services such as braille or audio materials; consultation and evaluation in facility design to accommodate people who are blind or visually impaired; and other related products and services.

American Council of the Blind
1155 15th Street, N.W., Suite 720
Washington, DC 20005
Telephone: (202) 467-5081;
(800) 424-8666
Fax: (202) 467-5085
E-mail: ncrabb@access.digex.net
http://www.acb.org
Promotes effective participation of blind people in all aspects of society. Provides information and referral, advocacy, consultation, and program development assistance.

American Foundation for the Blind
11 Penn Plaza, Suite 300
New York, NY 10001
Telephone: (212) 502-7600;
(800) 232-5463
TDD: (212) 502-7662
Fax: (212) 502-7777
E-mail: afbinfo@afb.net
http://www.afb.org
Acts as an information clearinghouse for people who are blind or visually impaired,

professionals, organizations, schools, and corporations. Operates a toll-free information line; provides information and referral services; advocates for services and legislation; and conducts research and mounts program initiatives to improve services to visually impaired persons. Operates the National Technology Program and the Careers and Technology Information Bank; publishes the *Directory of Services for Blind and Visually Impaired Persons in the United States and Canada,* the *Journal of Visual Impairment & Blindness,* and numerous books and videotapes. Maintains offices throughout the country in Chicago, Atlanta, Dallas, and San Francisco and a Governmental Relations Group in Washington, DC.

**Association for Education
and Rehabilitation of the Blind
and Visually Impaired**
4600 Duke Street, Suite 430
Alexandria, VA 22304

Telephone: (703) 823-9690
Fax: (703) 823-9695
E-mail: aernet@laser.net
Promotes all phases of education and work for people of all ages who are blind and visually impaired; strives to expand their opportunities to take a contributory place in society; and disseminates information. Subgroups include Division IX, Orientation and Mobility, which includes the Environmental Access Committee.

Guide Dog Users
14311 Astrodome Drive
Silver Spring, MD 20906
Telephone: (310) 598-2131
E-mail: jcsheehan@smart.net
Serves as a support group to provide education and advocacy for people who use dog guides.

National Association for Parents of the Visually Impaired (NAPVI)
P.O. Box 317
Watertown, MA 02272-0317
Telephone: (800) 562-6265
Fax: (617) 972-7444
Provides support to parents and families of children and youths who have visual impairments. Operates a national clearinghouse for information, education, and referral.

National Federation of the Blind
1800 Johnson Street
Baltimore, MD 21230
Telephone: (410) 659-9314
Fax: (410) 685-5653
http://www.nfb.org
Strives to improve social and economic conditions of blind persons, evaluates and assists in establishing programs, and provides public education.

CONSULTATION AND TECHNICAL ASSISTANCE
Consultation and Technical Assistance—General

AFB ADA Solution Center
11 Penn Plaza, Suite 300
New York, NY 10001
Telephone: (212) 502-7658
Fax: (212) 502-7771
E-mail: reginag@afb.net
http://www.afb.org

American Institute of Architects
1735 New York Avenue, N.W.
Washington, DC 20005
Telephone: (202) 626-7300
Fax: (202) 626-7587
Represents registered architects as membership organization. Maintains a resource library and archives and can perform information searches and research.

Disability and Business Technical Assistance Centers
ADA Technical Assistance Programs
National Institute on Disability and Rehabilitation Research

c/o KRA Corporation
8455 Colesville Road, Suite 935
Silver Spring, MD 20910-3319
Telephone: (301) 587-3555;
(800) 949-4232 for the location of the appropriate regional center
http://www.adata.org/
Assists parties covered by the ADA to understand and comply with the law and its regulations. Ten regional centers, funded by the National Institute on Disability and Rehabilitation Research, provide technical assistance, training, and resource referral on all aspects of the ADA. The centers also distribute a variety of ADA-related documents and publications.

International Code Council
5203 Leesburg Pike, Suite 708
Falls Church, VA 22041
Telephone: (703) 931-4533
Fax: (703) 379-1546
See listing under Consultation and Technical Assistance—Model Building Code Organizations

Job Accommodation Network (JAN)
West Virginia Rehabilitation Research
and Training Center
West Virginia University
P.O. Box 6080
Morgantown, WV 26506-6080
ADA Information: (800) 232-9675
Accommodation Information:
(800) 526-7234
Fax: (304) 293-5407
E-mail: Jan@jan.icdi.wvu.edu
http://www.jan.wvu.com
A project of the President's Committee on
Employment of People with Disabilities (see
listing under Federal Organizations), JAN
provides information on options for job
accommodations and employability issues
regarding people with functional limitations
to employers, rehabilitation professionals, and
people with disabilities throughout the United
States and Canada. Makes referrals to other
sources of information, services, and support.

National Alliance on Business
1201 New York Avenue, N.W.
Washington, DC 20005
Telephone: (202) 289-2905
TDD: (202) 289-2977

National Center for Access Unlimited
155 North Wacker Drive, Suite 315
Chicago, IL 60606
Telephone: (312) 369-0380
TDD: (312) 368-0179

**Project ACTION
(Accessible Community
Transportation in Our Nation)**
National Easter Seal Society
700 Thirteenth Street, N.W., Suite 200
Washington, DC 20005
Telephone: (800) 659-6428;
(202) 347-3066
TDD: (202) 347-7385
As a national program of the National Easter
Seal Society created by Congress and funded
by the Federal Transportation Administration, Project ACTION provides national
technical assistance, resources, and training
to disability organizations, individuals with
disabilities, and the transportation industry
to improve access to transportation for people with disabilities. Provides information
and technical assistance to help transportation operators implement the ADA. Promotes cooperation between the disability
community and the transportation industry.

Consultation and Technical Assistance—
Braille Signage

The organizations listed in this section all provide information about braille signage, its
installation in the built environment, and sources of products.

AFB ADA Solution Center
11 Penn Plaza, Suite 300
New York, NY 10001
Telephone: (212) 502-7658
Fax: (212) 502-7771
E-mail: reginag@afb.net
http://www.afb.org

Awards and Recognition Association
36 South State Street, Suite 1212
Chicago, IL 60603
Telephone: (800) 344-2148
Fax: (312) 236-1140
http://www.ara.org

Braille Authority of North America
c/o Associated Service for the Blind
919 Walnut Street
Philadelphia, PA 19107
Telephone: (215) 627-0600
Fax: (215) 922-0692

Duxbury Systems
435 King Street
P.O. Box 1504
Littleton, MA 04160
Telephone: (508) 486-9766
Fax: (508) 486-9712
E-mail: info@duxsys.com
http://world.std.com/~duxbury/

International Sign Association
801 North Fairfax Street, Suite 205
Alexandria, VA 22314
Telephone: (703) 836-4012
Fax: (703) 836-8353
http://www.signs.org
Represents sign companies as a membership association. Makes referrals to members who can produce accessible signage. The Governmental Relations Department provides information and answers questions about the ADA and signage. Publishes *Signs and the ADA: Americans with Disabilities Act Reference Manual.*

National Elevator Industry
185 Bridge Plaza North
Fort Lee, NJ 07024
Telephone: (201) 944-3211
Fax: (201) 944-5483

Society for Environmental Graphic Design
401 F Street N.W., Suite 333
Washington, DC 20001
Telephone: (202) 638-5555
Fax: (202) 638-0891
E-mail: segdoffice@aol.com

Consultation and Technical Assistance— Human Resources

The organizations listed in this section provide consultation related to the employment of people with disabilities.

AFB ADA Solution Center
11 Penn Plaza, Suite 300
New York, NY 10001
Telephone: (212) 502-7658
Fax: (212) 502-7771
E-mail: reginag@afb.net
http://www.afb.org

**AFB Careers
and Technology Information
Bank**
11 Penn Plaza, Suite 330
New York, NY 10001
Telephone: (212) 502-7660
Fax: (212) 502-7773
E-mail: techctr@afb.net
http://www.afb.org

Equal Employment Opportunity Commission
ADA Help Line
1801 L Street, N.W.
Washington, DC 20507
Telephone: (202) 663-4900;
(800) 669-4000
TDD: (202) 663-4494; (800) 669-6820

Publications: (800) 669-3362;
(800) 800-3302 (TDD)
http://www.eeoc.gov
See listing under Federal Agencies

Job Accommodation Network
West Virginia University
P.O. Box 6080
Morgantown, WV 26505-9901
ADA Information: (800) 232-9675
Accommodation Information:
(800) 526-7234
Fax: (304) 293-5407
E-mail: jan@jan.icdi.wvu.edu
See listing under General Consultation and Technical Assistance

**President's Committee
on Employment of People
with Disabilities**
1331 F Street, N.W., 3rd Floor
Washington, DC 20004
Telephone: (202) 376-6200
Fax: (202) 376-6219
E-mail: info@pcepd.gov
http://www50.pcepd.gov/pcepd
See listing under Federal Agencies

Rehabilitation Research and Training Center on Blindness and Low Vision
Mississippi State University
P.O. Drawer 6189
Mississippi State, MS 39762
Telephone: (601) 325-2001
Fax: (601) 325-8989
E-mail: rrtc@ra.msstate.edu
Information and Resource Referral
Center: (601) 325-2694 or
(800) 675-7782
TDD: (601) 325-8693
Fax: (601) 325-8989
http://www.msstate.edu/dept/rrtc/blind.html
Works to prevent or alleviate the vocational, economic, and personal effects of blindness and severe visual impairment. Conducts research and training programs to identify, assess, and augment services intended to facilitate the employment and career development of persons who are blind or severely visually impaired. Operates the Information and Resource Referral Center (I&RR) project, which provides information and state-by-state referrals to such services as rehabilitation, education, consumer organizations, low vision services, library and instructional services, and guide dog schools.

U.S. Department of Justice
Disability Rights Section
Civil Rights Division
P.O. Box 66738
Washington, DC 20035-6738
Telephone: (202) 514-0301 or
(800) 514-0301
http://www.dinf.org/crt/ada/adahom1.htm
See listing under Federal Agencies

Consultation and Technical Assistance— Model Building Code Organizations

The organizations listed in this section provide information about local building codes and access requirements for buildings and facilities in local jurisdictions. They are also involved in developing and providing model building codes.

American National Standards Institute A117.1 Committee
c/o International Code Council
5203 Leesburgh Pike, Suite 708
Falls Church, VA 22041-3401
Telephone: (703) 931-4533
Fax: (703) 379-1546
http://www.intlcode.org

Building Officials and Code Administrators International
4051 West Flossmoor Road
Country Club Hills, IL 60478-5795
Telephone: (708) 799-2300
Fax: (708) 799-4981
E-mail: boca@aecnet.com
http://www.bocai.org

International Code Council (formerly Council of American Building Officials)
5203 Leesburgh Pike, Suite 708
Falls Church, VA 22041
Telephone: (703) 931-4533
Fax: (703) 379-1546
http://www.intlcode.org

International Conference of Building Officials
5360 Workman Mill Road
Whittier, CA 90601-2298
Telephone: (562) 699-0541
Fax: (562) 699-4522
E-mail: johnson@icbo.org
http://www.icbo.org

National Conference of States on Building Codes and Standards
505 Huntmar Park Drive, Suite 210
Herndon, VA 22070
Telephone: (703) 437-0100
Fax: (703) 481-3596
http://www.ncsbcs.org

Southern Building Code Congress International
900 Montclair Road
Birmingham, AL 35236
Telephone: (205) 591-1853
Fax: (205) 591-0775

SOURCES OF PRODUCTS AND SERVICES

Selected Sources of Braille Materials

The organizations listed in this section are a sample of those that can help readers obtain braille translations of print documents. The *AFB Directory of Services for Blind and Visually Impaired Persons in the United States and Canada* provides more complete listings of sources. The National Library Service for the Blind and Physically Handicapped (see listing under Federal Agencies) supplies information on sources for braille transcription, braille books, equipment for writing braille, and the like.

American Printing House for the Blind
1839 Frankfort Avenue
P.O. Box 6085
Louisville, KY 40206-0085
Telephone: (502) 895-2405;
(800) 223-1839
Fax: (502) 899-2274
E-mail: info@aph.org
http://www.aph.org

Associated Services for the Blind
919 Walnut Street
Philadelphia, PA 19108
Telephone: (215) 627-0600
Fax: (215) 922-0692
E-mail: asbinfo@libertynet.org

Braille Inc.
184 Seapit Road
P.O. Box 457
East Falmouth, MA 02536-0457
Telephone: (508) 540-0800
Fax: (508) 548-6116
E-mail: braillinc@c2pecod.net

Braille International
3290 S.E. Slater Street
Stuart, FL 34997
Telephone: (407) 286-8366;
(800) 336-3142
Fax: (407) 286-8909

Howe Press of Perkins School for the Blind
175 North Beacon Street
Watertown, MA 02172
Telephone: (617) 924-3490
Fax: (617) 926-2027

Metrolina Association for the Blind
704 Louise Avenue
Charlotte, NC 28204
Telephone: (704) 372-3870;
(800) 926-5466
Fax: (704) 373-3872

National Braille Press
88 St. Stephen Street
Boston, MA 02115
Telephone: (617) 266-6160;
(800) 548-7323
Fax: (617) 437-0456
E-mail: orders@nbp.org

Print Access Center
The Lighthouse International
111 East 59th Street
New York, NY 10022
Telephone: (212) 821-9681
Fax: (212) 821-9707
E-mail: braille@lighthouse.org;
astevenson@lighthouse.org
http://www.lighthouse.org

Prose & Cons Braille Unit
P.O. Box 2500
Lincoln, NE 68542-2500
Telephone: (402) 471-3161, ext. 3373
Fax: (402) 471-3472

Sight Line Productions
505 Paradise Road, Suite 200
Swampscott, MA 01907

Telephone: (617) 595-9800
Fax: (617) 595-9800
E-mail: psudore@datablast.net

Visual Aid Volunteers
617 State Street
Garland, TX 75040
Telephone: (972) 272-1615
Fax: (972) 494-5002

Selected Sources of Recorded Materials

This section provides a selected listing of organizations that can help readers obtain recorded versions of their print materials. For additional listings, see the *AFB Directory of Services for Blind and Visually Impaired Persons in the United States and Canada.*

**American Printing House
for the Blind**
1839 Frankfort Avenue
P.O. Box 6085
Louisville, KY 40206-0085
Telephone: (502) 895-2405;
(800) 223-1839
Fax: (502) 899-2274
E-mail: info@aph.org
http://www.aph.org

**Audio Studio for the Reading
Impaired**
P.O. Box 23043
Anchorage, KY 40223
Telephone: (502) 245-5422

Cutting Corporation
4940 Hampden Lane, Suite 300
Bethesda, MD 20814
Telephone: (301) 654-2887
Fax: (301) 657-9057
E-mail: research@cutti.com

Evatone
4801 Ulmerton Road
Clearwater, FL 34622
Telephone: (813) 572-7000
Fax: (813) 572-6214
E-mail: pat.augustine@eva-tone.com

Magnetix
770 West Bay Street
Winter Garden, FL 37487
Telephone: (407) 656-4494
Fax: (407) 656-4825
E-mail: magnetix1@aol.com

Recording for the Blind and Dyslexic
20 Roszel Road
Princeton, NJ 08540
Telephone: (609) 452-0606;
(800) 221-4792
Fax: (609) 987-8116

RPL
1100 State Street
Camden, NJ 08102
Telephone: (609) 963-3000
Fax: (609) 963-3854
E-mail: rplmedia@rplmedia.com
http://www.rplmedia.com

Sun Sounds
7290 East Broadway
Tucson, AZ 85710
Telephone: (520) 296-2400 (Tucson);
(602) 231-0500 (Phoenix)
Fax: (520) 298-6676 (Tucson);
(602) 220-9335 (Phoenix)
E-mail: mtharin@aol.com (Tucson);
pasco@rio.maricopa.edu (Phoenix)

Talking Book Publishers
P.O. Box 1653
Englewood, CO 80150
Telephone: (303) 778-8606

TinMan
2800 Yellow Brick Road
St. Louis, MO 63129
Telephone: (314) 487-3735
Fax: (314) 487-1910

Selected Sources of Multimedia and Access Technology

The organizations listed here provide technical solutions for making information accessible using auditory output, audiodescription, and tactile displays. Some solutions involve interactive use of auditory, visual, and tactile media.

Acoustiguide Worldwide
1301 Avenue of the Americas,
32nd Floor
New York, NY 10019
Telephone: (212) 974-6600
Fax: (212) 974-6607
E-mail: acwwny@aol.com
Creates audiotours for cultural facilities and historic sites using a wide range of audio technologies and creative solutions.

Audio Description
Metropolitan Washington Ear
35 University Boulevard East
Silver Spring, MD 20901
Telephone: (301) 681-6636
Trains describers, guides, and docents in audiodescription; publishes a newsletter for individuals interested in audiodescription; and helps other organizations launch audiodescription services.

Computer Center for Visually Impaired People
Baruch College
City University of New York
151 East 25th Street
P.O. Box H 648
New York, NY 10010
Telephone: (212) 802-2140
Fax: (212) 802-2103
http://www.baruch.cuny.edu/ccvip
Offers services and tools to improve both physical and informational access to transit facilities, museums, and exhibits for patrons who are blind or visually impaired, including computerized audio/tactile computer graphic interfaces, computer-driven accessible kiosks, and raised-line and textured tactile graphics for wayfinding and explanatory materials.

Crane National Vendors
12955 Enterprise Way
Bridgeton, MO 63044-1200
Telephone: (314) 298-3500
Fax: (314) 298-3505
Manufactures and distributes "talking" vending machines.

Descriptive Video Service
WGBH-TV
125 Western Avenue
Boston, MA 02134
Telephone: (617) 492-2777
Fax: (617) 783-8668, ext. 3490
E-mail: laurie-everett@wgbh.org
http://www.boston.com.wgbh/dvs
Provides audiodescription for public and cable television as well as non-broadcast films and videos; provides description in IMAX and OMNI MAX movie theaters; operates a mail-order catalog of described movies and public television documentaries; and publishes a quarterly newsletter.

Narrative Television Networks
5840 South Memorial Drive, Suite 312
Tulsa, OK 74175
Telephone: (918) 627-1000

Fax: (918) 627-4101
E-mail: narrative@aol.com
Produces audiodescription for movies for cable television.

Talking Signs
812 North Boulevard
Baton Rouge, LA 70802
Telephone: (504) 344-2812
Fax: (504) 344-2811
Produces and supplies Talking Signs.

Trace Research and Development Center
University of Wisconsin–Madison
5901 Research Park Boulevard
Madison, WI 53719-1252
Telephone: (608) 262-6966
TTY: (608) 263-5408
Fax: (608) 262-8848
E-mail: web@trace.wisc.edu
http://trace.wisc.edu/
Provides EZ Access features to make accessible touchscreen information in such devices as kiosks, ATMs, building directories, and ticketing on fare machines.

Selected Sources of Assistive Technology and Computer Products

This section lists a representative sampling of manufacturers of assistive devices that enable people who are blind or visually impaired to obtain access to information available in print, frequently through computer technology, as well as the types of devices they generally provide. For more information on assistive technology and additional sources of products, contact the AFB National Technology Program; see the AFB listing under Organizations in the Field of Blindness.

Ai Squared
P.O. Box 669
Manchester Center, VT 05255
Telephone: (802) 362-3612
Fax: (802) 362-1670
E-mail: sales@aisquared.com;
@aisquared.com (support)
http://www.aisquared.com
Screen magnification software

Arkenstone
555 Oakmead Parkway
Sunnyvale, CA 94086
Telephone: (408) 245-5900;
(800) 444-4443
Fax: (408) 745-6739
http://www.arkenstone.org
OCR systems

Artic Technologies
55 Park Street

Troy, MI 48083
Telephone: (248) 588-7370
Fax: (248) 588-2650
E-mail: artic@ic.net
http://www.artictech.com
Screen magnification software

Blazie Engineering
105 East Jerretsville Road
Forest Hill, MD 21050
Telephone: (410) 836-5040
http://www.blazie.com
Braille printers and notetakers

Henter-Joyce
11800 31st Court North
St. Petersburg, FL 33716
Telephone: (800) 336-5658
Fax: (813) 803-8001
E-mail: info@hj.com
http://www.hj.com

Screen magnification software, synthetic speech systems

HumanWare
6245 King Road
Loomis, CA 95650
Telephone: (916) 652-7253;
(800) 722-3393
Fax: (916) 652-7296
E-mail: info@humanware.com
http://www.humanware.com
Braille printers and notetakers, braille display, synthetic speech systems, CCTVs, tactile image machines.

Kurzweil Educational Systems
411 Waverly Oaks Road
Waltham, MA 02154
Telephone: (617) 893-8200;
(800) 894-5374
Fax: (617) 893-4157
E-mail: info@kurzweiledu.com
http://www.kurzweiledu.com
Stand-alone or computer-based OCR systems

Optelec USA
4 Liberty Way
Westford, MA 01866
Telephone: (508) 392-0707;
(800) 828-1056
Fax: (508) 692-6073
E-mail: optelec@optelec.com
http://www.optelec.com
CCTV systems

TeleSensory Corporation
520 Almanor Avenue
Sunnyvale, CA 94086-3533
Telephone: (408) 616-8700;
(800) 286-8484
Fax: (408) 616-8753
E-mail: info@telesensory.com
http://www.telesensory.com
OCR systems, screen magnification systems, synthetic speech systems

Xerox Adaptive Products
9 Centennial Drive
Peabody, MA 01960
Telephone: (508) 977-2148,
(800) 248-6550
E-mail: doiron@xis.xerox.com
http://www.xerox.com
OCR and CCTV systems

Selected Sources of Products for Independent Living

The catalogs and businesses listed in this section offer a wide variety of products—such as talking clocks and calculators, large-print telephone keypads, signature guides, and communication aids—that help people who are blind or visually impaired carry on everyday activities. For a more complete listing, see the *AFB Directory of Products and Services for Blind and Visually Impaired Persons in the United States and Canada* (1997).

American Printing House for the Blind
P.O. Box 6085, Department 0086
Louisville, KY 40206-0085
Telephone: (800) 223-1839 (customer service); (800) 572-0844 (sales)
Fax: (502) 899-2274
E-mail: info@aph.org
http://www.aph.org

Ann Morris Enterprises, Inc.
890 Fams Court
East Meadow, NY 11554
Telephone: (516) 292-9232;
(800) 454-3175
Fax: (516) 292-2522
E-mail: annmor@netcom.com
http://tribeca.ios.com/tildaannm2

Enabling Technologies Company
3102 S.E. Jay Street
Stuart, FL 34997
Telephone: (407) 283-4817
Fax: (407) 220-2920

**Howe Press of Perkins School
for the Blind**
175 North Beacon Street
Watertown, MA 02172
Telephone: (617) 924-3490
Fax: (617) 926-2027

Independent Living Aids
27 East Mall
Plainview, NY 11803
Telephone: (800) 537-2118;
(516) 752-8080
Fax: (516) 752-3135
E-mail: indlivaids@aol.com
http://www.independentliving.com

Lighthouse Consumer Products
36-20 Northern Boulevard
Long Island City, NY 11101
Telephone: (718) 937-6959;
(800) 829-0500
E-mail: jjenkins@lighthouse.org
http://www.lighthouse.org

Lighthouse Low Vision Products
36-02 Northern Boulevard
Long Island City, NY 11101
Telephone: (718) 937-6959;
(800) 453-4293

LS&S Group, Inc.
P.O. Box 673
Northbrook, IL 60065
Telephone: (800) 468-4789;
(847) 498-9777
Fax: (847) 498-1482
E-mail: lssgrp@aol.com
http://www.lssgroup.com

Maxi-Aids
42 Executive Boulevard
P.O. Box 3209
Farmingdale, NY 11735
Telephone: (800) 522-6294;
(516) 752-0521
Fax: (516) 752-0689
E-mail: sales@maxiaids.com
http://www.maxiaids.com

**National Association
for Visually Handicapped**
22 West 21st Street, Sixth Floor
New York, NY 10010
Telephone: (212) 889-3141;
(415) 221-3201 (California only)
Fax: (212) 727-2931
E-mail: staff@navh.org
http://www.navh.org

National Federation of the Blind
1800 Johnson Street
Baltimore, MD 21230
Telephone: (410) 659-9314
Fax: (410) 685-5653
http://www.nfb.org

Science Products
P.O. Box 888
Southeastern, PA 19399
Telephone: (800) 888-7400;
(610) 296-2111
Fax: (610) 296-0488
Specializes in talking measuring tools and products used for commercial applications such as talking cash registers and talking scales.

Sense-Sations
Associated Services for the Blind
919 Walnut Street
Philadelphia, PA 19107
Telephone: (215) 627-0600, ext. 202

Recommended Reading

The materials listed in this bibliography will help readers to find further details on the topics discussed in this guide and to get information on other ADA-related topics that are not covered in this volume.

Accommodation and accessibility: Implementing ADA on a local level. (1992). New York: American Foundation for the Blind.

Accessible and usable buildings and facilities (ANSI 117.1, rev. ed.). (1998). Falls Church, VA: American National Standards Institute.

AFB ADA Consulting Group. (1992). *Making the ADA work for you: A video training seminar* [videotape]. New York: AFB Press.

AFB ADA Consulting Group. (1993). *Strategies for community access: Braille and raised large print facility signs* [videotape]. New York: American Foundation for the Blind.

ADAAG Review Advisory Committee. (September 1996). *Recommendations for a new ADAAG.* Washington, DC: U.S. Architectural and Transportation Barriers Compliance Board.

AFB directory of services for blind and visually impaired persons in the United States and Canada, 25th Edition (1997, book and CD-ROM). New York: AFB Press.

Barker, P., Barrick, J., & Wilson, R. (1995). *Building sight: A handbook of building and interior design solutions to include the needs of visually impaired people.* London: Royal National Institute for the Blind; distributed by AFB Press.

Bruyere, S. M., & Golden, T. P. (1996). *The job developer's guide to the Americans with Disabilities Act.* St. Augustine, FL: Training Resource Network.

Equal Employment Opportunity Commission. (January 1992). *A technical assistance manual on the employment provisions of the Americans with Disabilities Act,* Vols. I & II. Washington, DC: Government Printing Office.

Equal Employment Opportunity Commission. (1999). *Reasonable accommodation and undue hardship under the Americans with Disabilities Act (ADA).* Washington, DC: Author.

Equal Employment Opportunity Commission & U.S. Department of Justice. (October 1991). *Americans with Disabilities Act handbook.* Washington, DC: Government Printing Office.

Fersh, D., & Thomas, P. (1993). *Complying with the Americans with Disabilities Act: A guidebook for management and people with disabilities.* Westport, CT: Quorum Books.

Joffee, E. (1992, May-June). The ADA and public schools. *Journal of Visual Impairment & Blindness, 88* (3), 6–7.

Joffee, E., & Siller, M. A. (1997). *Reaching out: A creative access guide for designing exhibits and cultural programs for persons who are blind or visually impaired.* New York: AFB Press.

Morrissey, P. A. (1991). A primer for corporate America on civil rights for the disabled. Horsham, PA: LRP Publications.

National Council on Disability. (1995). *The Americans with Disabilities Act: Ensuring access to the American dream.* Washington, DC: Author.

National Council on Disability. (1997). *Equality of opportunity: The making of the Americans with Disabilities Act.* Washington, DC: Author.

Program on Employment and Disability. (1994.) *Working effectively with people who are blind or visually impaired.* New York: Cornell University.

Schroeder, P.W. (1993). *The Americans with Disabilities Act: A guide for people who are blind or visually impaired.* Washington, DC: American Council of the Blind.

U.S. Architectural and Transportation Barriers Compliance Board. (1992). *Americans with Disabilities Act accessibilities guidelines (ADAAG). Checklist for buildings and facilities.* Washington, DC: Author.

U.S. Architectural and Transportation Barriers Compliance Board. (1998). *Americans with Disabilities Act (ADA) accessibility guidelines for buildings and facilities; State and local government facilities.* Final Rule.

U.S. Department of Justice. (1998). *Enforcing the ADA: A status report.* Washington, DC: Author.

Uslan, M. M., Peck, A. F., Wiener, W. R., & Stern, A. (Eds.). (1990). *Access to mass transit for blind and visually impaired travelers.* New York: American Foundation for the Blind.

Welch, P. (Ed.). (1995). *Strategies for teaching universal design.* Boston: Adaptive Environments Center.

West, J. (Ed.). (1991). *The Americans with Disabilities Act: From policy to practice.* New York: Milbank Memorial Fund.

Americans with Disabilities Act of 1990

PUBLIC LAW 101–336 JULY 26, 1990
One Hundred First Congress of the United States of America
At the Second Session
Begun and held at the City of Washington on Tuesday, the twenty-third day of January, one thousand nine hundred and ninety.

AN ACT

To establish a clear and comprehensive prohibition of discrimination on the basis of disability.

Be it enacted by the Senate and House of Representatives of the United States of America in Congress assembled,

SECTION 1. SHORT TITLE; TABLE OF CONTENTS.

(a) Short Title. This Act may be cited as the "Americans with Disabilities Act of 1990."

(b) Table of Contents. The table of contents is as follows:

SEC. 2. FINDINGS AND PURPOSES

(a) Findings. The Congress finds that

(1) some 43,000,000 Americans have one or more physical or mental disabilities, and this number is increasing as the population as a whole is growing older;

(2) historically, society has tended to isolate and segregate individuals with disabilities, and, despite some improvements, such forms of discrimination against individuals with disabilities continue to be a serious and pervasive social problem;

(3) discrimination against individuals with disabilities persists in such critical areas as employment, housing, public accommodations, education, transportation, communication, recreation, institutionalization, health services, voting, and access to public services;

(4) unlike individuals who have experienced discrimination on the basis of race, color, sex, national origin, religion, or age, individuals who have experienced discrimination on the basis of disability have often had no legal recourse to redress such discrimination;

(5) individuals with disabilities continually encounter various forms of discrimination, including outright intentional exclusion, the discriminatory effects of architectural, transportation, and communication barriers, overprotective rules and policies, failure to make modifications to existing facilities and practices, exclusionary qualification standards and criteria, segregation, and relegation to lesser services, programs, activities, benefits, jobs, or other opportunities;

(6) census data, national polls, and other studies have documented that people with disabilities, as a group, occupy an inferior status in our society, and are severely disadvantaged socially, vocationally, economically, and educationally;

(7) individuals with disabilities are a discrete and insular minority who have been faced with restrictions and limitations, subjected to a history of purposeful unequal treatment, and relegated to a position of political powerlessness in our society, based on characteristics that are beyond the control of such individuals and resulting from stereotypic assumptions not truly indicative of the individual ability of such individuals to participate in, and contribute to, society;

(8) the Nation's proper goals regarding individuals with disabilities are to assure equality of opportunity, full participation, independent living, and economic self-sufficiency for such individuals; and

(9) the continuing existence of unfair and unnecessary discrimination and prejudice denies people with disabilities the opportunity to compete on an equal basis and to pursue those opportunities for which our free society is justifiably famous, and costs the United States billions of dollars in unnecessary expenses resulting from dependency and nonproductivity.

(b) Purpose. It is the purpose of this Act

(1) to provide a clear and comprehensive national mandate for the elimination of discrimination against individuals with disabilities;

(2) to provide clear, strong, consistent, enforceable standards addressing discrimination against individuals with disabilities;

(3) to ensure that the Federal Government plays a central role in enforcing the standards established in this Act on behalf of individuals with disabilities; and

(4) to invoke the sweep of congressional authority, including the power to enforce the fourteenth amendment and to regulate commerce, in order to address the major areas of discrimination faced day-to-day by people with disabilities.

SEC. 3. DEFINITIONS.

As used in this Act:

(1) Auxiliary aids and services. The term "auxiliary aids and services" includes—

(A) qualified interpreters or other effective methods of making aurally delivered materials available to individuals with hearing impairments;

(B) qualified readers, taped texts, or other effective methods of making visually delivered materials available to individuals with visual impairments;

(C) acquisition or modification of equipment or devices; and

(D) other similar services and actions.

(2) Disability. The term "disability" means, with respect to an individual—

(A) a physical or mental impairment that substantially limits one or more of the major life activities of such individual;

(B) a record of such an impairment; or

(C) being regarded as having such an impairment.

(3) State. The term "State" means each of the several States, the District of Columbia, the Commonwealth of Puerto Rico, Guam, American Samoa, the Virgin Islands, the Trust Territory of the Pacific Islands, and the Commonwealth of the Northern Mariana Islands.

TITLE I—EMPLOYMENT
SEC. 101. DEFINITIONS.

As used in this title:

(1) Commission. The term "Commission" means the Equal Employment Opportunity Commission established by section 705 of the Civil Rights Act of 1964 (42 U.S.C. 2000e-4).

(2) Covered entity. The term "covered entity" means an employer, employment agency, labor organization, or joint labor-management committee.

(3) Direct threat. The term "direct threat" means a significant risk to the health or safety of others that cannot be eliminated by reasonable accommodation.

(4) Employee. The term "employee" means an individual employed by an employer. With respect to employment in a foreign country, such term includes an individual who is a citizen of the United States.

(5) Employer.

(A) In general. The term "employer" means a person engaged in an industry affecting commerce who has 15 or more employees for each working day in each of 20 or more calendar weeks in the current or preceding calendar year, and any agent of such person, except that, for two years following the effective date of this title, an employer means a person engaged in an industry affecting commerce who has 25 or more employees for each working day in each of 20 or more calendar weeks in the current or preceding year, and any agent of such person.

(B) Exceptions. The term "employer" does not include (i) the United States, a corporation wholly owned by the government of the United States, or an Indian tribe; or (ii) a bona fide private membership club (other than a labor organization) that is exempt from taxation under section 501(c) of the Internal Revenue Code of 1986.

(6) Illegal use of drugs.

(A) In general. The term "illegal use of drugs" means the use of drugs, the possession or distribution of which is unlawful under the Controlled Substances Act (21 U.S.C. 812). Such term does not include the use of a drug taken under supervision by a licensed health care professional, or other uses authorized by the Controlled Substances Act or other provisions of Federal law.

(B) Drugs. The term "drug" means a controlled substance, as defined in schedules I through V of section 202 of the Controlled Substances Act.

(7) Person, etc. The terms "person," "labor organization," "employment agency," "commerce," and "industry affecting commerce," shall have the same meaning given such terms in section 701 of the Civil Rights Act of 1964 (42 U.S.C. 2000e).

(8) Qualified individual with a disability. The term "qualified individual with a disability" means an individual with a disability who, with or without reasonable accommodation, can perform the essential functions of the employment position that such individual holds or desires. For the purposes of this title, consideration shall be given to the employer's judgment as to what functions of a job are essential, and if an employer has prepared a written description before advertising or interviewing applicants for the job, this description shall be considered evidence of the essential functions of the job.

(9) Reasonable accommodation. The term "reasonable accommodation" may include

(A) making existing facilities used by employees readily accessible to and usable by individuals with disabilities; and

(B) job restructuring, part-time or modified work schedules, reassignment to a vacant position, acquisition or modification of equipment or devices, appropriate adjustment or modifications of examinations, training materials or policies, the provision of qualified readers or interpreters, and other similar accommodations for individuals with disabilities.

(10) Undue hardship.

(A) In general. The term "undue hardship" means an action requiring significant difficulty or expense, when considered in light of the factors set forth in subparagraph (B).

(B) Factors to be considered. In determining whether an accommodation would impose an undue hardship on a covered entity, factors to be considered include

(i) the nature and cost of the accommodation needed under this Act;

(ii) the overall financial resources of the facility or facilities involved in the provision of the reasonable accommodation; the number of persons employed at such facility; the effect on expenses and resources, or the impact otherwise of such accommodation upon the operation of the facility;

(iii) the overall financial resources of the covered entity; the overall size of the business of a covered entity with respect to the number of its employees; the number, type, and location of its facilities; and

(iv) the type of operation or operations of the covered entity, including the composition, structure, and functions of the workforce of such entity; the geographic separateness, administrative, or fiscal relationship of the facility or facilities in question to the covered entity.

SEC. 102. DISCRIMINATION.

(a) General Rule. No covered entity shall discriminate against a qualified individual with a disability because of the disability of such individual in regard to job application procedures, the hiring, advancement, or discharge of employees, employee compensation, job training, and other terms, conditions, and privileges of employment.

(b) Construction. As used in subsection (a), the term "discriminate" includes

(1) limiting, segregating, or classifying a job applicant or employee in a way that adversely affects the opportunities or status of such applicant or employee because of the disability of such applicant or employee;

(2) participating in a contractual or other arrangement or relationship that has the effect of subjecting a covered entity's qualified applicant or employee with a disability to the discrimination prohibited by this title (such relationship includes a relationship with an employment or referral agency, labor union, an organization providing fringe benefits to an employee of the covered entity, or an organization providing training and apprenticeship programs);

(3) utilizing standards, criteria, or methods of administration

(A) that have the effect of discrimination on the basis of disability; or

(B) that perpetuate the discrimination of others who are subject to common administrative control;

(4) excluding or otherwise denying equal jobs or benefits to a qualified individual because of the known disability of an individual with whom the qualified individual is known to have a relationship or association;

(5)

(A) not making reasonable accommodations to the known physical or mental limitations of an otherwise qualified individual with a disability who is an applicant or employee, unless such covered entity can demonstrate that the accommodation would impose an undue hardship on the operation of the business of such covered entity; or

(B) denying employment opportunities to a job applicant or employee who is an otherwise qualified individual with a disability, if such denial is based on the need of such covered entity to make reasonable accommodation to the physical or mental impairments of the employee or applicant;

(6) using qualification standards, employment tests or other selection criteria that screen out or tend to screen out an individual with a disability or a class of individuals with disabilities unless the standard, test or other selection criteria, as used by the covered entity, is shown to be job-related for the position in question and is consistent with business necessity; and

(7) failing to select and administer tests concerning employment in the most effective manner to ensure that, when such test is administered to a job applicant or employee who has a disability that impairs sensory, manual, or speaking skills, such test results accurately reflect the skills, aptitude, or whatever other factor of such applicant or employee that such test purports to measure, rather than reflecting the impaired sensory, manual, or speaking skills of such employee or applicant (except where such skills are the factors that the test purports to measure).

(c) Covered Entities in Foreign Countries.

(1) In general. It shall not be unlawful under this section for a covered entity to take any action that constitutes discrimination under this section with respect to an employee in a workplace in a foreign country if compliance with this section would cause such covered entity to violate the law of the foreign country in which such workplace is located.

(2) Control of Corporation.

(A) Presumption. If an employer controls a corporation whose place of incorporation is a foreign country, any practice that constitutes discrimination under this section and is engaged in by such corporation shall be presumed to be engaged in by such employer.

(B) Exception. This section shall not apply with respect to the foreign operations of an employer that is a foreign person not controlled by an American employer.

(C) Determination. For purposes of this paragraph, the determination of whether an employer controls a corporation shall be based on

(i) the interrelation of operations;

(ii) the common management;

(iii) the centralized control of labor relations; and

(iv) the common ownership or financial control of the employer and the corporation.

(d) Medical Examinations and Inquiries.

(1) In general. The prohibition against discrimination as referred to in subsection (a) shall include medical examinations and inquiries.

(2) Preemployment.

(A) Prohibited examination or inquiry. Except as provided in paragraph (3), a covered entity shall not conduct a medical examination or make inquiries of a job applicant as to whether such applicant is an individual with a disability or as to the nature or severity of such disability.

(B) Acceptable inquiry. A covered entity may make preemployment inquiries into the ability of an applicant to perform job-related functions.

(3) Employment entrance examination. A covered entity may require a medical examination after an offer of employment has been made to a job applicant and prior to the commencement of the employment duties of such applicant, and may condition an offer of employment on the results of such examination, if

(A) all entering employees are subjected to such an examination regardless of disability;

(B) information obtained regarding the medical condition or history of the applicant is collected and maintained on separate forms and in separate medical files and is treated as a confidential medical record, except that

(i) supervisors and managers may be informed regarding necessary restrictions on the work or duties of the employee and necessary accommodations;

(ii) first aid and safety personnel may be informed, when appropriate, if the disability might require emergency treatment; and

(iii) government officials investigating compliance with this Act shall be provided relevant information on request; and

(C) the results of such examination are used only in accordance with this title.

(4) Examination and inquiry.

(A) Prohibited examinations and inquiries. A covered entity shall not require a medical examination and shall not make inquiries of an employee as to whether such employee is an individual with a disability or as to the nature or severity of the disability, unless such examination or inquiry is shown to be job-related and consistent with business necessity.

(B) Acceptable examinations and inquiries. A covered entity may conduct voluntary medical examinations, including voluntary medical histories, which are part of an employee health program available to employees at that work site. A covered entity may make inquiries into the ability of an employee to perform job-related functions.

(C) Requirement. Information obtained under subparagraph (B) regarding the medical condition or history of any employee are subject to the requirements of subparagraphs (B) and (C) of paragraph (3).

SEC. 103. DEFENSES.

(a) In General. It may be a defense to a charge of discrimination under this Act that an alleged application of qualification standards, tests, or selection criteria that screen out or tend to screen out or otherwise deny a job or benefit to an individual with a disability has been shown to be job-related and consistent with business necessity, and such performance cannot be accomplished by reasonable accommodation, as required under this title.

(b) Qualification Standards. The term "qualification standards" may include a requirement that an individual shall not pose a direct threat to the health or safety of other individuals in the workplace.

(c) Religious Entities.

(1) In general. This title shall not prohibit a religious corporation, association, educational institution, or society from giving preference in employment to individuals of a particular religion to perform work connected with the carrying on by such corporation, association, educational institution, or society of its activities.

(2) Religious tenets requirement. Under this title, a religious organization may require that all applicants and employees conform to the religious tenets of such organization.

(d) List of Infectious and Communicable Diseases.

(1) In general. The Secretary of Health and Human Services, not later than 6 months after the date of enactment of this Act, shall

(A) review all infectious and communicable diseases which may be transmitted through handling the food supply;

(B) publish a list of infectious and communicable diseases which are transmitted through handling the food supply;

(C) publish the methods by which such diseases are transmitted; and

(D) widely disseminate such information regarding the list of diseases and their modes of transmissibility to the general public. Such list shall be updated annually.

(2) Applications. In any case in which an individual has an infectious or communicable disease that is transmitted to others through the handling of food, that is included on the list developed by the Secretary of Health and Human Services under paragraph (1), and which cannot be eliminated by reasonable accommodation, a covered entity may refuse to assign or continue to assign such individual to a job involving food handling.

(3) Construction. Nothing in this Act shall be construed to preempt, modify, or amend any State, county, or local law, ordinance, or regulation applicable to food handling which is designed to protect the public health from individuals who pose a significant risk to the health or safety of others, which cannot be eliminated by reasonable accommodation, pursuant to the list of infectious or communicable diseases and the modes of transmissibility published by the Secretary of Health and Human Services.

SEC. 104. ILLEGAL USE OF DRUGS AND ALCOHOL.

(a) Qualified Individual With a Disability. For purposes of this title, the term "qualified individual with a disability" shall not include any employee or applicant who is currently engaging in the illegal use of drugs, when the covered entity acts on the basis of such use.

(b) Rules of Construction. Nothing in subsection (a) shall be construed to exclude as a qualified individual with a disability an individual who

(1) has successfully completed a supervised drug rehabilitation program and is no longer engaging in the illegal use of drugs, or has otherwise been rehabilitated successfully and is no longer engaging in such use;

(2) is participating in a supervised rehabilitation program and is no longer engaging in such use; or

(3) is erroneously regarded as engaging in such use, but is not engaging in such use; except that it shall not be a violation of this Act for a covered entity to adopt or administer reasonable policies or procedures, including but not limited to drug testing, designed to ensure that an individual described in paragraph (1) or (2) is no longer engaging in the illegal use of drugs.

(c) Authority of Covered Entity. A covered entity

(1) may prohibit the illegal use of drugs and the use of alcohol at the workplace by all employees;

(2) may require that employees shall not be under the influence of alcohol or be engaging in the illegal use of drugs at the workplace;

(3) may require that employees behave in conformance with the requirements established under the Drug-Free Workplace Act of 1988 (41 U.S.C. 701 et seq.);

(4) may hold an employee who engages in the illegal use of drugs or who is an alcoholic to the same qualification standards for employment or job performance and behavior that such entity holds other employees, even if any unsatisfactory performance or behavior is related to the drug use or alcoholism of such employee; and

(5) may, with respect to Federal regulations regarding alcohol and the illegal use of drugs, require that

(A) employees comply with the standards established in such regulations of the Department of Defense, if the employees of the covered entity are employed in an industry subject to such regulations, including complying with regulations (if any) that apply to employment in sensitive positions in such an industry, in the case of employees of the covered entity who are employed in such positions (as defined in the regulations of the Department of Defense);

(B) employees comply with the standards established in such regulations of the Nuclear Regulatory Commission, if the employees of the covered entity are employed in an industry subject to such regulations, including complying with regulations (if any) that apply to employment in sensitive positions in such an industry, in the case of employees of the covered entity who are employed in such positions (as defined in the regulations of the Nuclear Regulatory Commission); and

(C) employees comply with the standards established in such regulations of the Department of Transportation, if the employees of the covered entity are employed in a transportation industry subject to such regulations, including complying with such regulations (if any) that apply to employment in sensitive positions in such an industry, in the case of employees of the covered entity who are employed in such positions (as defined in the regulations of the Department of Transportation).

(d) Drug Testing.

(1) In general. For purposes of this title, a test to determine the illegal use of drugs shall not be considered a medical examination.

(2) Construction. Nothing in this title shall be construed to encourage, prohibit, or authorize the conducting of drug testing for the illegal use of drugs by job applicants or employees or making employment decisions based on such test results.

(e) Transportation Employees. Nothing in this title shall be construed to encourage, prohibit, restrict, or authorize the otherwise lawful exercise by entities subject to the jurisdiction of the Department of Transportation of authority to

(1) test employees of such entities in, and applicants for, positions involving safety-sensitive duties for the illegal use of drugs and for on-duty impairment by alcohol; and

(2) remove such persons who test positive for illegal use of drugs and on-duty impairment by alcohol pursuant to paragraph (1) from safety-sensitive duties in implementing subsection (c).

SEC. 105. POSTING NOTICES.

Every employer, employment agency, labor organization, or joint labor-management committee covered under this title shall post notices in an accessible format to applicants, employees, and members describing the applicable provisions of this Act, in the manner prescribed by section 711 of the Civil Rights Act of 1964 (42 U.S.C. 2000e-10).

SEC. 106. REGULATIONS.

Not later than 1 year after the date of enactment of this Act, the Commission shall issue regulations in an accessible format to carry out this title in accordance with subchapter II of chapter 5 of title 5, United States Code.

SEC. 107. ENFORCEMENT.

(a) Powers, Remedies, and Procedures. The powers, remedies, and procedures set forth in sections 705, 706, 707, 709, and 710 of the Civil Rights Act of 1964 (42 U.S.C. 2000e-4, 2000e-5, 2000e-6, 2000e-8, and 2000e-9) shall be the powers, remedies, and procedures this title provides to the Commission, to the Attorney General, or to any person alleging discrimination on the basis of disability in violation of any provision of this Act, or regulations promulgated under section 106, concerning employment.

(b) Coordination. The agencies with enforcement authority for actions which allege employment discrimination under this title and under the Rehabilitation Act of 1973 shall develop procedures to ensure that administrative complaints filed under this title and under the Rehabilitation Act of 1973 are dealt with in a manner that avoids duplication of effort and prevents imposition of inconsistent or conflicting standards for the same requirements under this title and the Rehabilitation Act of 1973. The Commission, the Attorney General, and the Office of Federal Contract Compliance Programs shall establish such coordinating mechanisms (similar to provisions contained in the joint regulations promulgated by the Commission and the Attorney General at part 42 of title 28 and part 1691 of title 29, Code of Federal Regulations, and the Memorandum of Understanding between the Commission and the Office of Federal Contract Compliance Programs dated January 16, 1981 (46 Fed. Reg. 7435, January 23, 1981)) in regulations implementing this title and Rehabilitation Act of 1973 not later than 18 months after the date of enactment of this Act.

SEC. 108. EFFECTIVE DATE.

This title shall become effective 24 months after the date of enactment.

TITLE II—PUBLIC SERVICES

Subtitle A—Prohibition Against Discrimination and Other Generally Applicable Provisions

SEC. 201. DEFINITION.

As used in this title:

(1) Public entity. The term "public entity" means

(A) any State or local government;

(B) any department, agency, special purpose district, or other instrumentality of a State or States or local government; and

(C) the National Railroad Passenger Corporation, and any commuter authority (as defined in section 103(8) of the Rail Passenger Service Act).

(2) Qualified individual with a disability. The term "qualified individual with a disability" means an individual with a disability who, with or without reasonable modifications to rules, policies, or practices, the removal of architectural, communication, or transportation barriers, or the provision of auxiliary aids and services, meets the essential eligibility requirements for the receipt of services or the participation in programs or activities provided by a public entity.

SEC. 202. DISCRIMINATION.

Subject to the provisions of this title, no qualified individual with a disability shall, by reason of such disability, be excluded from participation in or be denied the benefits of the services, programs, or activities of a public entity, or be subjected to discrimination by any such entity.

SEC. 203. ENFORCEMENT.

The remedies, procedures, and rights set forth in section 505 of the Rehabilitation Act of 1973 (29 U.S.C. 794a) shall be the remedies, procedures, and rights this title provides to any person alleging discrimination on the basis of disability in violation of section 202.

SEC. 204. REGULATIONS.

(a) In General. Not later than 1 year after the date of enactment of this Act, the Attorney General shall promulgate regulations in an accessible format that implement this subtitle. Such regulations shall not include any matter within the scope of the authority of the Secretary of Transportation under section 223, 229, or 244.

(b) Relationship to Other Regulations. Except for "program accessibility, existing facilities," and "communications," regulations under subsection (a) shall be consistent with this Act and with the coordination regulations under part 41 of title 28, Code of Federal Regulations (as promulgated by the Department of Health, Education, and Welfare on January 13, 1978), applicable to recipients of Federal financial assistance under section 504 of the Rehabilitation Act of 1973 (29 U.S.C. 794). With respect to "program accessibility, existing facilities," and "communications," such regulations shall be consistent with regulations and analysis as in part 39 of title 28 of the Code of Federal Regulations, applicable to federally conducted activities under such section 504.

(c) Standards. Regulations under subsection (a) shall include standards applicable to facilities and vehicles covered by this subtitle, other than facilities, stations, rail passenger cars, and vehicles covered by subtitle B. Such standards shall be consistent with the minimum guidelines and requirements issued by the Architectural and Transportation Barriers Compliance Board in accordance with section 504(a) of this Act.

SEC. 205. EFFECTIVE DATE.

(a) General Rule. Except as provided in subsection (b), this subtitle shall become effective 18 months after the date of enactment of this Act.

(b) Exception. Section 204 shall become effective on the date of enactment of this Act.

Subtitle B—Actions Applicable to Public Transportation Provided by Public Entities Considered Discriminatory

PART I—PUBLIC TRANSPORTATION OTHER THAN BY AIRCRAFT OR CERTAIN RAIL OPERATIONS

SEC. 221. DEFINITIONS.

As used in this part:

(1) Demand responsive system. The term "demand responsive system" means any system of providing designated public transportation which is not a fixed route system.

(2) Designated public transportation. The term "designated public transportation" means transportation (other than public school transportation) by bus, rail, or any other conveyance (other than transportation by aircraft or intercity or commuter rail transportation (as defined in section 241)) that provides the general public with general or special service (including charter service) on a regular and continuing basis.

(3) Fixed route system. The term "fixed route system" means a system of providing designated public transportation on which a vehicle is operated along a prescribed route according to a fixed schedule.

(4) Operates. The term "operates," as used with respect to a fixed route system or demand responsive system, includes operation of such system by a person under a contractual or other arrangement or relationship with a public entity.

(5) Public school transportation. The term "public school transportation" means transportation by school bus vehicles of schoolchildren, personnel, and equipment to and from a public elementary or secondary school and school-related activities.

(6) Secretary. The term "Secretary" means the Secretary of Transportation.

SEC. 222. PUBLIC ENTITIES OPERATING FIXED ROUTE SYSTEMS.

(a) Purchase and Lease of New Vehicles. It shall be considered discrimination for purposes of section 202 of this Act and section 504 of the Rehabilitation Act of 1973 (29 U.S.C. 794) for a public entity which operates a fixed route system to purchase or lease a new bus, a new rapid rail vehicle, a new light rail vehicle, or any other new vehicle to be used on such system, if the solicitation for such purchase or lease is made after the 30th day following the effective date of this subsection and if such bus, rail vehicle, or other vehicle is not readily accessible to and usable by individuals with disabilities, including individuals who use wheelchairs.

(b) Purchase and Lease of Used Vehicles. Subject to subsection (c)(1), it shall be considered discrimination for purposes of section 202 of this Act and section 504 of the Rehabilitation Act of 1973 (29 U.S.C. 794) for a public entity which operates a fixed route system to purchase or lease, after the 30th day following the effective date of this subsection, a used vehicle for use on such system unless such entity makes demonstrated good faith efforts to purchase or lease a used vehicle for use on such system that is readily accessible to and usable by individuals with disabilities, including individuals who use wheelchairs.

(c) Remanufactured Vehicles.

(1) General rule. Except as provided in paragraph (2), it shall be considered discrimination for purposes of section 202 of this Act and section 504 of the Rehabilitation Act of 1973 (29 U.S.C. 794) for a public entity which operates a fixed route system

(A) to remanufacture a vehicle for use on such system so as to extend its usable life for 5 years or more, which remanufacture begins (or for which the solicitation is made) after the 30th day following the effective date of this subsection; or

(B) to purchase or lease for use on such system a remanufactured vehicle which has been remanufactured so as to extend its usable life for 5 years or more, which purchase or lease occurs after such 30th day and during the period in which the usable life is extended; unless, after remanufacture, the vehicle is, to the maximum extent feasible, readily accessible to and usable by individuals with disabilities, including individuals who use wheelchairs.

(2) Exception for historic vehicles.

(A) General rule. If a public entity operates a fixed route system any segment of which is included on the National Register of Historic Places and if making a vehicle of historic character to be used solely on such segment readily accessible to and usable by individuals with disabilities would significantly alter the historic character of such vehicle, the public entity only has to make (or to purchase or lease a remanufactured vehicle with) those modifications which are necessary to meet the requirements of paragraph (1) and which do not significantly alter the historic character of such vehicle.

(B) Vehicles of historic character defined by regulations. For purposes of this paragraph and section 228(b), a vehicle of historic character shall be defined by the regulations issued by the Secretary to carry out this subsection.

SEC. 223. PARATRANSIT AS A COMPLEMENT TO FIXED ROUTE SERVICE.

(a) General Rule. It shall be considered discrimination for purposes of section 202 of this Act and section 504 of the Rehabilitation Act of 1973 (29 U.S.C. 794) for a public entity which operates a fixed route system (other than a system which provides solely commuter bus service) to fail to provide with respect to the operations of its fixed route system, in accordance with this section, paratransit and other special transportation services to individuals with disabilities, including individuals who use wheelchairs, that are sufficient to provide to such individuals a level of service (1) which is comparable to the level of designated public transportation services provided to individuals without disabilities using such system; or (2) in the case of response time, which is comparable, to the extent practicable, to the level of designated public transportation services provided to individuals without disabilities using such system.

(b) Issuance of Regulations. Not later than 1 year after the effective date of this subsection, the Secretary shall issue final regulations to carry out this section.

(c) Required Contents of Regulations.

(1) Eligible recipients of service. The regulations issued under this section shall require each public entity which operates a fixed route system to provide the paratransit and other special transportation services required under this section

(A)(i) to any individual with a disability who is unable, as a result of a physical or mental impairment

(including a vision impairment) and without the assistance of another individual (except an operator of a wheelchair lift or other boarding assistance device), to board, ride, or disembark from any vehicle on the system which is readily accessible to and usable by individuals with disabilities;

(ii) to any individual with a disability who needs the assistance of a wheelchair lift or other boarding assistance device (and is able with such assistance) to board, ride, and disembark from any vehicle which is readily accessible to and usable by individuals with disabilities if the individual wants to travel on a route on the system during the hours of operation of the system at a time (or within a reasonable period of such time) when such a vehicle is not being used to provide designated public transportation on the route; and

(iii) to any individual with a disability who has a specific impairment-related condition which prevents such individual from traveling to a boarding location or from a disembarking location on such system;

(B) to one other individual accompanying the individual with the disability; and

(C) to other individuals, in addition to the one individual described in subparagraph (B), accompanying the individual with a disability provided that space for these additional individuals is available on the paratransit vehicle carrying the individual with a disability and that the transportation of such additional individuals will not result in a denial of service to individuals with disabilities. For purposes of clauses (i) and (ii) of subparagraph (A), boarding or disembarking from a vehicle does not include travel to the boarding location or from the disembarking location.

(2) Service area. The regulations issued under this section shall require the provision of paratransit and special transportation services required under this section in the service area of each public entity which operates a fixed route system, other than any portion of the service area in which the public entity solely provides commuter bus service.

(3) Service criteria. Subject to paragraphs (1) and (2), the regulations issued under this section shall establish minimum service criteria for determining the level of services to be required under this section.

(4) Undue financial burden limitation. The regulations issued under this section shall provide that, if the public entity is able to demonstrate to the satisfaction of the Secretary that the provision of paratransit and other special transportation services otherwise required under this section would impose an undue financial burden on the public entity, the public entity, notwithstanding any other provision of this section (other than paragraph (5)), shall only be required to provide such services to the extent that providing such services would not impose such a burden.

(5) Additional services. The regulations issued under this section shall establish circumstances under which the

Secretary may require a public entity to provide, notwithstanding paragraph (4), paratransit and other special transportation services under this section beyond the level of paratransit and other special transportation services which would otherwise be required under paragraph (4).

(6) Public participation. The regulations issued under this section shall require that each public entity which operates a fixed route system hold a public hearing, provide an opportunity for public comment, and consult with individuals with disabilities in preparing its plan under paragraph (7).

(7) Plans. The regulations issued under this section shall require that each public entity which operates a fixed route system

(A) within 18 months after the effective date of this subsection, submit to the Secretary, and commence implementation of, a plan for providing paratransit and other special transportation services which meets the requirements of this section; and

(B) on an annual basis thereafter, submit to the Secretary, and commence implementation of, a plan for providing such services.

(8) Provision of services by others. The regulations issued under this section shall

(A) require that a public entity submitting a plan to the Secretary under this section identify in the plan any person or other public entity which is providing a paratransit or other special transportation service for individuals with disabilities in the service area to which the plan applies; and

(B) provide that the public entity submitting the plan does not have to provide under the plan such service for individuals with disabilities.

(9) Other provisions. The regulations issued under this section shall include such other provisions and requirements as the Secretary determines are necessary to carry out the objectives of this section.

(d) Review of Plan.

(1) General rule. The Secretary shall review a plan submitted under this section for the purpose of determining whether or not such plan meets the requirements of this section, including the regulations issued under this section.

(2) Disapproval. If the Secretary determines that a plan reviewed under this subsection fails to meet the requirements of this section, the Secretary shall disapprove the plan and notify the public entity which submitted the plan of such disapproval and the reasons therefor.

(3) Modification of disapproved plan. Not later than 90 days after the date of disapproval of a plan under this subsection, the public entity which submitted the plan shall modify the plan to meet the requirements of this section and shall submit to the Secretary, and commence implementation of, such modified plan.

(e) Discrimination Defined. As used in subsection (a), the term "discrimination" includes

(1) a failure of a public entity to which the regulations issued under this section apply to submit, or commence implementation of, a plan in accordance with subsections (c)(6) and (c)(7);

(2) a failure of such entity to submit, or commence implementation of, a modified plan in accordance with subsection (d)(3);

(3) submission to the Secretary of a modified plan under subsection (d)(3) which does not meet the requirements of this section; or

(4) a failure of such entity to provide paratransit or other special transportation services in accordance with the plan or modified plan the public entity submitted to the Secretary under this section.

(f) Statutory Construction. Nothing in this section shall be construed as preventing a public entity

(1) from providing paratransit or other special transportation services at a level which is greater than the level of such services which are required by this section,

(2) from providing paratransit or other special transportation services in addition to those paratransit and special transportation services required by this section, or

(3) from providing such services to individuals in addition to those individuals to whom such services are required to be provided by this section.

SEC. 224. PUBLIC ENTITY OPERATING A DEMAND RESPONSIVE SYSTEM.

If a public entity operates a demand responsive system, it shall be considered discrimination, for purposes of section 202 of this Act and section 504 of the Rehabilitation Act of 1973 (29 U.S.C. 794), for such entity to purchase or lease a new vehicle for use on such system, for which a solicitation is made after the 30th day following the effective date of this section, that is not readily accessible to and usable by individuals with disabilities, including individuals who use wheelchairs, unless such system, when viewed in its entirety, provides a level of service to such individuals equivalent to the level of service such system provides to individuals without disabilities.

SEC. 225. TEMPORARY RELIEF WHERE LIFTS ARE UNAVAILABLE.

(a) Granting. With respect to the purchase of new buses, a public entity may apply for, and the Secretary may temporarily relieve such public entity from the obligation under section 222(a) or 224 to purchase new buses that are readily accessible to and usable by individuals with disabilities if such public entity demonstrates to the satisfaction of the Secretary

(1) that the initial solicitation for new buses made by the public entity specified that all new buses were to be lift-equipped and were to be otherwise accessible to and usable by individuals with disabilities;

(2) the unavailability from any qualified manufacturer of hydraulic, electromechanical, or other lifts for such new buses;

(3) that the public entity seeking temporary relief has made good faith efforts to locate a qualified manufacturer to supply the lifts to the manufacturer of such buses in sufficient time to comply with such solicitation; and

(4) that any further delay in purchasing new buses necessary to obtain such lifts would significantly impair transportation services in the community served by the public entity.

(b) Duration and Notice to Congress. Any relief granted under subsection (a) shall be limited in duration by a specified date, and the appropriate committees of Congress shall be notified of any such relief granted.

(c) Fraudulent Application. If, at any time, the Secretary has reasonable cause to believe that any relief granted under subsection (a) was fraudulently applied for, the Secretary shall

(1) cancel such relief if such relief is still in effect; and

(2) take such other action as the Secretary considers appropriate.

SEC. 226. NEW FACILITIES.

For purposes of section 202 of this Act and section 504 of the Rehabilitation Act of 1973 (29 U.S.C. 794), it shall be considered discrimination for a public entity to construct a new facility to be used in the provision of designated public transportation services unless such facility is readily accessible to and usable by individuals with disabilities, including individuals who use wheelchairs.

SEC. 227. ALTERATIONS OF EXISTING FACILITIES.

(a) General Rule. With respect to alterations of an existing facility or part thereof used in the provision of designated public transportation services that affect or could affect the usability of the facility or part thereof, it shall be considered discrimination, for purposes of section 202 of this Act and section 504 of the Rehabilitation Act of 1973 (29 U.S.C. 794), for a public entity to fail to make such alterations (or to ensure that the alterations are made) in such a manner that, to the maximum extent feasible, the altered portions of the facility are readily accessible to and usable by individuals with disabilities, including individuals who use wheelchairs, upon the completion of such alterations. Where the public entity is undertaking an alteration that affects or could affect usability of or access to an area of the facility containing a primary function, the entity shall also make the alterations in such a manner that, to the maximum extent feasible, the path of travel to the altered area and the bathrooms, telephones, and drinking fountains serving the altered area, are readily accessible to and usable by individuals with disabilities, including individuals who use wheelchairs, upon completion of such alterations, where such alterations to the path of travel or the bathrooms, telephones, and drinking fountains serving the altered area are not disproportionate to the overall alterations in terms of cost and scope (as determined under criteria established by the Attorney General).

(b) Special Rule for Stations.

(1) General rule. For purposes of section 202 of this Act and section 504 of the Rehabilitation Act of 1973 (29 U.S.C. 794), it shall be considered discrimination for a public entity that provides designated public transportation to fail, in accordance with the provisions of this subsection, to make key stations (as determined under criteria established by the Secretary by regulation) in rapid rail and light rail systems readily accessible to and usable by individuals with disabilities, including individuals who use wheelchairs.

(2) Rapid rail and light rail key stations.

(A) Accessibility. Except as otherwise provided in this paragraph, all key stations (as determined under criteria established by the Secretary by regulation) in rapid rail and light rail systems shall be made readily accessible to and usable by individuals with disabilities, including individuals who use wheelchairs, as soon as practicable but in no event later than the last day of the 3-year period beginning on the effective date of this paragraph.

(B) Extension for extraordinarily expensive structural changes. The Secretary may extend the 3-year period under subparagraph (A) up to a 30-year period for key stations in a rapid rail or light rail system which stations need extraordinarily expensive structural changes to, or replacement of, existing facilities; except that by the last day of the 20th year following the date of the enactment of this Act at least 2/3 of such key stations must be readily accessible to and usable by individuals with disabilities.

(3) Plans and milestones. The Secretary shall require the appropriate public entity to develop and submit to the Secretary a plan for compliance with this subsection

(A) that reflects consultation with individuals with disabilities affected by such plan and the results of a public hearing and public comments on such plan, and

(B) that establishes milestones for achievement of the requirements of this subsection.

SEC. 228. PUBLIC TRANSPORTATION PROGRAMS AND ACTIVITIES IN EXISTING FACILITIES AND ONE CAR PER TRAIN RULE.

(a) Public Transportation Programs and Activities in Existing Facilities.

(1) In general. With respect to existing facilities used in the provision of designated public transportation services, it shall be considered discrimination, for purposes of section 202 of this Act and section 504 of the Rehabilitation Act of 1973 (29 U.S.C. 794), for a public entity to fail to operate a designated public transportation program or activity conducted in such facilities so that, when viewed in the entirety, the program or activity is readily accessible to and usable by individuals with disabilities.

(2) Exception. Paragraph (1) shall not require a public entity to make structural changes to existing facilities in order to make such facilities accessible to individuals who

use wheelchairs, unless and to the extent required by section 227(a) (relating to alterations) or section 227(b) (relating to key stations).

(3) Utilization. Paragraph (1) shall not require a public entity to which paragraph (2) applies, to provide to individuals who use wheelchairs services made available to the general public at such facilities when such individuals could not utilize or benefit from such services provided at such facilities.

(b) One Car Per Train Rule.

(1) General rule. Subject to paragraph (2), with respect to 2 or more vehicles operated as a train by a light or rapid rail system, for purposes of section 202 of this Act and section 504 of the Rehabilitation Act of 1973 (29 U.S.C. 794), it shall be considered discrimination for a public entity to fail to have at least 1 vehicle per train that is accessible to individuals with disabilities, including individuals who use wheelchairs, as soon as practicable but in no event later than the last day of the 5-year period beginning on the effective date of this section.

(2) Historic trains. In order to comply with paragraph (1) with respect to the remanufacture of a vehicle of historic character which is to be used on a segment of a light or rapid rail system which is included on the National Register of Historic Places, if making such vehicle readily accessible to and usable by individuals with disabilities would significantly alter the historic character of such vehicle, the public entity which operates such system only has to make (or to purchase or lease a remanufactured vehicle with) those modifications which are necessary to meet the requirements of section 222(c)(1) and which do not significantly alter the historic character of such vehicle.

SEC. 229. REGULATIONS.

(a) In General. Not later than 1 year after the date of enactment of this Act, the Secretary of Transportation shall issue regulations, in an accessible format, necessary for carrying out this part (other than section 223).

(b) Standards. The regulations issued under this section and section 223 shall include standards applicable to facilities and vehicles covered by this subtitle. The standards shall be consistent with the minimum guidelines and requirements issued by the Architectural and Transportation Barriers Compliance Board in accordance with section 504 of this Act.

SEC. 230. INTERIM ACCESSIBILITY REQUIREMENTS.

If final regulations have not been issued pursuant to section 229, for new construction or alterations for which a valid and appropriate State or local building permit is obtained prior to the issuance of final regulations under such section, and for which the construction or alteration authorized by such permit begins within one year of the receipt of such permit and is completed under the terms of such permit, compliance with the Uniform Federal Accessibility Standards in

effect at the time the building permit is issued shall suffice to satisfy the requirement that facilities be readily accessible to and usable by persons with disabilities as required under sections 226 and 227, except that, if such final regulations have not been issued one year after the Architectural and Transportation Barriers Compliance Board has issued the supplemental minimum guidelines required under section 504(a) of this Act, compliance with such supplemental minimum guidelines shall be necessary to satisfy the requirement that facilities be readily accessible to and usable by persons with disabilities prior to issuance of the final regulations.

SEC. 231. EFFECTIVE DATE.

(a) General Rule. Except as provided in subsection (b), this part shall become effective 18 months after the date of enactment of this Act.

(b) Exception. Sections 222, 223 (other than subsection (a)), 224, 225, 227(b), 228(b), and 229 shall become effective on the date of enactment of this Act.

PART II—PUBLIC TRANSPORTATION BY INTERCITY AND COMMUTER RAIL

SEC. 241. Definitions.

As used in this part:

(1) Commuter authority. The term "commuter authority" has the meaning given such term in section 103(8) of the Rail Passenger Service Act (45 U.S.C. 502(8)).

(2) Commuter rail transportation. The term "commuter rail transportation" has the meaning given the term "commuter service" in section 103(9) of the Rail Passenger Service Act (45 U.S.C. 502(9)).

(3) Intercity rail transportation. The term "intercity rail transportation" means transportation provided by the National Railroad Passenger Corporation.

(4) Rail passenger car. The term "rail passenger car" means, with respect to intercity rail transportation, single-level and bi-level coach cars, single-level and bi-level dining cars, single-level and bi-level sleeping cars, single-level and bi-level lounge cars, and food service cars.

(5) Responsible person. The term "responsible person" means

(A) in the case of a station more than 50 percent of which is owned by a public entity, such public entity;

(B) in the case of a station more than 50 percent of which is owned by a private party, the persons providing intercity or commuter rail transportation to such station, as allocated on an equitable basis by regulation by the Secretary of Transportation; and

(C) in a case where no party owns more than 50 percent of a station, the persons providing intercity or commuter rail transportation to such station and the owners of the station, other than private party owners, as allocated on an equitable basis by regulation by the Secretary of Transportation.

(6) Station. The term "station" means the portion of a property located appurtenant to a right-of-way on which intercity

or commuter rail transportation is operated, where such portion is used by the general public and is related to the provision of such transportation, including passenger platforms, designated waiting areas, ticketing areas, restrooms, and, where a public entity providing rail transportation owns the property, concession areas, to the extent that such public entity exercises control over the selection, design, construction, or alteration of the property, but such term does not include flag stops.

SEC. 242. INTERCITY AND COMMUTER RAIL ACTIONS CONSIDERED DISCRIMINATORY.

(a) Intercity Rail Transportation.

(1) One car per train rule. It shall be considered discrimination for purposes of section 202 of this Act and section 504 of the Rehabilitation Act of 1973 (29 U.S.C. 794) for a person who provides intercity rail transportation to fail to have at least one passenger car per train that is readily accessible to and usable by individuals with disabilities, including individuals who use wheelchairs, in accordance with regulations issued under section 244, as soon as practicable, but in no event later than 5 years after the date of enactment of this Act.

(2) New intercity cars.

(A) General rule. Except as otherwise provided in this subsection with respect to individuals who use wheelchairs, it shall be considered discrimination for purposes of section 202 of this Act and section 504 of the Rehabilitation Act of 1973 (29 U.S.C. 794) for a person to purchase or lease any new rail passenger cars for use in intercity rail transportation, and for which a solicitation is made later than 30 days after the effective date of this section, unless all such rail cars are readily accessible to and usable by individuals with disabilities, including individuals who use wheelchairs, as prescribed by the Secretary of Transportation in regulations issued under section 244.

(B) Special rule for single-level passenger coaches for individuals who use wheelchairs. Single-level passenger coaches shall be required to

(i) be able to be entered by an individual who uses a wheelchair;

(ii) have space to park and secure a wheelchair;

(iii) have a seat to which a passenger in a wheelchair can transfer, and a space to fold and store such passenger's wheelchair; and

(iv) have a restroom usable by an individual who uses a wheelchair, only to the extent provided in paragraph (3).

(C) Special rule for single-level dining cars for individuals who use wheelchairs. Single-level dining cars shall not be required to

(i) be able to be entered from the station platform by an individual who uses a wheelchair; or

(ii) have a restroom usable by an individual who uses a wheelchair if no restroom is provided in such car for any passenger.

(D) Special rule for bi-level dining cars for individuals who use wheelchairs. Bi-level dining cars shall not be required to

(i) be able to be entered by an individual who uses a wheelchair;

(ii) have space to park and secure a wheelchair;

(iii) have a seat to which a passenger in a wheelchair can transfer, or a space to fold and store such passenger's wheelchair; or

(iv) have a restroom usable by an individual who uses a wheelchair.

(3) Accessibility of single-level coaches.

(A) General rule. It shall be considered discrimination for purposes of section 202 of this Act and section 504 of the Rehabilitation Act of 1973 (29 U.S.C. 794) for a person who provides intercity rail transportation to fail to have on each train which includes one or more single-level rail passenger coaches

(i) a number of spaces

(I) to park and secure wheelchairs (to accommodate individuals who wish to remain in their wheelchairs) equal to not less than one-half of the number of single-level rail passenger coaches in such train; and

(II) to fold and store wheelchairs (to accommodate individuals who wish to transfer to coach seats) equal to not less than one-half of the number of single-level rail passenger coaches in such train, as soon as practicable, but in no event later than 5 years after the date of enactment of this Act; and

(ii) a number of spaces

(I) to park and secure wheelchairs (to accommodate individuals who wish to remain in their wheelchairs) equal to not less than the total number of single-level rail passenger coaches in such train; and

(II) to fold and store wheelchairs (to accommodate individuals who wish to transfer to coach seats) equal to not less than the total number of single-level rail passenger coaches in such train, as soon as practicable, but in no event later than 10 years after the date of enactment of this Act.

(B) Location. Spaces required by subparagraph (A) shall be located in single-level rail passenger coaches or food service cars.

(C) Limitation. Of the number of spaces required on a train by subparagraph (A), not more than two spaces to park and secure wheelchairs nor more than two spaces to fold and store wheelchairs shall be located in any one coach or food service car.

(D) Other accessibility features. Single-level rail passenger coaches and food service cars on which the spaces required by subparagraph (A) are located shall have a restroom usable by an individual who uses a wheelchair and shall be able to be entered from the station platform by an individual who uses a wheelchair.

(4) Food service.

(A) Single-level dining cars. On any train in which a single-level dining car is used to provide food service

(i) if such single-level dining car was purchased after the date of enactment of this Act, table service in such car shall be provided to a passenger who uses a wheelchair if

(I) the car adjacent to the end of the dining car through which a wheelchair may enter is itself accessible to a wheelchair;

(II) such passenger can exit to the platform from the car such passenger occupies, move down the platform, and enter the adjacent accessible car described in subclause (I) without the necessity of the train being moved within the station; and

(III) space to park and secure a wheelchair is available in the dining car at the time such passenger wishes to eat (if such passenger wishes to remain in a wheelchair), or space to store and fold a wheelchair is available in the dining car at the time such passenger wishes to eat (if such passenger wishes to transfer to a dining car seat); and

(ii) appropriate auxiliary aids and services, including a hard surface on which to eat, shall be provided to ensure that other equivalent food service is available to individuals with disabilities, including individuals who use wheelchairs, and to passengers traveling with such individuals. Unless not practicable, a person providing intercity rail transportation shall place an accessible car adjacent to the end of a dining car described in clause (i) through which an individual who uses a wheelchair may enter.

(B) Bi-level dining cars. On any train in which a bi-level dining car is used to provide food service

(i) if such train includes a bi-level lounge car purchased after the date of enactment of this Act, table service in such lounge car shall be provided to individuals who use wheelchairs and to other passengers; and

(ii) appropriate auxiliary aids and services, including a hard surface on which to eat, shall be provided to ensure that other equivalent food service is available to individuals with disabilities, including individuals who use wheelchairs, and to passengers traveling with such individuals.

(b) Commuter Rail Transportation.

(1) One car per train rule. It shall be considered discrimination for purposes of section 202 of this Act and section 504 of the Rehabilitation Act of 1973 (29 U.S.C. 794) for a person who provides commuter rail transportation to fail to have at least one passenger car per train that is readily accessible to and usable by individuals with disabilities, including individuals who use wheelchairs, in accordance with regulations issued under section 244, as soon as practicable, but in no event later than 5 years after the date of enactment of this Act.

(2) New commuter rail cars.

(A) General rule. It shall be considered discrimination for purposes of section 202 of this Act and section 504 of the Rehabilitation Act of 1973 (29 U.S.C. 794) for a person to purchase or lease any new rail passenger cars for use in commuter rail transportation, and for which a solicitation is made later than 30 days after the effective date of this section, unless all such rail cars are readily accessible to and usable by individuals with disabilities, including individuals who use wheelchairs, as prescribed by the Secretary of Transportation in regulations issued under section 244.

(B) Accessibility. For purposes of section 202 of this Act and section 504 of the Rehabilitation Act of 1973 (29 U.S.C. 794), a requirement that a rail passenger car used in commuter rail transportation be accessible to or readily accessible to and usable by individuals with disabilities, including individuals who use wheelchairs, shall not be construed to require

(i) a restroom usable by an individual who uses a wheelchair if no restroom is provided in such car for any passenger;

(ii) space to fold and store a wheelchair; or

(iii) a seat to which a passenger who uses a wheelchair can transfer.

(c) Used Rail Cars. It shall be considered discrimination for purposes of section 202 of this Act and section 504 of the Rehabilitation Act of 1973 (29 U.S.C. 794) for a person to purchase or lease a used rail passenger car for use in intercity or commuter rail transportation, unless such person makes demonstrated good faith efforts to purchase or lease a used rail car that is readily accessible to and usable by individuals with disabilities, including individuals who use wheelchairs, as prescribed by the Secretary of Transportation in regulations issued under section 244.

(d) Remanufactured Rail Cars.

(1) Remanufacturing. It shall be considered discrimination for purposes of section 202 of this Act and section 504 of the Rehabilitation Act of 1973 (29 U.S.C. 794) for a person to remanufacture a rail passenger car for use in intercity or commuter rail transportation so as to extend its usable life for 10 years or more, unless the rail car, to the maximum extent feasible, is made readily accessible to and usable by individuals with disabilities, including individuals who use wheelchairs, as prescribed by the Secretary of Transportation in regulations issued under section 244.

(2) Purchase or lease. It shall be considered discrimination for purposes of section 202 of this Act and section 504 of the Rehabilitation Act of 1973 (29 U.S.C. 794) for a person to purchase or lease a remanufactured rail passenger car for use in intercity or commuter rail transportation unless such car was remanufactured in accordance with paragraph (1).

(e) Stations.

(1) New stations. It shall be considered discrimination for purposes of section 202 of this Act and section 504 of the Rehabilitation Act of 1973 (29 U.S.C. 794) for a person to build a new station for use in intercity or commuter rail transportation that is not readily accessible to and usable by individuals with disabilities, including individuals who use wheelchairs, as prescribed by the Secretary of Transportation in regulations issued under section 244.

(2) Existing stations.

(A) Failure to make readily accessible.

(i) General rule. It shall be considered discrimination for purposes of section 202 of this Act and section 504 of the Rehabilitation Act of 1973 (29 U.S.C. 794) for a responsible person to fail to make existing stations in the intercity rail transportation system, and existing key stations in commuter rail transportation systems, readily accessible to and usable by individuals with disabilities, including individuals who use wheelchairs, as prescribed by the Secretary of Transportation in regulations issued under section 244.

(ii) Period for compliance.

(I) Intercity rail. All stations in the intercity rail transportation system shall be made readily accessible to and usable by individuals with disabilities, including individuals who use wheelchairs, as soon as practicable, but in no event later than 20 years after the date of enactment of this Act.

(II) Commuter rail. Key stations in commuter rail transportation systems shall be made readily accessible to and usable by individuals with disabilities, including individuals who use wheelchairs, as soon as practicable but in no event later than 3 years after the date of enactment of this Act, except that the time limit may be extended by the Secretary of Transportation up to 20 years after the date of enactment of this Act in a case where the raising of the entire passenger platform is the only means available of attaining accessibility or where other extraordinarily expensive structural changes are necessary to attain accessibility.

(iii) Designation of key stations. Each commuter authority shall designate the key stations in its commuter rail transportation system, in consultation with individuals with disabilities and organizations representing such individuals, taking into consideration such factors as high ridership and whether such station serves as a transfer or feeder station. Before the final designation of key stations under this clause, a commuter authority shall hold a public hearing.

(iv) Plans and milestones. The Secretary of Transportation shall require the appropriate person to develop a plan for carrying out this subparagraph that reflects consultation with individuals with disabilities affected by such plan and that establishes milestones for achievement of the requirements of this subparagraph.

(B) Requirement when making alterations.

(i) General rule. It shall be considered discrimination, for purposes of section 202 of this Act and section 504 of the Rehabilitation Act of 1973 (29 U.S.C. 794), with respect to alterations of an existing station or part thereof in the intercity or commuter rail transportation systems that affect or could affect the usability of the station or part thereof, for the responsible person, owner, or person in control of the station to fail to make the alterations in such a manner that, to the maximum extent feasible, the altered portions of the station are readily accessible to and usable by individuals with disabilities, including individuals who use wheelchairs, upon completion of such alterations.

(ii) Alterations to a primary function area. It shall be considered discrimination, for purposes of section 202 of this Act and section 504 of the Rehabilitation Act of 1973 (29 U.S.C. 794), with respect to alterations that affect or could affect the usability of or access to an area of the station containing a primary function, for the responsible person, owner, or person in control of the station to fail to make the alterations in such a manner that, to the maximum extent feasible, the path of travel to the altered area, and the bathrooms, telephones, and drinking fountains serving the altered area, are readily accessible to and usable by individuals with disabilities, including individuals who use wheelchairs, upon completion of such alterations, where such alterations to the path of travel or the bathrooms, telephones, and drinking fountains serving the altered area are not disproportionate to the overall alterations in terms of cost and scope (as determined under criteria established by the Attorney General).

(C) Required cooperation. It shall be considered discrimination for purposes of section 202 of this Act and section 504 of the Rehabilitation Act of 1973 (29 U.S.C. 794) for an owner, or person in control, of a station governed by subparagraph (A) or (B) to fail to provide reasonable cooperation to a responsible person with respect to such station in that responsible person's efforts to comply with such subparagraph. An owner, or person in control, of a station shall be liable to a responsible person for any failure to provide reasonable cooperation as required by this subparagraph. Failure to receive reasonable cooperation required by this subparagraph shall not be a defense to a claim of discrimination under this Act.

SEC. 243. CONFORMANCE OF ACCESSIBILITY STANDARDS.

Accessibility standards included in regulations issued under this part shall be consistent with the minimum guidelines issued by the Architectural and Transportation Barriers Compliance Board under section 504(a) of this Act.

SEC. 244. REGULATIONS.

Not later than 1 year after the date of enactment of this Act, the Secretary of Transportation shall issue regulations, in an accessible format, necessary for carrying out this part.

SEC. 245. INTERIM ACCESSIBILITY REQUIREMENTS.

(a) Stations. If final regulations have not been issued pursuant to section 244, for new construction or alterations for which a valid and appropriate State or local building permit is obtained prior to the issuance of final regulations under such section, and for which the construction or alteration authorized by such permit begins within one year of the receipt of such permit and is completed under the terms of such permit, compliance with the Uniform Federal Accessibility Standards in effect at the time the building permit is issued shall suffice to satisfy the requirement that stations be readily accessible to and usable by persons with disabilities as required under section 242(e), except that, if such final regulations have not ben issued one year after the Architectural and Transportation Barriers Compliance Board has issued the supplemental minimum guidelines required under section 504(a) of this Act, compliance with such supplemental minimum guidelines shall be necessary to satisfy the requirement that stations be readily accessible to and usable by persons with disabilities prior to issuance of the final regulations.

(b) Rail Passenger Cars. If final regulations have not been issued pursuant to section 244, a person shall be considered to have complied with the requirements of section 242 (a) through (d) that a rail passenger car be readily accessible to and usable by individuals with disabilities, if the design for such car complies with the laws and regulations (including the Minimum Guidelines and Requirements for Accessible Design and such supplemental minimum guidelines as are issued under section 504(a) of this Act) governing accessibility of such cars, to the extent that such laws and regulations are not inconsistent with this part and are in effect at the time such design is substantially completed.

SEC. 246. EFFECTIVE DATE.

(a) General Rule. Except as provided in subsection (b), this part shall become effective 18 months after the date of enactment of this Act.

(b) Exception. Sections 242 and 244 shall become effective on the date of enactment of this Act.

TITLE III—PUBLIC ACCOMMODATIONS AND SERVICES OPERATED BY PRIVATE ENTITIES

SEC. 301. DEFINITIONS.

As used in this title:

(1) Commerce. The term "commerce" means travel, trade, traffic, commerce, transportation, or communication

(A) among the several States;

(B) between any foreign country or any territory or possession and any State; or

(C) between points in the same State but through another State or foreign country.

(2) Commercial facilities. The term "commercial facilities" means facilities

(A) that are intended for nonresidential use; and

(B) whose operations will affect commerce. Such term shall not include railroad locomotives, railroad freight cars, railroad cabooses, railroad cars described in section 242 or covered under this title, railroad rights-of-way, or facilities that are covered or expressly exempted from coverage under the Fair Housing Act of 1968 (42 U.S.C. 3601 et seq.).

(3) Demand responsive system. The term "demand responsive system" means any system of providing transportation of individuals by a vehicle, other than a system which is a fixed route system.

(4) Fixed route system. The term "fixed route system" means a system of providing transportation of individuals (other than by aircraft) on which a vehicle is operated along a prescribed route according to a fixed schedule.

(5) Over-the-road bus. The term "over-the-road bus" means a bus characterized by an elevated passenger deck located over a baggage compartment.

(6) Private entity. The term "private entity" means any entity other than a public entity (as defined in section 201(1)).

(7) Public accommodation. The following private entities are considered public accommodations for purposes of this title, if the operations of such entities affect commerce

(A) an inn, hotel, motel, or other place of lodging, except for an establishment located within a building that contains not more than five rooms for rent or hire and that is actually occupied by the proprietor of such establishment as the residence of such proprietor;

(B) a restaurant, bar, or other establishment serving food or drink;

(C) a motion picture house, theater, concert hall, stadium, or other place of exhibition or entertainment;

(D) an auditorium, convention center, lecture hall, or other place of public gathering;

(E) a bakery, grocery store, clothing store, hardware store, shopping center, or other sales or rental establishment;

(F) a laundromat, dry-cleaner, bank, barber shop, beauty shop, travel service, shoe repair service, funeral parlor, gas station, office of an accountant or lawyer, pharmacy, insurance office, professional office of a health care provider, hospital, or other service establishment;

(G) a terminal, depot, or other station used for specified public transportation;

(H) a museum, library, gallery, or other place of public display or collection;

(I) a park, zoo, amusement park, or other place of recreation;

(J) a nursery, elementary, secondary, undergraduate, or postgraduate private school, or other place of education;

(K) a day care center, senior citizen center, homeless shelter, food bank, adoption agency, or other social service center establishment; and

(L) a gymnasium, health spa, bowling alley, golf course, or other place of exercise or recreation.

(8) Rail and railroad. The terms "rail" and "railroad" have the meaning given the term "railroad" in section 202(e) of the Federal Railroad Safety Act of 1970 (45 U.S.C. 431(e)).

(9) Readily achievable. The term "readily achievable" means easily accomplishable and able to be carried out without much difficulty or expense. In determining whether an action is readily achievable, factors to be considered include

(A) the nature and cost of the action needed under this Act;

(B) the overall financial resources of the facility or facilities involved in the action; the number of persons employed at such facility; the effect on expenses and resources, or the impact otherwise of such action upon the operation of the facility;

(C) the overall financial resources of the covered entity; the overall size of the business of a covered entity with respect to the number of its employees; the number, type, and location of its facilities; and

(D) the type of operation or operations of the covered entity, including the composition, structure, and functions of the workforce of such entity; the geographic separateness, administrative or fiscal relationship of the facility or facilities in question to the covered entity.

(10) Specified public transportation. The term "specified public transportation" means transportation by bus, rail, or any other conveyance (other than by aircraft) that provides the general public with general or special service (including charter service) on a regular and continuing basis.

(11) Vehicle. The term "vehicle" does not include a rail passenger car, railroad locomotive, railroad freight car, railroad caboose, or a railroad car described in section 242 or covered under this title.

SEC. 302. PROHIBITION OF DISCRIMINATION BY PUBLIC ACCOMMODATIONS.

(a) General Rule. No individual shall be discriminated against on the basis of disability in the full and equal enjoyment of the goods, services, facilities, privileges, advantages, or accommodations of any place of public accommodation by any person who owns, leases (or leases to), or operates a place of public accommodation.

(b) Construction.

(1) General prohibition.

(A) Activities.

(i) Denial of participation. It shall be discriminatory to subject an individual or class of individuals on the basis of a disability or disabilities of such individual or class, directly, or through contractual, licensing, or other arrangements, to a denial of the opportunity of the individual or class to participate in or benefit from the goods, services, facilities, privileges, advantages, or accommodations of an entity.

(ii) Participation in unequal benefit. It shall be discriminatory to afford an individual or class of individuals, on the basis of a disability or disabilities of such individual or class, directly, or through contractual, licensing, or other arrangements with the opportunity to participate in or benefit from a good, service, facility, privilege, advantage, or accommodation that is not equal to that afforded to other individuals.

(iii) Separate benefit. It shall be discriminatory to provide an individual or class of individuals, on the basis of a disability or disabilities of such individual or class, directly, or through contractual, licensing, or other arrangements with a good, service, facility, privilege, advantage, or accommodation that is different or separate from that provided to other individuals, unless such action is necessary to provide the individual or class of individuals with a good, service, facility, privilege, advantage, or accommodation, or other opportunity that is as effective as that provided to others.

(iv) Individual or class of individuals. For purposes of clauses (i) through (iii) of this subparagraph, the term "individual or class of individuals" refers to the clients or customers of the covered public accommodation that enters into the contractual, licensing or other arrangement.

(B) Integrated settings. Goods, services, facilities, privileges, advantages, and accommodations shall be afforded to an individual with a disability in the most integrated setting appropriate to the needs of the individual.

(C) Opportunity to participate. Notwithstanding the existence of separate or different programs or activities provided in accordance with this section, an individual with a disability shall not be denied the opportunity to participate in such programs or activities that are not separate or different.

(D) Administrative methods. An individual or entity shall not, directly or through contractual or other arrangements, utilize standards or criteria or methods of administration

(i) that have the effect of discriminating on the basis of disability; or

(ii) that perpetuate the discrimination of others who are subject to common administrative control.

(E) Association. It shall be discriminatory to exclude or otherwise deny equal goods, services, facilities, privileges, advantages, accommodations, or other opportunities to an individual or entity because of the known disability of an individual with whom the individual or entity is known to have a relationship or association.

(2) Specific prohibitions.

(A) Discrimination. For purposes of subsection (a), discrimination includes

(i) the imposition or application of eligibility criteria that screen out or tend to screen out an individual with a disability or any class of individuals with disabilities from fully and equally enjoying any goods, services, facilities, privileges, advantages, or accommodations, unless such criteria can be shown to be necessary for the provision of the goods, services, facilities, privileges, advantages, or accommodations being offered;

(ii) a failure to make reasonable modifications in policies, practices, or procedures, when such modifications are necessary to afford such goods, services, facilities, privileges, advantages, or accommodations to individuals with disabilities, unless the entity can demonstrate that making such modifications would fundamentally alter the nature of such goods, services, facilities, privileges, advantages, or accommodations;

(iii) a failure to take such steps as may be necessary to ensure that no individual with a disability is excluded, denied services, segregated or otherwise treated differently than other individuals because of the absence of auxiliary aids and services, unless the entity can demonstrate that taking such steps would fundamentally alter the nature of the good, service, facility, privilege, advantage, or accommodation being offered or would result in an undue burden;

(iv) a failure to remove architectural barriers, and communication barriers that are structural in nature, in existing facilities, and transportation barriers in existing vehicles and rail passenger cars used by an establishment for transporting individuals (not including barriers that can only be removed through the retrofitting of vehicles or rail passenger cars by the installation of a hydraulic or other lift), where such removal is readily achievable; and

(v) where an entity can demonstrate that the removal of a barrier under clause (iv) is not readily achievable, a failure to make such goods, services, facilities, privileges, advantages, or accommodations available through alternative methods if such methods are readily achievable.

(B) Fixed route system.

(i) Accessibility. It shall be considered discrimination for a private entity which operates a fixed route system and which is not subject to section 304 to purchase or lease a vehicle with a seating capacity in excess of 16 passengers (including the driver) for use on such system, for which a solicitation is made after the 30th day following the effective date of this subparagraph, that is not readily accessible to and usable by individuals with disabilities, including individuals who use wheelchairs.

(ii) Equivalent service. If a private entity which operates a fixed route system and which is not subject to section 304 purchases or leases a vehicle with a seating capacity of 16 passengers or less (including the driver) for use on such system after the effective date of

this subparagraph that is not readily accessible to or usable by individuals with disabilities, it shall be considered discrimination for such entity to fail to operate such system so that, when viewed in its entirety, such system ensures a level of service to individuals with disabilities, including individuals who use wheelchairs, equivalent to the level of service provided to individuals without disabilities.

(C) Demand responsive system. For purposes of subsection (a), discrimination includes

(i) a failure of a private entity which operates a demand responsive system and which is not subject to section 304 to operate such system so that, when viewed in its entirety, such system ensures a level of service to individuals with disabilities, including individuals who use wheelchairs, equivalent to the level of service provided to individuals without disabilities; and

(ii) the purchase or lease by such entity for use on such system of a vehicle with a seating capacity in excess of 16 passengers (including the driver), for which solicitations are made after the 30th day following the effective date of this subparagraph, that is not readily accessible to and usable by individuals with disabilities (including individuals who use wheelchairs) unless such entity can demonstrate that such system, when viewed in its entirety, provides a level of service to individuals with disabilities equivalent to that provided to individuals without disabilities.

(D) Over-the-road buses.

(i) Limitation on applicability. Subparagraphs (B) and (C) do not apply to over-the-road buses.

(ii) Accessibility requirements. For purposes of subsection (a), discrimination includes (I) the purchase or lease of an over-the-road bus which does not comply with the regulations issued under section 306(a)(2) by a private entity which provides transportation of individuals and which is not primarily engaged in the business of transporting people, and (II) any other failure of such entity to comply with such regulations.

(3) Specific Construction. Nothing in this title shall require an entity to permit an individual to participate in or benefit from the goods, services, facilities, privileges, advantages and accommodations of such entity where such individual poses a direct threat to the health or safety of others. The term "direct threat" means a significant risk to the health or safety of others that cannot be eliminated by a modification of policies, practices, or procedures or by the provision of auxiliary aids or services.

SEC. 303. NEW CONSTRUCTION AND ALTERATIONS IN PUBLIC ACCOMMODATIONS AND COMMERCIAL FACILITIES.

(a) Application of Term. Except as provided in subsection (b), as applied to public accommodations and commercial facilities, discrimination for purposes of section 302(a) includes

(1) a failure to design and construct facilities for first occupancy later than 30 months after the date of enactment of this Act that are readily accessible to and usable by individuals with disabilities, except where an entity can demonstrate that it is structurally impracticable to meet the requirements of such subsection in accordance with standards set forth or incorporated by reference in regulations issued under this title; and

(2) with respect to a facility or part thereof that is altered by, on behalf of, or for the use of an establishment in a manner that affects or could affect the usability of the facility or part thereof, a failure to make alterations in such a manner that, to the maximum extent feasible, the altered portions of the facility are readily accessible to and usable by individuals with disabilities, including individuals who use wheelchairs. Where the entity is undertaking an alteration that affects or could affect usability of or access to an area of the facility containing a primary function, the entity shall also make the alterations in such a manner that, to the maximum extent feasible, the path of travel to the altered area and the bathrooms, telephones, and drinking fountains serving the altered area, are readily accessible to and usable by individuals with disabilities where such alterations to the path of travel or the bathrooms, telephones, and drinking fountains serving the altered area are not disproportionate to the overall alterations in terms of cost and scope (as determined under criteria established by the Attorney General).

(b) Elevator. Subsection (a) shall not be construed to require the installation of an elevator for facilities that are less than three stories or have less than 3,000 square feet per story unless the building is a shopping center, a shopping mall, or the professional office of a health care provider or unless the Attorney General determines that a particular category of such facilities requires the installation of elevators based on the usage of such facilities.

SEC. 304. PROHIBITION OF DISCRIMINATION IN SPECIFIED PUBLIC TRANSPORTATION SERVICES PROVIDED BY PRIVATE ENTITIES.

(a) General Rule. No individual shall be discriminated against on the basis of disability in the full and equal enjoyment of specified public transportation services provided by a private entity that is primarily engaged in the business of transporting people and whose operations affect commerce.

(b) Construction. For purposes of subsection (a), discrimination includes

(1) the imposition or application by a entity described in subsection (a) of eligibility criteria that screen out or tend to screen out an individual with a disability or any class of individuals with disabilities from fully enjoying the specified public transportation services provided by the entity, unless such criteria can be shown to be necessary for the provision of the services being offered;

(2) the failure of such entity to

(A) make reasonable modifications consistent with those required under section 302(b)(2)(A)(ii);

(B) provide auxiliary aids and services consistent with the requirements of section 302(b)(2)(A)(iii); and

(C) remove barriers consistent with the requirements of section 302(b)(2)(A) and with the requirements of section 303(a)(2);

(3) the purchase or lease by such entity of a new vehicle (other than an automobile, a van with a seating capacity of less than 8 passengers, including the driver, or an over-the-road bus) which is to be used to provide specified public transportation and for which a solicitation is made after the 30th day following the effective date of this section, that is not readily accessible to and usable by individuals with disabilities, including individuals who use wheelchairs; except that the new vehicle need not be readily accessible to and usable by such individuals if the new vehicle is to be used solely in a demand responsive system and if the entity can demonstrate that such system, when viewed in its entirety, provides a level of service to such individuals equivalent to the level of service provided to the general public;

(4)

(A) the purchase or lease by such entity of an over-the- road bus which does not comply with the regulations issued under section 306(a)(2); and

(B) any other failure of such entity to comply with such regulations; and

(5) the purchase or lease by such entity of a new van with a seating capacity of less than 8 passengers, including the driver, which is to be used to provide specified public transportation and for which a solicitation is made after the 30th day following the effective date of this section that is not readily accessible to or usable by individuals with disabilities, including individuals who use wheelchairs; except that the new van need not be readily accessible to and usable by such individuals if the entity can demonstrate that the system for which the van is being purchased or leased, when viewed in its entirety, provides a level of service to such individuals equivalent to the level of service provided to the general public;

(6) the purchase or lease by such entity of a new rail passenger car that is to be used to provide specified public transportation, and for which a solicitation is made later than 30 days after the effective date of this paragraph, that is not readily accessible to and usable by individuals with disabilities, including individuals who use wheelchairs; and

(7) the remanufacture by such entity of a rail passenger car that is to be used to provide specified public transportation so as to extend its usable life for 10 years or more, or the purchase or lease by such entity of such a rail car, unless the rail car, to the maximum extent feasible, is made readily accessible to and usable by individuals with disabilities, including individuals who use wheelchairs.

(c) Historical or Antiquated Cars.

(1) Exception. To the extent that compliance with subsection (b)(2)(C) or (b)(7) would significantly alter the historic or antiquated character of a historical or antiquated rail passenger car, or a rail station served exclusively by such cars, or would result in violation of any rule, regulation, standard, or order issued by the Secretary of Transportation under the Federal Railroad Safety Act of 1970, such compliance shall not be required.

(2) Definition. As used in this subsection, the term "historical or antiquated rail passenger car" means a rail passenger car

(A) which is not less than 30 years old at the time of its use for transporting individuals;

(B) the manufacturer of which is no longer in the business of manufacturing rail passenger cars; and

(C) which

(i) has a consequential association with events or persons significant to the past; or

(ii) embodies, or is being restored to embody, the distinctive characteristics of a type of rail passenger car used in the past, or to represent a time period which has passed.

SEC. 305. STUDY.

(a) Purposes. The Office of Technology Assessment shall undertake a study to determine

(1) the access needs of individuals with disabilities to over-the-road buses and over-the-road bus service; and

(2) the most cost-effective methods for providing access to over-the-road buses and over-the-road bus service to individuals with disabilities, particularly individuals who use wheelchairs, through all forms of boarding options.

(b) Contents. The study shall include, at a minimum, an analysis of the following:

(1) The anticipated demand by individuals with disabilities for accessible over-the-road buses and over-the-road bus service.

(2) The degree to which such buses and service, including any service required under sections 304(b)(4) and 306(a)(2), are readily accessible to and usable by individuals with disabilities.

(3) The effectiveness of various methods of providing accessibility to such buses and service to individuals with disabilities.

(4) The cost of providing accessible over-the-road buses and bus service to individuals with disabilities, including consideration of recent technological and cost saving developments in equipment and devices.

(5) Possible design changes in over-the-road buses that could enhance accessibility, including the installation of accessible restrooms which do not result in a loss of seating capacity.

(6) The impact of accessibility requirements on the continuation of over-the-road bus service, with particu-

lar consideration of the impact of such requirements on such service to rural communities.

(c) Advisory Committee. In conducting the study required by subsection (a), the Office of Technology Assessment shall establish an advisory committee, which shall consist of

(1) members selected from among private operators and manufacturers of over-the-road buses;

(2) members selected from among individuals with disabilities, particularly individuals who use wheelchairs, who are potential riders of such buses; and

(3) members selected for their technical expertise on issues included in the study, including manufacturers of boarding assistance equipment and devices.

The number of members selected under each of paragraphs (1) and (2) shall be equal, and the total number of members selected under paragraphs (1) and (2) shall exceed the number of members selected under paragraph (3).

(d) Deadline. The study required by subsection (a), along with recommendations by the Office of Technology Assessment, including any policy options for legislative action, shall be submitted to the President and Congress within 36 months after the date of the enactment of this Act. If the President determines that compliance with the regulations issued pursuant to section 306(a)(2)(B) on or before the applicable deadlines specified in section 306(a)(2)(B) will result in a significant reduction in intercity over-the-road bus service, the President shall extend each such deadline by 1 year.

(e) Review. In developing the study required by subsection (a), the Office of Technology Assessment shall provide a preliminary draft of such study to the Architectural and Transportation Barriers Compliance Board established under section 502 of the Rehabilitation Act of 1973 (29 U.S.C. 792). The Board shall have an opportunity to comment on such draft study, and any such comments by the Board made in writing within 120 days after the Board's receipt of the draft study shall be incorporated as part of the final study required to be submitted under subsection (d).

SEC. 306. REGULATIONS.

(a) Transportation Provisions.

(1) General rule. Not later than 1 year after the date of the enactment of this Act, the Secretary of Transportation shall issue regulations in an accessible format to carry out sections 302(b)(2) (B) and (C) and to carry out section 304 (other than subsection (b)(4)).

(2) Special rules for providing access to over-the-road buses.

(A) Interim requirements.

(i) Issuance. Not later than 1 year after the date of the enactment of this Act, the Secretary of Transportation shall issue regulations in an accessible format to carry out sections 304(b)(4) and 302(b)(2)(D)(ii) that require each private entity which uses an over-the-road bus to provide transportation of individuals to provide accessibility to such bus; except that such regulations shall not require any structural changes in over-the-road buses in order to provide access to individuals who use wheelchairs during the effective period of such regulations and shall not require the purchase of boarding assistance devices to provide access to such individuals.

(ii) Effective period. The regulations issued pursuant to this subparagraph shall be effective until the effective date of the regulations issued under subparagraph (B).

(B) Final requirement.

(i) Review of study and interim requirements. The Secretary shall review the study submitted under section 305 and the regulations issued pursuant to subparagraph (A).

(ii) Issuance. Not later than 1 year after the date of the submission of the study under section 305, the Secretary shall issue in an accessible format new regulations to carry out sections 304(b)(4) and 302(b)(2)(D)(ii) that require, taking into account the purposes of the study under section 305 and any recommendations resulting from such study, each private entity which uses an over-the-road bus to provide transportation to individuals to provide accessibility to such bus to individuals with disabilities, including individuals who use wheelchairs.

(iii) Effective period. Subject to section 305(d), the regulations issued pursuant to this subparagraph shall take effect

(I) with respect to small providers of transportation (as defined by the Secretary), 7 years after the date of the enactment of this Act; and

(II) with respect to other providers of transportation, 6 years after such date of enactment.

(C) Limitation on requiring installation of accessible restrooms. The regulations issued pursuant to this paragraph shall not require the installation of accessible restrooms in over-the-road buses if such installation would result in a loss of seating capacity.

(3) Standards. The regulations issued pursuant to this subsection shall include standards applicable to facilities and vehicles covered by sections 302(b)(2) and 304.

(b) Other Provisions. Not later than 1 year after the date of the enactment of this Act, the Attorney General shall issue regulations in an accessible format to carry out the provisions of this title not referred to in subsection (a) that include standards applicable to facilities and vehicles covered under section 302.

(c) Consistency With ATBCB Guidelines. Standards included in regulations issued under subsections (a) and (b) shall be consistent with the minimum guidelines and requirements issued by the Architectural and Transportation Barriers Compliance Board in accordance with section 504 of this Act.

(d) Interim Accessibility Standards.

(1) Facilities. If final regulations have not been issued pursuant to this section, for new construction or alterations for which a valid and appropriate State or local building permit is obtained prior to the issuance of final regulations under this section, and for which the construction or alteration authorized by such permit begins within one year of the receipt of such permit and is completed under the terms of such permit, compliance with the Uniform Federal Accessibility Standards in effect at the time the building permit is issued shall suffice to satisfy the requirement that facilities be readily accessible to and usable by persons with disabilities as required under section 303, except that, if such final regulations have not been issued one year after the Architectural and Transportation Barriers Compliance Board has issued the supplemental minimum guidelines required under section 504(a) of this Act, compliance with such supplemental minimum guidelines shall be necessary to satisfy the requirement that facilities be readily accessible to and usable by persons with disabilities prior to issuance of the final regulations.

(2) Vehicles and rail passenger cars. If final regulations have not been issued pursuant to this section, a private entity shall be considered to have complied with the requirements of this title, if any, that a vehicle or rail passenger car be readily accessible to and usable by individuals with disabilities, if the design for such vehicle or car complies with the laws and regulations (including the Minimum Guidelines and Requirements for Accessible Design and such supplemental minimum guidelines as are issued under section 504(a) of this Act) governing accessibility of such vehicles or cars, to the extent that such laws and regulations are not inconsistent with this title and are in effect at the time such design is substantially completed.

SEC. 307. EXEMPTIONS FOR PRIVATE CLUBS AND RELIGIOUS ORGANIZATIONS.

The provisions of this title shall not apply to private clubs or establishments exempted from coverage under title II of the Civil Rights Act of 1964 (42 U.S.C. 2000-a(e)) or to religious organizations or entities controlled by religious organizations, including places of worship.

SEC. 308. ENFORCEMENT.

(a) In General.

(1) Availability of remedies and procedures. The remedies and procedures set forth in section 204(a) of the Civil Rights Act of 1964 (42 U.S.C. 2000a-3(a)) are the remedies and procedures this title provides to any person who is being subjected to discrimination on the basis of disability in violation of this title or who has reasonable grounds for believing that such person is about to be subjected to discrimination in violation of section 303. Nothing in this section shall require a person with a disability to engage in a futile gesture if such person has actual notice that a person or organization covered by this title does not intend to comply with its provisions.

(2) Injunctive relief. In the case of violations of sections 302(b)(2)(A)(iv) and section 303(a), injunctive relief shall

include an order to alter facilities to make such facilities readily accessible to and usable by individuals with disabilities to the extent required by this title. Where appropriate, injunctive relief shall also include requiring the provision of an auxiliary aid or service, modification of a policy, or provision of alternative methods, to the extent required by this title.

(b) Enforcement by the Attorney General.

    (1) Denial of rights.

      (A) Duty to investigate.

        (i) In general. The Attorney General shall investigate alleged violations of this title, and shall undertake periodic reviews of compliance of covered entities under this title.

        (ii) Attorney General certification. On the application of a State or local government, the Attorney General may, in consultation with the Architectural and Transportation Barriers Compliance Board, and after prior notice and a public hearing at which persons, including individuals with disabilities, are provided an opportunity to testify against such certification, certify that a State law or local building code or similar ordinance that establishes accessibility requirements meets or exceeds the minimum requirements of this Act for the accessibility and usability of covered facilities under this title. At any enforcement proceeding under this section, such certification by the Attorney General shall be rebuttable evidence that such State law or local ordinance does meet or exceed the minimum requirements of this Act.

      (B) Potential violation. If the Attorney General has reasonable cause to believe that

        (i) any person or group of persons is engaged in a pattern or practice of discrimination under this title; or

        (ii) any person or group of persons has been discriminated against under this title and such discrimination raises an issue of general public importance, the Attorney General may commence a civil action in any appropriate United States district court.

    (2) Authority of court. In a civil action under paragraph (1)(B), the court

      (A) may grant any equitable relief that such court considers to be appropriate, including, to the extent required by this title

        (i) granting temporary, preliminary, or permanent relief;

        (ii) providing an auxiliary aid or service, modification of policy, practice, or procedure, or alternative method; and

        (iii) making facilities readily accessible to and usable by individuals with disabilities;

      (B) may award such other relief as the court considers to be appropriate, including monetary damages to persons aggrieved when requested by the Attorney General; and

      (C) may, to vindicate the public interest, assess a civil penalty against the entity in an amount

        (i) not exceeding $50,000 for a first violation; and

        (ii) not exceeding $100,000 for any subsequent violation.

    (3) Single violation. For purposes of paragraph (2)(C), in determining whether a first or subsequent violation has occurred, a determination in a single action, by judgment or settlement, that the covered entity has engaged in more than one discriminatory act shall be counted as a single violation.

    (4) Punitive damages. For purposes of subsection (b)(2)(B), the term "monetary damages" and "such other relief" does not include punitive damages.

    (5) Judicial consideration. In a civil action under paragraph (1)(B), the court, when considering what amount of civil penalty, if any, is appropriate, shall give consideration to any good faith effort or attempt to comply with this Act by the entity. In evaluating good faith, the court shall consider, among other factors it deems relevant, whether the entity could have reasonably anticipated the need for an appropriate type of auxiliary aid needed to accommodate the unique needs of a particular individual with a disability.

SEC. 309. EXAMINATIONS AND COURSES.

Any person that offers examinations or courses related to applications, licensing, certification, or credentialing for secondary or postsecondary education, professional, or trade purposes shall offer such examinations or courses in a place and manner accessible to persons with disabilities or offer alternative accessible arrangements for such individuals.

SEC. 310. EFFECTIVE DATE.

(a) General Rule. Except as provided in subsections (b) and (c), this title shall become effective 18 months after the date of the enactment of this Act.

(b) Civil Actions. Except for any civil action brought for a violation of section 303, no civil action shall be brought for any act or omission described in section 302 which occurs

    (1) during the first 6 months after the effective date, against businesses that employ 25 or fewer employees and have gross receipts of $1,000,000 or less; and

    (2) during the first year after the effective date, against businesses that employ 10 or fewer employees and have gross receipts of $500,000 or less.

(c) Exception. Sections 302(a) for purposes of section 302(b)(2) (B) and (C) only, 304(a) for purposes of section 304(b)(3) only, 304(b)(3), 305, and 306 shall take effect on the date of the enactment of this Act.

TITLE IV—TELECOMMUNICATIONS

SEC. 401. TELECOMMUNICATIONS RELAY SERVICES FOR HEARING-IMPAIRED AND SPEECH-IMPAIRED INDIVIDUALS.

(a) Telecommunications. Title II of the Communications Act of 1934 (47 U.S.C. 201 et seq.) is amended by adding at the end thereof the following new section:

"SEC. 225. TELECOMMUNICATIONS SERVICES FOR HEARING-IMPAIRED AND SPEECH-IMPAIRED INDIVIDUALS.

"(a) Definitions. As used in this section

"(1) Common carrier or carrier. The term 'common carrier' or 'carrier' includes any common carrier engaged in interstate communication by wire or radio as defined in section 3(h) and any common carrier engaged in intrastate communication by wire or radio, notwithstanding sections 2(b) and 221(b).

"(2) TDD. The term 'TDD' means a Telecommunications Device for the Deaf, which is a machine that employs graphic communication in the transmission of coded signals through a wire or radio communication system.

"(3) Telecommunications relay services. The term 'telecommunications relay services' means telephone transmission services that provide the ability for an individual who has a hearing impairment or speech impairment to engage in communication by wire or radio with a hearing individual in a manner that is functionally equivalent to the ability of an individual who does not have a hearing impairment or speech impairment to communicate using voice communication services by wire or radio. Such term includes services that enable two-way communication between an individual who uses a TDD or other nonvoice terminal device and an individual who does not use such a device.

"(b) Availability of Telecommunications Relay Services.

"(1) In general. In order to carry out the purposes established under section 1, to make available to all individuals in the United States a rapid, efficient nationwide communication service, and to increase the utility of the telephone system of the Nation, the Commission shall ensure that interstate and intrastate telecommunications relay services are available, to the extent possible and in the most efficient manner, to hearing-impaired and speech-impaired individuals in the United States.

"(2) Use of General Authority and Remedies. For the purposes of administering and enforcing the provisions of this section and the regulations prescribed thereunder, the Commission shall have the same authority, power, and functions with respect to common carriers engaged in intrastate communication as the Commission has in administering and enforcing the provisions of this title with respect to any common carrier engaged in interstate communication. Any violation of this section by any common carrier engaged in intrastate communication shall be subject to the same remedies, penalties, and procedures as are applicable to a violation of this Act by a common carrier engaged in interstate communication.

"(c) Provision of Services. Each common carrier providing telephone voice transmission services shall, not later than 3 years after the date of enactment of this section, provide in compliance with the regulations prescribed under this section, throughout the area in which it offers service, telecom-

munications relay services, individually, through designees, through a competitively selected vendor, or in concert with other carriers. A common carrier shall be considered to be in compliance with such regulations

"(1) with respect to intrastate telecommunications relay services in any State that does not have a certified program under subsection (f) and with respect to interstate telecommunications relay services, if such common carrier (or other entity through which the carrier is providing such relay services) is in compliance with the Commission's regulations under subsection (d); or

"(2) with respect to intrastate telecommunications relay services in any State that has a certified program under subsection (f) for such State, if such common carrier (or other entity through which the carrier is providing such relay services) is in compliance with the program certified under subsection (f) for such State.

"(d) Regulations.

"(1) In general. The Commission shall, not later than 1 year after the date of enactment of this section, prescribe regulations to implement this section, including regulations that

"(A) establish functional requirements, guidelines, and operations procedures for telecommunications relay services;

"(B) establish minimum standards that shall be met in carrying out subsection (c);

"(C) require that telecommunications relay services operate every day for 24 hours per day;

"(D) require that users of telecommunications relay services pay rates no greater than the rates paid for functionally equivalent voice communication services with respect to such factors as the duration of the call, the time of day, and the distance from point of origination to point of termination;

"(E) prohibit relay operators from failing to fulfill the obligations of common carriers by refusing calls or limiting the length of calls that use telecommunications relay services;

"(F) prohibit relay operators from disclosing the content of any relayed conversation and from keeping records of the content of any such conversation beyond the duration of the call; and

"(G) prohibit relay operators from intentionally altering a relayed conversation.

"(2) Technology. The Commission shall ensure that regulations prescribed to implement this section encourage, consistent with section 7(a) of this Act, the use of existing technology and do not discourage or impair the development of improved technology.

"(3) Jurisdictional separation of costs.

"(A) In general. Consistent with the provisions of section 410 of this Act, the Commission shall prescribe regulations governing the jurisdictional separation of costs for the services provided pursuant to this section.

"(B) Recovering costs. Such regulations shall generally provide that costs caused by interstate telecommunications relay services shall be recovered from all subscribers for every interstate service and costs caused by intrastate telecommunications relay services shall be recovered from the intrastate jurisdiction. In a State that has a certified program under subsection (f), a State commission shall permit a common carrier to recover the costs incurred in providing intrastate telecommunications relay services by a method consistent with the requirements of this section.

"(e) Enforcement.

"(1) In general. Subject to subsections (f) and (g), the Commission shall enforce this section.

"(2) Complaint. The Commission shall resolve, by final order, a complaint alleging a violation of this section within 180 days after the date such complaint is filed.

"(f) Certification.

"(1) State documentation. Any State desiring to establish a State program under this section shall submit documentation to the Commission that describes the program of such State for implementing intrastate telecommunications relay services and the procedures and remedies available for enforcing any requirements imposed by the State program.

"(2) Requirements for certification. After review of such documentation, the Commission shall certify the State program if the Commission determines that

"(A) the program makes available to hearing-impaired and speech-impaired individuals, either directly, through designees, through a competitively selected vendor, or through regulation of intrastate common carriers, intrastate telecommunications relay services in such State in a manner that meets or exceeds the requirements of regulations prescribed by the Commission under subsection (d); and

"(B) the program makes available adequate procedures and remedies for enforcing the requirements of the State program.

"(3) Method of funding. Except as provided in subsection (d), the Commission shall not refuse to certify a State program based solely on the method such State will implement for funding intrastate telecommunication relay services.

"(4) Suspension or revocation of certification. The Commission may suspend or revoke such certification if, after notice and opportunity for hearing, the Commission determines that such certification is no longer warranted. In a State whose program has been suspended or revoked, the Commission shall take such steps as may be necessary, consistent with this section, to ensure continuity of telecommunications relay services.

"(g) Complaint.

"(1) Referral of complaint. If a complaint to the Commission alleges a violation of this section with respect to intrastate telecommunications relay services within a State and certification of the program of such State under subsection (f) is in effect, the Commission shall refer such complaint to such State.

"(2) Jurisdiction of commission. After referring a complaint to a State under paragraph (1), the Commission shall exercise jurisdiction over such complaint only if

"(A) final action under such State program has not been taken on such complaint by such State

"(i) within 180 days after the complaint is filed with such State; or

"(ii) within a shorter period as prescribed by the regulations of such State; or

"(B) the Commission determines that such State program is no longer qualified for certification under subsection (f)."

(b) Conforming Amendments. The Communications Act of 1934 (47 U.S.C. 151 et seq.) is amended

(1) in section 2(b) (47 U.S.C. 152(b)), by striking section 224 and inserting sections 224 and 225 ; and

(2) in section 221(b) (47 U.S.C. 221(b)), by striking section 301 and inserting sections 225 and 301.

SEC. 402. CLOSED-CAPTIONING OF PUBLIC SERVICE ANNOUNCEMENTS.

Section 711 of the Communications Act of 1934 is amended to read as follows:

"SEC. 711. CLOSED-CAPTIONING OF PUBLIC SERVICE ANNOUNCEMENTS.

"Any television public service announcement that is produced or funded in whole or in part by any agency or instrumentality of Federal Government shall include closed captioning of the verbal content of such announcement. A television broadcast station licensee

"(1) shall not be required to supply closed captioning for any such announcement that fails to include it; and

"(2) shall not be liable for broadcasting any such announcement without transmitting a closed caption unless the licensee intentionally fails to transmit the closed caption that was included with the announcement."

TITLE V—MISCELLANEOUS PROVISIONS
SEC. 501. CONSTRUCTION.

(a) In General. Except as otherwise provided in this Act, nothing in this Act shall be construed to apply a lesser standard than the standards applied under title V of the Rehabilitation Act of 1973 (29 U.S.C. 790 et seq.) or the regulations issued by Federal agencies pursuant to such title.

(b) Relationship to Other Laws. Nothing in this Act shall be construed to invalidate or limit the remedies, rights, and procedures of any Federal law or law of any State or political subdivision of any State or jurisdiction that provides greater or equal protection for the rights of individuals with disabilities than are afforded by this Act. Nothing in this Act shall be construed to preclude the prohibition of, or the imposition of restrictions on, smoking in places of employment covered by title I, in transportation covered by title II or III, or in places of public accommodation covered by title III.

(c) Insurance. Titles I through IV of this Act shall not be construed to prohibit or restrict

(1) an insurer, hospital or medical service company, health maintenance organization, or any agent, or entity that administers benefit plans, or similar organizations from underwriting risks, classifying risks, or administering such risks that are based on or not inconsistent with State law; or

(2) a person or organization covered by this Act from establishing, sponsoring, observing or administering the terms of a bona fide benefit plan that are based on underwriting risks, classifying risks, or administering such risks that are based on or not inconsistent with State law; or

(3) a person or organization covered by this Act from establishing, sponsoring, observing or administering the terms of a bona fide benefit plan that is not subject to State laws that regulate insurance.

Paragraphs (1), (2), and (3) shall not be used as a subterfuge to evade the purposes of title I and III.

(d) Accommodations and Services. Nothing in this Act shall be construed to require an individual with a disability to accept an accommodation, aid, service, opportunity, or benefit which such individual chooses not to accept.

SEC. 502. STATE IMMUNITY.

A State shall not be immune under the eleventh amendment to the Constitution of the United States from an action in Federal or State court of competent jurisdiction for a violation of this Act. In any action against a State for a violation of the requirements of this Act, remedies (including remedies both at law and in equity) are available for such a violation to the same extent as such remedies are available for such a violation in an action against any public or private entity other than a State.

SEC. 503. PROHIBITION AGAINST RETALIATION AND COERCION.

(a) Retaliation. No person shall discriminate against any individual because such individual has opposed any act or practice made unlawful by this Act or because such individual made a charge, testified, assisted, or participated in any manner in an investigation, proceeding, or hearing under this Act.

(b) Interference, Coercion, or Intimidation. It shall be unlawful to coerce, intimidate, threaten, or interfere with any individual in the exercise or enjoyment of, or on account of his or her having exercised or enjoyed, or on account of his or her having aided or encouraged any other individual in the exercise or enjoyment of, any right granted or protected by this Act.

(c) Remedies and Procedures. The remedies and procedures available under sections 107, 203, and 308 of this Act shall be available to aggrieved persons for violations of sub-

sections (a) and (b), with respect to title I, title II and title III, respectively.

SEC. 504. REGULATIONS BY THE ARCHITECTURAL AND TRANSPORTATION BARRIERS COMPLIANCE BOARD.

(a) Issuance of Guidelines. Not later than 9 months after the date of enactment of this Act, the Architectural and Transportation Barriers Compliance Board shall issue minimum guidelines that shall supplement the existing Minimum Guidelines and Requirements for Accessible Design for purposes of titles II and III of this Act.

(b) Contents of Guidelines. The supplemental guidelines issued under subsection (a) shall establish additional requirements, consistent with this Act, to ensure that buildings, facilities, rail passenger cars, and vehicles are accessible, in terms of architecture and design, transportation, and communication, to individuals with disabilities.

(c) Qualified Historic Properties.

(1) In general. The supplemental guidelines issued under subsection (a) shall include procedures and requirements for alterations that will threaten or destroy the historic significance of qualified historic buildings and facilities as defined in 4.1.7(1)(a) of the Uniform Federal Accessibility Standards.

(2) Sites eligible for listing in National Register. With respect to alterations of buildings or facilities that are eligible for listing in the National Register of Historic Places under the National Historic Preservation Act (16 U.S.C. 470 et seq.), the guidelines described in paragraph (1) shall, at a minimum, maintain the procedures and requirements established in 4.1.7 (1) and (2) of the Uniform Federal Accessibility Standards.

(3) Other sites. With respect to alterations of buildings or facilities designated as historic under State or local law, the guidelines described in paragraph (1) shall establish procedures equivalent to those established by 4.1.7(1) (b) and (c) of the Uniform Federal Accessibility Standards, and shall require, at a minimum, compliance with the requirements established in 4.1.7(2) of such standards.

SEC. 505. ATTORNEY'S FEES.

In any action or administrative proceeding commenced pursuant to this Act, the court or agency, in its discretion, may allow the prevailing party, other than the United States, a reasonable attorney's fee, including litigation expenses, and costs, and the United States shall be liable for the foregoing the same as a private individual.

SEC. 506. TECHNICAL ASSISTANCE.

(a) Plan for Assistance.

(1) In general. Not later than 180 days after the date of enactment of this Act, the Attorney General, in consultation with the Chair of the Equal Employment Opportunity Commission, the Secretary of Transportation, the

Chair of the Architectural and Transportation Barriers Compliance Board, and the Chairman of the Federal Communications Commission, shall develop a plan to assist entities covered under this Act, and other Federal agencies, in understanding the responsibility of such entities and agencies under this Act.

(2) Publication of plan. The Attorney General shall publish the plan referred to in paragraph (1) for public comment in accordance with subchapter II of chapter 5 of title 5, United States Code (commonly known as the Administrative Procedure Act).

(b) Agency and Public Assistance. The Attorney General may obtain the assistance of other Federal agencies in carrying out subsection (a), including the National Council on Disability, the President's Committee on Employment of People with Disabilities, the Small Business Administration, and the Department of Commerce.

(c) Implementation.

(1) Rendering assistance. Each Federal agency that has responsibility under paragraph (2) for implementing this Act may render technical assistance to individuals and institutions that have rights or duties under the respective title or titles for which such agency has responsibility.

(2) Implementation of titles.

(A) Title I. The Equal Employment Opportunity Commission and the Attorney General shall implement the plan for assistance developed under subsection (a), for title I.

(B) Title II.

(i) Subtitle A. The Attorney General shall implement such plan for assistance for subtitle A of title II.

(ii) Subtitle B. The Secretary of Transportation shall implement such plan for assistance for subtitle B of title II.

(C) Title III. The Attorney General, in coordination with the Secretary of Transportation and the Chair of the Architectural Transportation Barriers Compliance Board, shall implement such plan for assistance for title III, except for section 304, the plan for assistance for which shall be implemented by the Secretary of Transportation.

(D) Title IV. The Chairman of the Federal Communications Commission, in coordination with the Attorney General, shall implement such plan for assistance for title IV.

(3) Technical assistance manuals. Each Federal agency that has responsibility under paragraph (2) for implementing this Act shall, as part of its implementation responsibilities, ensure the availability and provision of appropriate technical assistance manuals to individuals or entities with rights or duties under this Act no later than six months after applicable final regulations are published under titles I, II, III, and IV.

(d) Grants and Contracts.

(1) In general. Each Federal agency that has responsibility under subsection (c)(2) for implementing this Act may make grants or award contracts to effectuate the purposes of this section, subject to the availability of appropriations. Such grants and contracts may be awarded to individuals, institutions not organized for profit and no part of the net earnings of which inures to the benefit of any private shareholder or individual (including educational institutions), and associations representing individuals who have rights or duties under this Act. Contracts may be awarded to entities organized for profit, but such entities may not be the recipients of grants described in this paragraph.

(2) Dissemination of information. Such grants and contracts, among other uses, may be designed to ensure wide dissemination of information about the rights and duties established by this Act and to provide information and technical assistance about techniques for effective compliance with this Act.

(e) Failure to Receive Assistance. An employer, public accommodation, or other entity covered under this Act shall not be excused from compliance with the requirements of this Act because of any failure to receive technical assistance under this section, including any failure in the development or dissemination of any technical assistance manual authorized by this section.

SEC. 507. FEDERAL WILDERNESS AREAS.

(a) Study. The National Council on Disability shall conduct a study and report on the effect that wilderness designations and wilderness land management practices have on the ability of individuals with disabilities to use and enjoy the National Wilderness Preservation System as established under the Wilderness Act (16 U.S.C. 1131 et seq.).

(b) Submission of Report. Not later than 1 year after the enactment of this Act, the National Council on Disability shall submit the report required under subsection (a) to Congress.

(c) Specific Wilderness Access.

(1) In general. Congress reaffirms that nothing in the Wilderness Act is to be construed as prohibiting the use of a wheelchair in a wilderness area by an individual whose disability requires use of a wheelchair, and consistent with the Wilderness Act no agency is required to provide any form of special treatment or accommodation, or to construct any facilities or modify any conditions of lands within a wilderness area in order to facilitate such use.

(2) Definition. For purposes of paragraph (1), the term "wheelchair" means a device designed solely for use by a mobility-impaired person for locomotion, that is suitable for use in an indoor pedestrian area.

SEC. 508. TRANSVESTITES.

For the purposes of this Act, the term "disabled" or "disability" shall not apply to an individual solely because that individual is a transvestite.

SEC. 509. COVERAGE OF CONGRESS AND THE AGENCIES OF THE LEGISLATIVE BRANCH.

(a) Coverage of the Senate.

(1) Commitment to Rule XLII. The Senate reaffirms its commitment to Rule XLII of the Standing Rules of the Senate which provides as follows:

"No member, officer, or employee of the Senate shall, with respect to employment by the Senate or any office thereof

"(a) fail or refuse to hire an individual;

"(b) discharge an individual; or

"(c) otherwise discriminate against an individual with respect to promotion, compensation, or terms, conditions, or privileges of employment on the basis of such individual's race, color, religion, sex, national origin, age, or state of physical handicap."

(2) Application to Senate employment. The rights and protection provided pursuant to this Act, the Civil Rights Act of 1990 (S. 2104, 101st Congress), the Civil Rights Act of 1964, the Age Discrimination in Employment Act of 1967, and the Rehabilitation Act of 1973 shall apply with respect to employment by the United States Senate.

(3) Investigation and adjudication of claims. All claims raised by any individual with respect to Senate employment, pursuant to the Acts referred to in paragraph (2), shall be investigated and adjudicated by the Select Committee on Ethics, pursuant to S. Res. 338, 88th Congress, as amended, or such other entity as the Senate may designate.

(4) Rights of employees. The Committee on Rules and Administration shall ensure that Senate employees are informed of their rights under the Acts referred to in paragraph (2).

(5) Applicable Remedies. When assigning remedies to individuals found to have a valid claim under the Acts referred to in paragraph (2), the Select Committee on Ethics, or such other entity as the Senate may designate, should to the extent practicable apply the same remedies applicable to all other employees covered by the Acts referred to in paragraph (2). Such remedies shall apply exclusively.

(6) Matters Other Than Employment.

(A) In General. The rights and protection under this Act shall, subject to subparagraph (B), apply with respect to the conduct of the Senate regarding matters other than employment.

(B) Remedies. The Architect of the Capitol shall establish remedies and procedures to be utilized with respect to the rights and protections provided pursuant to subparagraph (A). Such remedies and procedures shall apply exclusively, after approval in accordance with subparagraph (C).

(C) Proposed remedies and procedures. For purposes of subparagraph (B), the Architect of the Capitol shall submit proposed remedies and procedures to the Senate Committee on Rules and Administration. The remedies and procedures shall be effective upon the approval of the Committee on Rules and Administration.

(7) Exercise of rulemaking power. Notwithstanding any other provision of law, enforcement and adjudication of the rights and protections referred to in paragraph (2) and (6)(A) shall be within the exclusive jurisdiction of the United States Senate. The provisions of paragraph (1), (3), (4), (5), (6)(B), and (6)(C) are enacted by the Senate as an exercise of the rulemaking power of the Senate, with full recognition of the right of the Senate to change its rules, in the same manner, and to the same extent, as in the case of any other rule of the Senate.

(b) Coverage of the House of Representatives.

(1) In general. Notwithstanding any other provision of this Act or of law, the purposes of this Act shall, subject to paragraphs (2) and (3), apply in their entirety to the House of Representatives.

(2) Employment in the House.

(A) Application. The rights and protections under this Act shall, subject to subparagraph (B), apply with respect to any employee in an employment position in the House of Representatives and any employing authority of the House of Representatives.

(B) Administration.

(i) In general. In the administration of this paragraph, the remedies and procedures made applicable pursuant to the resolution described in clause (ii) shall apply exclusively.

(ii) Resolution. The resolution referred to in clause (i) is House Resolution 15 of the One Hundred First Congress, as agreed to January 3, 1989, or any other provision that continues in effect the provisions of, or is a successor to, the Fair Employment Practices Resolution (House Resolution 558 of the One Hundredth Congress, as agreed to October 4, 1988).

(C) Exercise of rulemaking power. The provisions of subparagraph (B) are enacted by the House of Representatives as an exercise of the rulemaking power of the House of Representatives, with full recognition of the right of the House to change its rules, in the same manner, and to the same extent as in the case of any other rule of the House.

(3) Matters other than employment.

(A) In general. The rights and protection under this Act shall, subject to subparagraph (B), apply with respect to the conduct of the House of Representatives regarding matters other than employment.

(B) Remedies. The Architect of the Capitol shall establish remedies and procedures to be utilized with respect to the rights and protections provided pursuant to subparagraph (A). Such remedies and procedures shall apply exclusively, after approval in accordance with subparagraph (C).

(C) Approval. For purposes of subparagraph (B), the Architect of the Capitol shall submit proposed remedies and procedures to the Speaker of the House of Representatives. The remedies and procedures shall be effective upon the approval of the Speaker, after consultation with the House Office Building Commission.

(c) Instrumentalities of Congress.

(1) In general. The rights and protection under this Act shall, subject to paragraph (2), apply with respect to the conduct of each instrumentality of the Congress.

(2) Establishment of remedies and procedures by instrumentalities. The chief official of each instrumentality of the Congress shall establish remedies and procedures to be utilized with respect to the rights and protections provided pursuant to paragraph (1). Such remedies and procedures shall apply exclusively.

(3) Report to Congress. The chief official of each instrumentality of the Congress shall, after establishing remedies and procedures for purposes of paragraph (2), submit to the Congress a report describing the remedies and procedures.

(4) Definition of instrumentalities. For purposes of this section, instrumentalities of the Congress include the following: the Architect of the Capitol, the Congressional Budget Office, the General Accounting Office, the Government Printing Office, the Library of Congress, the Office of Technology Assessment, and the United States Botanic Garden.

(5) Construction. Nothing in this section shall alter the enforcement procedures for individuals with disabilities provided in the General Accounting Office Personnel Act of 1980 and regulations promulgated pursuant to that Act.

SEC. 510. ILLEGAL USE OF DRUGS.

(a) In General. For purposes of this Act, the term "individual with a disability" does not include an individual who is currently engaging in the illegal use of drugs, when the covered entity acts on the basis of such use.

(b) Rules of Construction. Nothing in subsection (a) shall be construed to exclude as an individual with a disability an individual who

(1) has successfully completed a supervised drug rehabilitation program and is no longer engaging in the illegal use of drugs, or has otherwise been rehabilitated successfully and is no longer engaging in such use;

(2) is participating in a supervised rehabilitation program and is no longer engaging in such use; or

(3) is erroneously regarded as engaging in such use, but is not engaging in such use;

except that it shall not be a violation of this Act for a covered entity to adopt or administer reasonable policies or procedures, including but not limited to drug testing, designed to ensure that an individual described in paragraph (1) or (2) is no longer engaging in the illegal use of drugs; however, nothing in this section shall be construed to encourage, prohibit,

restrict, or authorize the conducting of testing for the illegal use of drugs.

(c) Health and Other Services. Notwithstanding subsection (a) and section 511(b)(3), an individual shall not be denied health services, or services provided in connection with drug rehabilitation, on the basis of the current illegal use of drugs if the individual is otherwise entitled to such services.

(d) Definition of Illegal use of drugs.

(1) In general. The term "illegal use of drugs" means the use of drugs, the possession or distribution of which is unlawful under the Controlled Substances Act (21 U.S.C. 812). Such term does not include the use of a drug taken under supervision by a licensed health care professional, or other uses authorized by the Controlled Substances Act or other provisions of Federal law.

(2) Drugs. The term "drug" means a controlled substance, as defined in schedules I through V of section 202 of the Controlled Substances Act.

SEC. 511. DEFINITIONS.

(a) Homosexuality and Bisexuality. For purposes of the definition of "disability" in section 3(2), homosexuality and bisexuality are not impairments and as such are not disabilities under this Act.

(b) Certain Conditions. Under this Act, the term "disability" shall not include

(1) transvestism, transsexualism, pedophilia, exhibitionism, voyeurism, gender identity disorders not resulting from physical impairments, or other sexual behavior disorders;

(2) compulsive gambling, kleptomania, or pyromania; or

(3) psychoactive substance use disorders resulting from current illegal use of drugs.

SEC. 512. AMENDMENTS TO THE REHABILITATION ACT.

(a) Definition of Handicapped Individual. Section 7(8) of the Rehabilitation Act of 1973 (29 U.S.C. 706(8)) is amended by redesignating subparagraph (C) as subparagraph (D), and by inserting after subparagraph (B) the following subparagraph:

"(C)

"(i) For purposes of title V, the term 'individual with handicaps' does not include an individual who is currently engaging in the illegal use of drugs, when a covered entity acts on the basis of such use.

"(ii) Nothing in clause (i) shall be construed to exclude as an individual with handicaps an individual who

"(I) has successfully completed a supervised drug rehabilitation program and is no longer engaging in the illegal use of drugs, or has otherwise been rehabilitated successfully and is no longer engaging in such use;

"(II) is participating in a supervised rehabilitation program and is no longer engaging in such use; or

"(III) is erroneously regarded as engaging in such use, but is not engaging in such use;

except that it shall not be a violation of this Act for a covered entity to adopt or administer reasonable policies or procedures, including but not limited to drug testing, designed to ensure that an individual described in subclause (I) or (II) is no longer engaging in the illegal use of drugs.

"(iii) Notwithstanding clause (i), for purposes of programs and activities providing health services and services provided under titles I, II and III, an individual shall not be excluded from the benefits of such programs or activities on the basis of his or her current illegal use of drugs if he or she is otherwise entitled to such services.

"(iv) For purposes of programs and activities providing educational services, local educational agencies may take disciplinary action pertaining to the use or possession of illegal drugs or alcohol against any handicapped student who currently is engaging in the illegal use of drugs or in the use of alcohol to the same extent that such disciplinary action is taken against nonhandicapped students. Furthermore, the due process procedures at 34 CFR 104.36 shall not apply to such disciplinary actions.

"(v) For purposes of sections 503 and 504 as such sections relate to employment, the term individual with handicaps does not include any individual who is an alcoholic whose current use of alcohol prevents such individual from performing the duties of the job in question or whose employment, by reason of such current alcohol abuse, would constitute a direct threat to property or the safety of others."

(b) Definition of Illegal Drugs. Section 7 of the Rehabilitation Act of 1973 (29 U.S.C. 706) is amended by adding at the end the following new paragraph:

"(22)(A) The term 'drug' means a controlled substance, as defined in schedules I through V of section 202 of the Controlled Substances Act (21 U.S.C. 812).

"(B) The term 'illegal use of drugs' means the use of drugs, the possession or distribution of which is unlawful under the Controlled Substances Act. Such term does not include the use of a drug taken under supervision by a licensed health care professional, or other uses authorized by the Controlled Substances Act or other provisions of Federal law."

(c) Conforming Amendments. Section 7(8)(B) of the Rehabilitation Act of 1973 (29 U.S.C. 706(8)(B)) is amended

(1) in the first sentence, by striking

"Subject to the second sentence of this subparagraph," and inserting "Subject to subparagraphs (C) and (D),"; and

(2) by striking the second sentence.

SEC. 513. ALTERNATIVE MEANS OF DISPUTE RESOLUTION.

Where appropriate and to the extent authorized by law, the use of alternative means of dispute resolution, including settlement negotiations, conciliation, facilitation, mediation, factfinding, minitrials, and arbitration, is encouraged to resolve disputes arising under this Act.

SEC. 514. SEVERABILITY.

Should any provision in this Act be found to be unconstitutional by a court of law, such provision shall be severed from the remainder of the Act, and such action shall not affect the enforceability of the remaining provisions of the Act.
Approved July 26, l990.

LEGISLATIVE HISTORY—S. 933 (H.R. 2273):
HOUSE REPORTS: No. 101- 485, Pt. 1 (Comm. on Public Works and Transportation), Pt. 2 (Comm. on Education and Labor), Pt. 3 (Comm. on the Judiciary), and Pt. 4 (Comm. on Energy and Commerce) all accompanying H.R. 2273; and No. 101-558 and No. 101-569 both from (Comm. of Conference).
SENATE REPORTS: No. 101-116 (Comm. on Labor and Human Resources).
CONGRESSIONAL RECORD:
Vol. 135 (1989): Sept. 7, considered and passed by Senate.
Vol. 136 (1990): May 17, 22, H.R. 2273 considered and passed House; S. 933 passed in lieu.
July 11, Senate recommitted conference report.
July 12, House agreed to conference report.
July 13, Senate agreed to conference report.
WEEKLY COMPILATION OF PRESIDENTIAL DOCUMENTS, Vol. 26 (1990): July 26, Presidential remarks and statement.

Excerpts from the Americans with Disabilities Act Accessibility Guidelines (ADAAG) for Buildings and Facilities

I. PURPOSE.

This document contains scoping and technical requirements for accessibility to buildings and facilities by individuals with disabilities under the Americans with Disabilities Act (ADA) of 1990. These scoping and technical requirements are to be applied during the design, construction, and alteration of buildings and facilities covered by Titles II and III of the ADA to the extent required by regulations issued by Federal agencies, including the Department of Justice and the Department of Transportation, under the ADA.

. . . . .

Paragraphs marked with an asterisk have related, non-mandatory material in the Appendix. In the Appendix, the corresponding paragraph numbers are preceded by an A. [Paragraphs from the appendix included in this excerpt immediately follow the sections to which they refer.]

2. GENERAL.
2.1 PROVISIONS FOR ADULTS AND CHILDREN.

The specifications in these guidelines are based upon adult dimensions and anthropometrics. These guidelines also contain alternate specifications based on children's dimensions and anthropometrics for drinking fountains, water closets, toilet stalls, lavatories, sinks, and fixed or built-in seating and tables.

2.2* EQUIVALENT FACILITATION.

Departures from particular technical and scoping requirements of this guideline by the use of other designs and technologies are permitted where the alternative designs and technologies used will provide substantially equivalent or greater access to and usability of the facility.

3. MISCELLANEOUS INSTRUCTIONS AND DEFINITIONS.
3.1 GRAPHIC CONVENTIONS.

Graphic conventions are shown in Table 1 [not included here]. Dimensions that are not marked minimum or maximum are absolute, unless otherwise indicated in the text or captions.

3.2 DIMENSIONAL TOLERANCES.

All dimensions are subject to conventional building industry tolerances for field conditions.

3.3 NOTES.

The text of these guidelines does not contain notes or footnotes. Additional information, explanations, and advisory materials are located in the Appendix. Paragraphs marked with an asterisk have related, nonmandatory material in the Appendix. In the Appendix, the corresponding paragraph numbers are preceded by an A.

3.4 GENERAL TERMINOLOGY.

comply with. Meet one or more specifications of these guidelines.

if, if ... then. Denotes a specification that applies only when the conditions described are present.

may. Denotes an option or alternative.

shall. Denotes a mandatory specification or requirement.

should. Denotes an advisory specification or recommendation.

3.5 DEFINITIONS.

Access Aisle. An accessible pedestrian space between elements, such as parking spaces, seating, and desks, that provides clearances appropriate for use of the elements.

Accessible. Describes a site, building, facility, or portion thereof that complies with these guidelines.

Accessible Element. An element specified by these guidelines (for example, telephone, controls, and the like).

Accessible Route. A continuous unobstructed path connecting all accessible elements and spaces of a building or facility. Interior accessible routes may include corridors, floors, ramps, elevators, lifts, and clear floor space at fixtures. Exterior accessible routes may include parking access aisles, curb ramps, crosswalks at vehicular ways, walks, ramps, and lifts.

Accessible Space. Space that complies with these guidelines.

Adaptability. The ability of certain building spaces and elements, such as kitchen counters, sinks, and grab bars, to be added or altered so as to accommodate the needs of individuals with or without disabilities or to accommodate the needs of persons with different types or degrees of disability.

Addition. An expansion, extension, or increase in the gross floor area of a building or facility.

Administrative Authority. A governmental agency that adopts or enforces regulations and guidelines for the design, construction, or alteration of buildings and facilities.

Alteration. An alteration is a change to a building or facility that affects or could affect the usability of the building or facility or part thereof. Alterations include, but are not limited to, remodeling, renovation, rehabilitation, reconstruction, historic restoration, resurfacing of circulation paths or vehicular ways, changes or rearrangement of the structural parts or elements, and changes or rearrangement in the plan configuration of walls and full-height partitions. Normal maintenance, reroofing, painting or wallpapering, or changes to mechanical and electrical systems are not alterations unless they affect the usability of the building or facility.

Area of Rescue Assistance. An area, which has direct access to an exit, where people who are unable to use stairs may remain temporarily in safety to await further instructions or assistance during emergency evacuation.

Assembly Area. A room or space accommodating a group of individuals for recreational, educational, political, social, civic, or amusement purposes, or for the consumption of food and drink.

Building. Any structure used and intended for supporting or sheltering any use or occupancy.

Circulation Path. An exterior or interior way of passage from one place to another for pedestrians, including, but not limited to, walks, hallways, courtyards, stairways, and stair landings.

Clear. Unobstructed.

Clear Floor Space. The minimum unobstructed floor or ground space required to accommodate a single, stationary wheelchair and occupant.

Closed Circuit Telephone. A telephone with dedicated line(s) such as a house phone, courtesy phone or phone that must be used to gain entrance to a facility.

Common Use. Refers to those interior and exterior rooms, spaces, or elements that are made available for the use of a restricted group of people (for example, occupants of a homeless shelter, the occupants of an office building, or the guests of such occupants).

Cross Slope. The slope that is perpendicular to the direction of travel (see running slope).

Curb Ramp. A short ramp cutting through a curb or built up to it.

Detectable Warning. A standardized surface feature built in or applied to walking surfaces or other elements to warn visually impaired people of hazards on a circulation path.

Dwelling Unit. A single unit which provides a kitchen or food preparation area, in addition to rooms and spaces for living, bathing, sleeping, and the like. Dwelling units include a single family home or a townhouse used as a transient group home; an apartment building used as a shelter; guestrooms in a hotel that provide sleeping accommodations and food preparation areas; and other similar facilities used on a transient basis. For purposes of these guidelines, use of the term "Dwelling Unit" does not imply the unit is used as a residence.

Egress, Means of. A continuous and unobstructed way of exit travel from any point in a building or facility to a public way. A means of egress comprises vertical and horizontal travel and may include intervening room spaces, doorways, hallways, corridors, passageways, balconies, ramps, stairs, enclosures, lobbies, horizontal exits, courts and yards. An accessible means of egress is one that complies with these guidelines and does not include stairs, steps, or escalators. Areas of rescue assistance or evacuation elevators may be included as part of accessible means of egress.

Element. An architectural or mechanical component of a building, facility, space, or site, e.g., telephone, curb ramp, door, drinking fountain, seating, or water closet.

Entrance. Any access point to a building or portion of a building or facility used for the purpose of entering. An entrance includes the approach walk, the vertical access leading to the entrance platform, the entrance platform itself, vestibules if provided, the entry door(s) or gate(s), and the hardware of the entry door(s) or gate(s).

Facility. All or any portion of buildings, structures, site improvements, complexes, equipment, roads, walks, passageways, parking lots, or other real or personal property located on a site.

Ground Floor. Any occupiable floor less than one story above or below grade with direct access to grade. A building or facility always has at least one ground floor and may have more than one ground floor as where a split level entrance has been provided or where a building is built into a hillside.

Mezzanine or Mezzanine Floor. That portion of a story which is an intermediate floor level placed within the story and having occupiable space above and below its floor.

Marked Crossing. A crosswalk or other identified path intended for pedestrian use in crossing a vehicular way.

Multifamily Dwelling. Any building containing more than two dwelling units.

Occupiable. A room or enclosed space designed for human occupancy in which individuals congregate for amusement, educational or similar purposes, or in which occupants are engaged at labor, and which is equipped with means of egress, light, and ventilation.

Operable Part. A part of a piece of equipment or appliance used to insert or withdraw objects, or to activate, deactivate, or adjust the equipment or appliance (for example, coin slot, pushbutton, handle).

Path of Travel. (Reserved).

Power-assisted Door. A door used for human passage with a mechanism that helps to open the door, or relieves the opening resistance of a door, upon the activation of a switch or a continued force applied to the door itself.

Private Facility. A place of public accommodation or a commercial facility subject to title III of the ADA and 28 CFR part 36 or a transportation facility subject to title III of the ADA and 49 CFR 37.45.

Public Facility. A facility or portion of a facility constructed by, on behalf of, or for the use of a public entity subject to title II of the ADA and 28 CFR part 35 or to title II of the ADA and 49 CFR 37.41 or 37.43.

Public Use. Describes interior or exterior rooms or spaces that are made available to the general public. Public use may be provided at a building or facility that is privately or publicly owned.

Ramp. A walking surface which has a running slope greater than 1:20.

Running Slope. The slope that is parallel to the direction of travel (see Cross Slope).

Service Entrance. An entrance intended primarily for delivery of goods or services.

Signage. Displayed verbal, symbolic, tactile, and pictorial information.

Site. A parcel of land bounded by a property line or a designated portion of a public right-of-way.

Site Improvement. Landscaping, paving for pedestrian and vehicular ways, outdoor lighting, recreational facilities, and the like, added to a site.

Sleeping Accommodations. Rooms in which people sleep; for example, dormitory and hotel or motel guest rooms or suites.

Space. A definable area, e.g., room, toilet room, hall, assembly area, entrance, storage room, alcove, courtyard, or lobby.

Story. That portion of a building included between the upper surface of a floor and upper surface of the floor or roof next above. If such portion of a building does not include occupiable space, it is not considered a story for purposes of these guidelines. There may be more than one floor level within a story as in the case of a mezzanine or mezzanines.

Structural Frame. The structural frame shall be considered to be the columns and the girders, beams, trusses and spandrels having direct connections to the columns and all other members which are essential to the stability of the building as a whole.

Tactile. Describes an object that can be perceived using the sense of touch.

TDD (Telecommunication Devices for the Deaf). See Text Telephone.

Technically Infeasible. See 4.1.6(1)(j) EXCEPTION.

Text Telephone (TTY). Machinery or equipment that employs interactive text based communications through the transmission of coded signals across the standard telephone network. Text telephones can include, for example, devices known as TDDs (telecommunication display devices or telecommunication devices for deaf persons) or computers with special modems. Text telephones are also called TTYs, an abbreviation for tele-typewriter.

Transient Lodging.* A building, facility, or portion thereof, excluding inpatient medical care facilities and residential facilities, that contains sleeping accommodations. Transient lodging may include, but is not limited to, resorts, group homes, hotels, motels, and dormitories.

TTY (Tele-Typewriter). See Text Telephone.

Vehicular Way. A route intended for vehicular traffic, such as a street, driveway, or parking lot.

Walk. An exterior pathway with a prepared surface intended for pedestrian use, including general pedestrian areas such as plazas and courts.

4. ACCESSIBLE ELEMENTS AND SPACES: SCOPE AND TECHNICAL REQUIREMENTS.
4.1 MINIMUM REQUIREMENTS.

4.1.1* Application.

(1) General. All areas of newly designed or newly constructed buildings and facilities and altered portions of existing buildings and facilities shall comply with section 4, unless otherwise provided in this section or as modified in a special application section.

(2) Application Based on Building Use. Special application sections provide additional requirements based on building use. When a building or facility contains more than one use covered by a special application section, each portion shall comply with the requirements for that use.

(3)* Areas Used Only by Employees as Work Areas. Areas that are used only as work areas shall be designed and constructed so that individuals with disabilities can approach, enter, and exit the areas. These guidelines do not require that any areas used only as work areas be constructed to permit maneuvering within the work area or be constructed or equipped (i.e., with racks or shelves) to be accessible.

A4.1.1(3) Areas Used Only by Employees as Work Areas. Where there are a series of individual work stations of the same type (e.g., laboratories, service counters, ticket booths), 5%, but not less than one, of each type of work station should be constructed so that an individual with disabilities can maneuver within the work stations. Rooms housing individual offices in a typical office building must meet the requirements of the guidelines concerning doors, accessible routes, etc. but do not need to allow for maneuvering space around individual desks. Modifications required to permit maneuvering within the work area may be accomplished as a reasonable accommodation to individual employees with disabilities under Title I of the ADA. Consideration should also be given to placing shelves in employee work areas at a convenient height for accessibility or installing commercially available shelving that is adjustable so that reasonable accommodations can be made in the future.

If work stations are made accessible they should comply with the applicable provisions of 4.2 through 4.35.

(4) Temporary Structures. These guidelines cover temporary buildings or facilities as well as permanent facilities. Temporary buildings and facilities are not of permanent construction but are extensively used or are essential for public use for a period of time. Examples of temporary buildings or facilities covered by these guidelines include, but are not limited to: reviewing stands, temporary classrooms, bleacher areas, exhibit areas, temporary banking facilities, temporary health screening services, or temporary safe pedestrian passageways around a construction site. Structures, sites and equipment directly associated with the actual processes of construction, such as scaffolding, bridging, materials hoists, or construction trailers are not included.

(5) General Exceptions.

(a) In new construction, a person or entity is not required to meet fully the requirements of these guidelines where that person or entity can demonstrate that it is structurally impracticable to do so. Full compliance will be considered structurally impracticable only in those rare circumstances when the unique characteristics of terrain prevent the incorporation of accessibility features. If full compliance with the requirements of these guidelines is structurally impracticable, a person or entity shall comply with the requirements to the extent it is not structurally impracticable. Any portion of the building or facility which can be made accessible shall comply to the extent that it is not structurally impracticable.

(b) Accessibility is not required to or in:

(i) raised areas used primarily for purposes of security or life or fire safety, including, but not limited to, observation or lookout galleries, prison guard towers, fire towers, or fixed life guard stands;

(ii) non-occupiable spaces accessed only by ladders, catwalks, crawl spaces, very narrow passageways, tunnels, or freight (non-passenger) elevators, and frequented only by service personnel for maintenance, repair, or occasional monitoring of equipment; such spaces may include, but are not limited to, elevator pits, elevator penthouses, piping or equipment catwalks, water or sewage treatment pump rooms and stations, electric substations and transformer vaults, and highway and tunnel utility facilities; or

(iii) single occupant structures accessed only by a passageway that is below grade or that is elevated above standard curb height, including, but not limited to, toll booths accessed from underground tunnels.

4.1.3 Accessible Buildings: New Construction. Accessible buildings and facilities shall meet the following minimum requirements:

(2) All objects that overhang or protrude into circulation paths shall comply with 4.4.

(5)* One passenger elevator complying with 4.10 shall serve each level, including mezzanines, in all multi-story buildings and facilities unless exempted below. If more than one elevator is provided, each passenger elevator shall comply with 4.10.

EXCEPTION 1: Elevators are not required in:

(a) private facilities that are less than three stories or that have less than 3000 square feet per story unless the building is a shopping center, a shopping mall, or the professional office of a health care provider, or another type of facility as determined by the Attorney General; or

(b) public facilities that are less than three stories and that are not open to the general public if the story above or below the accessible ground floor houses no more than five persons and is less than 500 square feet. Examples may include, but are not limited to, drawbridge towers and boat traffic towers, lock and dam control stations, and train dispatching towers.

The elevator exemptions set forth in paragraphs (a) and (b) do not obviate or limit in any way the obligation to comply with the other accessibility requirements established in section 4.1.3. For example, floors above or below the accessible ground floor must meet the requirements of this section except for elevator service. If toilet or bathing facilities are provided on a level not served by an elevator, then toilet or bathing facilities must be provided on the accessible ground floor. In new construction, if a building or facility is eligible for exemption but a passenger elevator is nonetheless planned, that elevator shall meet the requirements of 4.10 and shall serve each level in the building. A passenger elevator that provides service from a garage to only one level of a building or facility is not required to serve other levels.

EXCEPTION 2: Elevator pits, elevator penthouses, mechanical rooms, piping or equipment catwalks are exempted from this requirement.

EXCEPTION 3: Accessible ramps complying with 4.8 may be used in lieu of an elevator.

EXCEPTION 4: Platform lifts (wheelchair lifts) complying with 4.11 of this guideline and applicable State or local codes may be used in lieu of an elevator only under the following conditions:

(a) To provide an accessible route to a performing area in an assembly occupancy.

(b) To comply with the wheelchair viewing position line-of-sight and dispersion requirements of 4.33.3.

(c) To provide access to incidental occupiable spaces and rooms which are not open to the general public and which house no more than five persons, including but not limited to equipment control rooms and projection booths.

(d) To provide access where existing site constraints or other constraints make use of a ramp or an elevator infeasible.

(e) To provide access to raised judges' benches, clerks' stations, speakers' platforms, jury boxes and witness stands or to depressed areas such as the well of a court.

EXCEPTION 5: Elevators located in air traffic control towers are not required to serve the cab and the floor immediately below the cab.

A4.1.3(5) Only passenger elevators are covered by the accessibility provisions of 4.10. Materials and equipment hoists, freight elevators not intended for passenger use, dumbwaiters, and construction elevators are not covered by these guidelines. If a building is exempt from the elevator requirement, it is not necessary to provide a platform lift or other means of vertical access in lieu of an elevator.

Under **Exception 4**, platform lifts are allowed where existing conditions make it impractical to install a ramp or elevator. Such conditions generally occur where it is essential to provide access to small raised or lowered areas where space may not be available for a ramp. Examples include, but are not limited to, raised pharmacy platforms, commercial offices raised above a sales floor, or radio and news booths.

(16) Building Signage:

(a) Signs which designate permanent rooms and spaces shall comply with 4.30.1, 4.30.4, 4.30.5 and 4.30.6.

(b) Other signs which provide direction to or information about functional spaces of the building shall comply with 4.30.1, 4.30.2, 4.30.3, and 4.30.5.

EXCEPTION: Building directories, menus, and all other signs which are temporary are not required to comply.

4.3 ACCESSIBLE ROUTE.

4.3.1* General. All walks, halls, corridors, aisles, skywalks, tunnels, and other spaces that are part of an accessible route shall comply with 4.3.

4.3.2 Location.

(1) At least one accessible route within the boundary of the site shall be provided from public transportation stops, accessible parking, and accessible passenger loading zones, and public streets or sidewalks to the accessible building entrance they serve. The accessible route shall, to the maximum extent feasible, coincide with the route for the general public.

(2) At least one accessible route shall connect accessible buildings, facilities, elements, and spaces that are on the same site.

(3) At least one accessible route shall connect accessible building or facility entrances with all accessible spaces and elements and with all accessible dwelling units within the building or facility.

(4) An accessible route shall connect at least one accessible entrance of each accessible dwelling unit with those exte-

rior and interior spaces and facilities that serve the accessible dwelling unit.

4.3.3 Width. The minimum clear width of an accessible route shall be 36 in (915 mm) except at doors (see 4.13.5 and 4.13.6). If a person in a wheelchair must make a turn around an obstruction, the minimum clear width of the accessible route shall be as shown in Fig. 7(a) and (b) [not included here].

4.3.4 Passing Space. If an accessible route has less than 60 in (1525 mm) clear width, then passing spaces at least 60 in by 60 in (1525 mm by 1525 mm) shall be located at reasonable intervals not to exceed 200 ft (61 m). A T-intersection of two corridors or walks is an acceptable passing place.

4.3.5 Head Room. Accessible routes shall comply with 4.4.2.

4.3.6 Surface Textures. The surface of an accessible route shall comply with 4.5.

4.3.7 Slope. An accessible route with a running slope greater than 1:20 is a ramp and shall comply with 4.8. Nowhere shall the cross slope of an accessible route exceed 1:50.

4.3.8 Changes in Levels. Changes in levels along an accessible route shall comply with 4.5.2. If an accessible route has changes in level greater than ½ in (13 mm), then a curb ramp, ramp, elevator, or platform lift (as permitted in 4.1.3 and 4.1.6) shall be provided that complies with 4.7, 4.8, 4.10, or 4.11, respectively. An accessible route does not include stairs, steps, or escalators. See definition of "egress, means of" in 3.5.

4.3.9 Doors. Doors along an accessible route shall comply with 4.13.

4.3.10* Egress. Accessible routes serving any accessible space or element shall also serve as a means of egress for emergencies or connect to an accessible area of rescue assistance.

A4.3.10 Egress. Because people with disabilities may visit, be employed or be a resident in any building, emergency management plans with specific provisions to ensure their safe evacuation also play an essential role in fire safety and life safety.

4.3.11 Areas of Rescue Assistance.

4.3.11.1 Location and Construction. An area of rescue assistance shall be one of the following:

(1) A portion of a stairway landing within a smokeproof enclosure (complying with local requirements).

(2) A portion of an exterior exit balcony located immediately adjacent to an exit stairway when the balcony complies with local requirements for exterior exit balconies. Openings to the interior of the building located within 20 feet (6 m) of the area of rescue assistance shall be protected with fire assemblies having a three-fourths hour fire protection rating.

(3) A portion of a one-hour fire-resistive corridor (complying with local requirements for fire-resistive construc-

tion and for openings) located immediately adjacent to an exit enclosure.

(4) A vestibule located immediately adjacent to an exit enclosure and constructed to the same fire-resistive standards as required for corridors and openings.

(5) A portion of a stairway landing within an exit enclosure which is vented to the exterior and is separated from the interior of the building with not less than one-hour fire-resistive doors.

(6) When approved by the appropriate local authority, an area or a room which is separated from other portions of the building by a smoke barrier. Smoke barriers shall have a fire-resistive rating of not less than one hour and shall completely enclose the area or room. Doors in the smoke barrier shall be tight-fitting smoke- and draft-control assemblies having a fire-protection rating of not less than 20 minutes and shall be self-closing or automatic closing. The area or room shall be provided with an exit directly to an exit enclosure. Where the room or area exits into an exit enclosure which is required to be of more than one-hour fire-resistive construction, the room or area shall have the same fire-resistive construction, including the same opening protection, as required for the adjacent exit enclosure.

(7) An elevator lobby when elevator shafts and adjacent lobbies are pressurized as required for smokeproof enclosures by local regulations and when complying with requirements herein for size, communication, and signage. Such pressurization system shall be activated by smoke detectors on each floor located in a manner approved by the appropriate local authority. Pressurization equipment and its duct work within the building shall be separated from other portions of the building by a minimum two-hour fire-resistive construction.

4.3.11.2 Size. Each area of rescue assistance shall provide at least two accessible areas each being not less than 30 inches by 48 inches (760 mm by 1220 mm). The area of rescue assistance shall not encroach on any required exit width. The total number of such 30-inch by 48-inch (760 mm by 1220 mm) areas per story shall be not less than one for every 200 persons of calculated occupant load served by the area of rescue assistance.

EXCEPTION: The appropriate local authority may reduce the minimum number of 30-inch by 48-inch (760 mm by 1220 mm) areas to one for each area of rescue assistance on floors where the occupant load is less than 200.

4.3.11.3* Stairway Width. Each stairway adjacent to an area of rescue assistance shall have a minimum clear width of 48 inches between handrails.

4.3.11.4* Two-way Communication. A method of two-way communication, with both visible and audible signals, shall be provided between each area of rescue assistance and the primary entry. The fire department or appropriate local authority may approve a location other than the primary entry.

4.3.11.5 Identification. Each area of rescue assistance shall be identified by a sign which states "AREA OF RESCUE ASSISTANCE" and displays the international symbol of accessibility. The sign shall be illuminated when exit sign illumination is required. Signage shall also be installed at all inaccessible exits and where otherwise necessary to clearly indicate the direction to areas of rescue assistance. In each area of rescue assistance, instructions on the use of the area under emergency conditions shall be posted adjoining the two-way communication system.

4.4 PROTRUDING OBJECTS.

4.4.1* General. Objects projecting from walls (for example, telephones) with their leading edges between 27 in and 80 in (685 mm and 2030 mm) above the finished floor shall protrude no more than 4 in (100 mm) into walks, halls, corridors, passageways, or aisles. Objects mounted with their leading edges at or below 27 in (685 mm) above the finished floor may protrude any amount. Free-standing objects mounted on posts or pylons may overhang 12 in (305 mm) maximum from 27 in to 80 in (685 mm to 2030 mm) above the ground or finished floor. Protruding objects shall not reduce the clear width of an accessible route or maneuvering space.

A4.4.1 General. Service animals are trained to recognize and avoid hazards. However, most people with severe impairments of vision use the long cane as an aid to mobility. The two principal cane techniques are the touch technique, where the cane arcs from side to side and touches points outside both shoulders; and the diagonal technique, where the cane is held in a stationary position diagonally across the body with the cane tip touching or just above the ground at a point outside one shoulder and the handle or grip extending to a point outside the other shoulder. The touch technique is used primarily in uncontrolled areas, while the diagonal technique is used primarily in certain limited, controlled, and familiar environments. Cane users are often trained to use both techniques.

Potential hazardous objects are noticed only if they fall within the detection range of canes. Visually impaired people walking toward an object can detect an overhang if its lowest surface is not higher than 27 in (685 mm). When walking alongside protruding objects, they cannot detect overhangs. Since proper cane and service animal techniques keep people away from the edge of a path or from walls, a slight overhang of no more than 4 in (100 mm) is not hazardous.

4.4.2 Head Room.

Walks, halls, corridors, passageways, aisles, or other circulation spaces shall have 80 in (2030 mm) minimum clear head room. If vertical clearance of an area adjoining an accessible route is reduced to less than 80 in (nominal dimension), a barrier to warn blind or visually-impaired persons shall be provided.

4.5 GROUND AND FLOOR SURFACES.

4.5.1* General.

Ground and floor surfaces along accessible routes and in accessible rooms and spaces including floors, walks, ramps, stairs, and curb ramps, shall be stable, firm, slip-resistant, and shall comply with 4.5.

A4.5.1 General. People who have difficulty walking or maintaining balance or who use crutches, canes, or walkers, and those with restricted gaits are particularly sensitive to slipping and tripping hazards. For such people, a stable and regular surface is necessary for safe walking, particularly on stairs. Wheelchairs can be propelled most easily on surfaces that are hard, stable, and regular. Soft loose surfaces such as shag carpet, loose sand or gravel, wet clay, and irregular surfaces such as cobblestones can significantly impede wheelchair movement.

Slip resistance is based on the frictional force necessary to keep a shoe heel or crutch tip from slipping on a walking surface under conditions likely to be found on the surface. While the dynamic coefficient of friction during walking varies in a complex and non-uniform way, the static coefficient of friction, which can be measured in several ways, provides a close approximation of the slip resistance of a surface. Contrary to popular belief, some slippage is necessary to walking, especially for persons with restricted gaits; a truly "non-slip" surface could not be negotiated.

The Occupational Safety and Health Administration recommends that walking surfaces have a static coefficient of friction of 0.5. A research project sponsored by the Architectural and Transportation Barriers Compliance Board (Access Board) conducted tests with persons with disabilities and concluded that a higher coefficient of friction was needed by such persons. A static coefficient of friction of 0.6 is recommended for accessible routes and 0.8 for ramps.

It is recognized that the coefficient of friction varies considerably due to the presence of contaminants, water, floor finishes, and other factors not under the control of the designer or builder and not subject to design and construction guidelines and that compliance would be difficult to measure on the building site. Nevertheless, many common building materials suitable for flooring are now labeled with information on the static coefficient of friction. While it may not be possible to compare one product directly with another, or to guarantee a constant measure, builders and designers are encouraged to specify materials with appropriate values. As more products include information on slip resistance, improved uniformity in measurement and specification is likely. The Access Board's advisory guidelines on Slip Resistant Surfaces provides additional information on this subject.

Cross slopes on walks and ground or floor surfaces can cause considerable difficulty in propelling a wheelchair in a straight line.

4.5.2 Changes in Level. Changes in level up to ¼ in (6 mm) may be vertical and without edge treatment. Changes in level between ¼ in and ½ in (6 mm and 13 mm) shall be beveled with a slope no greater than 1:2. Changes in level greater than ½ in (13 mm) shall be accomplished by means of a ramp that complies with 4.7 or 4.8.

4.5.3* Carpet. If carpet or carpet tile is used on a ground or floor surface, then it shall be securely attached; have a firm cushion, pad, or backing, or no cushion or pad; and have a level loop, textured loop, level cut pile, or level cut/uncut pile texture. The maximum pile thickness shall be ½ in (13 mm). Exposed edges of carpet shall be fastened to floor surfaces and have trim along the entire length of the exposed edge. Carpet edge trim shall comply with 4.5.2.

A4.5.3 Carpet. Much more needs to be done in developing both quantitative and qualitative criteria for carpeting (i.e., problems associated with texture and weave need to be studied). However, certain functional characteristics are well established. When both carpet and padding are used, it is desirable to have minimum movement (preferably none) between the floor and the pad and the pad and the carpet which would allow the carpet to hump or warp. In heavily trafficked areas, a thick, soft (plush) pad or cushion, particularly in combination with long carpet pile, makes it difficult for individuals in wheelchairs and those with other ambulatory disabilities to get about. Firm carpeting can be achieved through proper selection and combination of pad and carpet, sometimes with the elimination of the pad or cushion, and with proper installation. Carpeting designed with a weave that causes a zigzag effect when wheeled across is strongly discouraged.

4.5.4 Gratings. If gratings are located in walking surfaces, then they shall have spaces no greater than ½ in (13 mm) wide in one direction. If gratings have elongated openings, then they shall be placed so that the long dimension is perpendicular to the dominant direction of travel.

4.7 CURB RAMPS.

4.7.1 Location. Curb ramps complying with 4.7 shall be provided wherever an accessible route crosses a curb.

4.7.2 Slope. Slopes of curb ramps shall comply with 4.8.2. Transitions from ramps to walks, gutters, or streets shall be flush and free of abrupt changes. Maximum slopes of adjoining gutters, road surface immediately adjacent to the curb ramp, or accessible route shall not exceed 1:20.

4.7.3 Width. The minimum width of a curb ramp shall be 36 in (915 mm), exclusive of flared sides.

4.7.4 Surface. Surfaces of curb ramps shall comply with 4.5.

4.7.5 Sides of Curb Ramps. If a curb ramp is located where pedestrians must walk across the ramp, or where it is not protected by handrails or guardrails, it shall have flared sides; the maximum slope of the flare shall be 1:10. Curb ramps with returned curbs may be used where pedestrians would not normally walk across the ramp.

4.7.6 Built-up Curb Ramps. Built-up curb ramps shall be located so that they do not project into vehicular traffic lanes.

4.7.7 Detectable Warnings. [Provision suspended until July 26, 2001] A curb ramp shall have a detectable warning complying with 4.29.2. The detectable warning shall extend the full width and depth of the curb ramp.

4.7.8 Obstructions. Curb ramps shall be located or protected to prevent their obstruction by parked vehicles.

4.7.9 Location at Marked Crossings. Curb ramps at marked crossings shall be wholly contained within the markings, excluding any flared sides.

4.7.10 Diagonal Curb Ramps. If diagonal (or corner type) curb ramps have returned curbs or other well-defined edges, such edges shall be parallel to the direction of pedestrian flow. The bottom of diagonal curb ramps shall have 48 in (1220 mm) minimum clear space. If diagonal curb ramps are provided at marked crossings, the 48 in (1220 mm) clear space shall be within the markings. If diagonal curb ramps have flared sides, they shall also have at least a 24 in (610 mm) long segment of straight curb located on each side of the curb ramp and within the marked crossing.

4.7.11 Islands. Any raised islands in crossings shall be cut through level with the street or have curb ramps at both sides and a level area at least 48 in (1220 mm) long between the curb ramps in the part of the island intersected by the crossings.

4.8 RAMPS.

4.8.1* General. Any part of an accessible route with a slope greater than 1:20 shall be considered a ramp and shall comply with 4.8.

4.8.2* Slope and Rise. The least possible slope shall be used for any ramp. The maximum slope of a ramp in new construction shall be 1:12. The maximum rise for any run shall be 30 in (760 mm). Curb ramps and ramps to be constructed on existing sites or in existing buildings or facilities may have slopes and rises as allowed in 4.1.6(3)(a) if space limitations prohibit the use of a 1:12 slope or less.

4.8.3 Clear Width. The minimum clear width of a ramp shall be 36 in (915 mm).

4.8.4* Landings. Ramps shall have level landings at bottom and top of each ramp and each ramp run. Landings shall have the following features:

(1) The landing shall be at least as wide as the ramp run leading to it.

(2) The landing length shall be a minimum of 60 in (1525 mm) clear.

(3) If ramps change direction at landings, the minimum landing size shall be 60 in by 60 in (1525 mm by 1525 mm).

(4) If a doorway is located at a landing, then the area in front of the doorway shall comply with 4.13.6.

4.8.5* Handrails. If a ramp run has a rise greater than 6 in (150 mm) or a horizontal projection greater than 72 in (1830 mm), then it shall have handrails on both sides. Handrails are not required on curb ramps or adjacent to seating in assembly areas. Handrails shall comply with 4.26 and shall have the following features:

(1) Handrails shall be provided along both sides of ramp segments. The inside handrail on switchback or dogleg ramps shall always be continuous.

(2) If handrails are not continuous, they shall extend at least 12 in (305 mm) beyond the top and bottom of the ramp segment and shall be parallel with the floor or ground surface.

(3) The clear space between the handrail and the wall shall be 1½ in (38 mm).

(4) Gripping surfaces shall be continuous.

(5) Top of handrail gripping surfaces shall be mounted between 34 in and 38 in (865 mm and 965 mm) above ramp surfaces.

(6) Ends of handrails shall be either rounded or returned smoothly to floor, wall, or post.

(7) Handrails shall not rotate within their fittings.

A4.8.5 Handrails. The requirements for stair and ramp handrails in this guideline are for adults. When children are principal users in a building or facility (e.g. elementary schools), a second set of handrails at an appropriate height can assist them and aid in preventing accidents. A maximum height of 28 inches measured to the top of the gripping surface from the ramp surface or stair nosing is recommended for handrails designed for children. Sufficient vertical clearance between upper and lower handrails (9 inches minimum) should be provided to help prevent entrapment.

4.8.6 Cross Slope and Surfaces. The cross slope of ramp surfaces shall be no greater than 1:50. Ramp surfaces shall comply with 4.5.

4.8.7 Edge Protection. Ramps and landings with drop-offs shall have curbs, walls, railings, or projecting surfaces that prevent people from slipping off the ramp. Curbs shall be a minimum of 2 in (50 mm) high.

4.8.8 Outdoor Conditions. Outdoor ramps and their approaches shall be designed so that water will not accumulate on walking surfaces.

4.9 STAIRS.

4.9.1* Minimum Number. Stairs required to be accessible by 4.1 shall comply with 4.9.

A4.9.1 Minimum Number. Only interior and exterior stairs connecting levels that are not connected by an elevator, ramp, or other accessible means of vertical access have to comply with 4.9.

4.9.2 Treads and Risers. On any given flight of stairs, all steps shall have uniform riser heights and uniform tread widths. Stair treads shall be no less than 11 in (280 mm) wide, measured from riser to riser. Open risers are not permitted.

4.9.3 Nosings. The undersides of nosings shall not be abrupt. The radius of curvature at the leading edge of the tread shall be no greater than ½ in (13 mm). Risers shall be sloped or the underside of the nosing shall have an angle not less than 60 degrees from the horizontal. Nosings shall project no more than 1½ in (38 mm).

4.9.4 Handrails. Stairways shall have handrails at both sides of all stairs. Handrails shall comply with 4.26 and shall have the following features:

(1) Handrails shall be continuous along both sides of stairs. The inside handrail on switchback or dogleg stairs shall always be continuous.

(2) If handrails are not continuous, they shall extend at least 12 in (305 mm) beyond the top riser and at least 12 in (305 mm) plus the width of one tread beyond the bottom riser. At the top, the extension shall be parallel with the floor or ground surface. At the bottom, the handrail shall continue to slope for a distance of the width of one tread from the bottom riser; the remainder of the extension shall be horizontal. Handrail extensions shall comply with 4.4.

(3) The clear space between handrails and wall shall be 1½ in (38 mm).

(4) Gripping surfaces shall be uninterrupted by newel posts, other construction elements, or obstructions.

(5) Top of handrail gripping surface shall be mounted between 34 in and 38 in (865 mm and 965 mm) above stair nosings.

(6) Ends of handrails shall be either rounded or returned smoothly to floor, wall or post.

(7) Handrails shall not rotate within their fittings.

4.9.5 Detectable Warnings at Stairs. (Reserved).

4.9.6 Outdoor Conditions. Outdoor stairs and their approaches shall be designed so that water will not accumulate on walking surfaces.

4.10 ELEVATORS.

4.10.1 General. Accessible elevators shall be on an accessible route and shall comply with 4.10 and with the ASME A17.1-1990, Safety Code for Elevators and Escalators. Freight elevators shall not be considered as meeting the requirements of this section unless the only elevators provided are used as combination passenger and freight elevators for the public and employees.

4.10.2 Automatic Operation. Elevator operation shall be automatic. Each car shall be equipped with a self-leveling feature that will automatically bring the car to floor landings within a tolerance of ½ in (13 mm) under rated loading to zero loading conditions. This self-leveling feature shall be automatic and independent of the operating device and shall correct the overtravel or undertravel.

4.10.3 Hall Call Buttons. Call buttons in elevator lobbies and halls shall be centered at 42 in (1065 mm) above the floor. Such call buttons shall have visual signals to indicate when each call is registered and when each call is answered. Call buttons shall be a minimum of ¾ in (19 mm) in the smallest dimension. The button designating the up direction shall be on top. Buttons shall be raised or flush. Objects mounted beneath hall call buttons shall not project into the elevator lobby more than 4 in (100 mm).

4.10.4 Hall Lanterns. A visible and audible signal shall be provided at each hoistway entrance to indicate which car is answering a call. Audible signals shall sound once for the up direction and twice for the down direction or shall have verbal annunciators that say "up" or "down." Visible signals shall have the following features:

(1) Hall lantern fixtures shall be mounted so that their centerline is at least 72 in (1830 mm) above the lobby floor.

(2) Visual elements shall be at least 2½ in (64 mm) in the smallest dimension.

(3) Signals shall be visible from the vicinity of the hall call button. In-car lanterns located in cars, visible from the vicinity of hall call buttons, and conforming to the above requirements, shall be acceptable.

4.10.5 Raised and Braille Characters on Hoistway Entrances. All elevator hoistway entrances shall have raised and Braille floor designations provided on both jambs. The centerline of the characters shall be 60 in (1525 mm) above finish floor. Such characters shall be 2 in (50 mm) high and shall comply with 3:4.30.4. Permanently applied plates are acceptable if they are permanently fixed to the jambs.

4.10.6* Door Protective and Reopening Device. Elevator doors shall open and close automatically. They shall be provided with a reopening device that will stop and reopen a car door and hoistway door automatically if the door becomes obstructed by an object or person. The device shall be capable of completing these operations without requiring contact for an obstruction passing through the opening at heights of 5 in and 29 in (125 mm and 735 mm) above finish floor. Door reopening devices shall remain effective for at least 20 seconds. After such an interval, doors may close in accordance with the requirements of ASME A17.1-1990.

4.10.7* Door and Signal Timing for Hall Calls. The minimum acceptable time from notification that a car is answering a call until the doors of that car start to close shall be calculated from the following equation:

$$T = D/(1.5 \text{ ft/s}) \text{ or } T = D/(445 \text{ mm/s})$$

where T total time in seconds and D distance (in feet or millimeters) from a point in the lobby or corridor 60 in (1525 mm) directly in front of the farthest call button controlling that car to the centerline of its hoistway door. For cars with in-car lanterns, T begins when the lantern is visible from the vicinity of hall call buttons and an audible signal is sounded. The minimum acceptable notification time shall be 5 seconds.

4.10.8 Door Delay for Car Calls. The minimum time for elevator doors to remain fully open in response to a car call shall be 3 seconds.

4.10.9 Floor Plan of Elevator Cars. The floor area of elevator cars shall provide space for wheelchair users to enter the car, maneuver within reach of controls, and exit from the car. The clearance between the car platform sill and the edge of any hoistway landing shall be no greater than 1¼ in (32 mm).

4.10.10 Floor Surfaces. Floor surfaces shall comply with 4.5.

4.10.11 Illumination Levels. The level of illumination at the car controls, platform, and car threshold and landing sill shall be at least 5 footcandles (53.8 lux).

4.10.12* Car Controls. Elevator control panels shall have the following features:

(1) Buttons. All control buttons shall be at least ¾ in (19 mm) in their smallest dimension. They shall be raised or flush.

(2) Tactile, Braille, and Visual Control Indicators. All control buttons shall be designated by Braille and by raised standard alphabet characters for letters, arabic characters for numerals, or standard symbols and as required in ASME A17.1-1990. Raised and Braille characters and symbols shall comply with 4.30. The call button for the main entry floor shall be designated by a raised star at the left of the floor designation. All raised designations for control buttons shall be placed immediately to the left of the button to which they apply. Applied plates, permanently attached, are an acceptable means to provide raised control designations. Floor buttons shall be provided with visual indicators to show when each call is registered. The visual indicators shall be extinguished when each call is answered.

(3) Height. All floor buttons shall be no higher than 54 in (1370 mm) above the finish floor for side approach and 48 in (1220 mm) for front approach. Emergency controls, including the emergency alarm and emergency stop, shall be grouped at the bottom of the panel and shall have their centerlines no less than 35 in (890 mm) above the finish floor.

(4) Location. Controls shall be located on a front wall if cars have center opening doors, and at the side wall or at the front wall next to the door if cars have side opening doors.

A4.10.12 Car Controls. Industry-wide standardization of elevator control panel design would make all elevators significantly more convenient for use by people with severe visual impairments. In many cases, it will be possible to locate the highest control on elevator panels within 48 in (1220 mm) from the floor.

4.10.13* Car Position Indicators. In elevator cars, a visual car position indicator shall be provided above the car control panel or over the door to show the position of the elevator in the hoistway. As the car passes or stops at a floor served by the elevators, the corresponding numerals shall illuminate, and an audible signal shall sound. Numerals shall be a minimum of ½ in (13 mm) high. The audible signal shall be no less than 20 decibels with a frequency no higher than 1500 Hz. An automatic verbal announcement of the floor number at which a car stops or which a car passes may be substituted for the audible signal.

A4.10.13 Car Position Indicators. A special button may be provided that would activate the audible signal within the given elevator only for the desired trip, rather than maintaining the audible signal in constant operation.

4.10.14* Emergency Communications. If provided, emergency two-way communication systems between the elevator and a point outside the hoistway shall comply with ASME A17.1-1990. The highest operable part of a two-way communication system shall be a maximum of 48 in (1220 mm) from the floor of the car. It shall be identified by a raised symbol and lettering complying with 4.30 and located adjacent to the device. If the system uses a handset then the length of the cord from the panel to the handset shall be at least 29 in (735 mm). If the system is located in a closed compartment the compartment door hardware shall conform to 4.27, Controls and Operating Mechanisms. The emergency intercommunication system shall not require voice communication.

4.26 HANDRAILS, GRAB BARS, AND TUB AND SHOWER SEATS.

4.26.1* General. All handrails, grab bars, and tub and shower seats required to be accessible by 4.1, 4.8, 4.9, 4.16, 4.17, 4.20 or 4.21 shall comply with 4.26.

4.26.2* Size and Spacing of Grab Bars and Handrails. The diameter or width of the gripping surfaces of a handrail or grab bar shall be 1¼ in to 1½ in (32 mm to 38 mm), or the shape shall provide an equivalent gripping surface. If handrails or grab bars are mounted adjacent to a wall, the space between the wall and the grab bar shall be 1½ in (38 mm). Handrails may be located in a recess if the recess is a maximum of 3 in (75 mm) deep and extends at least 18 in (455 mm) above the top of the rail.

4.26.3 Structural Strength. The structural strength of grab bars, tub and shower seats, fasteners, and mounting devices shall meet the following specification:

(1) Bending stress in a grab bar or seat induced by the maximum bending moment from the application of 250 lbf (1112N) shall be less than the allowable stress for the material of the grab bar or seat.

(2) Shear stress induced in a grab bar or seat by the application of 250 lbf (1112N) shall be less than the allowable

shear stress for the material of the grab bar or seat. If the connection between the grab bar or seat and its mounting bracket or other support is considered to be fully restrained, then direct and torsional shear stresses shall be totaled for the combined shear stress, which shall not exceed the allowable shear stress.

(3) Shear force induced in a fastener or mounting device from the application of 250 lbf (1112N) shall be less than the allowable lateral load of either the fastener or mounting device or the supporting structure, whichever is the smaller allowable load.

(4) Tensile force induced in a fastener by a direct tension force of 250 lbf (1112N) plus the maximum moment from the application of 250 lbf (1112N) shall be less than the allowable withdrawal load between the fastener and the supporting structure.

(5) Grab bars shall not rotate within their fittings.

4.26.4 Eliminating Hazards. A handrail or grab bar and any wall or other surface adjacent to it shall be free of any sharp or abrasive elements. Edges shall have a minimum radius of 1/8 in (3.2 mm).

4.27 CONTROLS AND OPERATING MECHANISMS.

4.27.1 General. Controls and operating mechanisms required to be accessible by 4.1 shall comply with 4.27.

4.27.2 Clear Floor Space. Clear floor space complying with 4.2.4 that allows a forward or a parallel approach by a person using a wheelchair shall be provided at controls, dispensers, receptacles, and other operable equipment.

4.27.3* Height. The highest operable part of controls, dispensers, receptacles, and other operable equipment shall be placed within at least one of the reach ranges specified in 4.2.5 and 4.2.6. Electrical and communications system receptacles on walls shall be mounted no less than 15 in (380 mm) above the floor.

EXCEPTION: These requirements do not apply where the use of special equipment dictates otherwise or where electrical and communications systems receptacles are not normally intended for use by building occupants.

4.27.4 Operation. Controls and operating mechanisms shall be operable with one hand and shall not require tight grasping, pinching, or twisting of the wrist. The force required to activate controls shall be no greater than 5 lbf (22.2 N).

4.28 ALARMS.

4.28.1 General. Alarm systems required to be accessible by 4.1 shall comply with 4.28. At a minimum, visual signal appliances shall be provided in buildings and facilities in each of the following areas: restrooms and any other general usage areas (e.g., meeting rooms), hallways, lobbies, and any other area for common use.

4.28.2* Audible Alarms. If provided, audible emergency alarms shall produce a sound that exceeds the prevailing equivalent sound level in the room or space by at least 15 dBA or exceeds any maximum sound level with a duration of 60 seconds by 5 dBA, whichever is louder. Sound levels for alarm signals shall not exceed 120 dbA.

A4.28.2 Audible Alarms. Audible emergency signals must have an intensity and frequency that can attract the attention of individuals who have partial hearing loss. People over 60 years of age generally have difficulty perceiving frequencies higher than 10,000 Hz. An alarm signal which has a periodic element to its signal, such as single stroke bells (clang-pause-clang-pause), hi-low (up-down-up-down) and fast whoop (on-off-on-off) are best. Avoid continuous or reverberating tones. Select a signal which has a sound characterized by three or four clear tones without a great deal of "noise" in between.

4.28.3* Visual Alarms. Visual alarm signal appliances shall be integrated into the building or facility alarm system. If single station audible alarms are provided then single station visual alarm signals shall be provided. Visual alarm signals shall have the following minimum photometric and location features:

(1) The lamp shall be a xenon strobe type or equivalent.

(2) The color shall be clear or nominal white (i.e., unfiltered or clear filtered white light).

(3) The maximum pulse duration shall be two-tenths of one second (0.2 sec) with a maximum duty cycle of 40 percent. The pulse duration is defined as the time interval between initial and final points of 10 percent of maximum signal.

(4) The intensity shall be a minimum of 75 candela.

(5) The flash rate shall be a minimum of 1 Hz and a maximum of 3 Hz.

(6) The appliance shall be placed 80 in (2030 mm) above the highest floor level within the space or 6 in (152 mm) below the ceiling, whichever is lower.

(7) In general, no place in any room or space required to have a visual signal appliance shall be more than 50 ft (15 m) from the signal (in the horizontal plane). In large rooms and spaces exceeding 100 ft (30 m) across, without obstructions 6 ft (2 m) above the finish floor, such as auditoriums, devices may be placed around the perimeter, spaced a maximum 100 ft (30 m) apart, in lieu of suspending appliances from the ceiling.

(8) No place in common corridors or hallways in which visual alarm signalling appliances are required shall be more than 50 ft (15 m) from the signal.

A4.28.3 Visual Alarms. The specifications in this section do not preclude the use of zoned or coded alarm systems.

4.28.4* Auxiliary Alarms. Units and sleeping accommodations shall have a visual alarm connected to the building emergency alarm system or shall have a standard 110-volt electrical receptacle into which such an alarm can be connected and a means by which a signal from the building emergency alarm system can trigger such an auxiliary alarm. When visual alarms are in place the signal shall be visible in all areas of the unit or room. Instructions for use of the auxiliary alarm or receptacle shall be provided.

A4.28.4 Auxiliary Alarms. Locating visual emergency alarms in rooms where persons who are deaf may work or reside alone can ensure that they will always be warned when an emergency alarm is activated. To be effective, such devices must be located and oriented so that they will spread signals and reflections throughout a space or raise the overall light level sharply. However, visual alarms alone are not necessarily the best means to alert sleepers. A study conducted by Underwriters Laboratory (UL) concluded that a flashing light more than seven times brighter was required (110 candela v. 15 candela, at the same distance) to awaken sleepers as was needed to alert awake subjects in a normal daytime illuminated room.

For hotel and other rooms where people are likely to be asleep, a signal-activated vibrator placed between mattress and box spring or under a pillow was found by UL to be much more effective in alerting sleepers. Many readily available devices are sound-activated so that they could respond to an alarm clock, clock radio, wake-up telephone call or room smoke detector. Activation by a building alarm system can either be accomplished by a separate circuit activating an auditory alarm which would, in turn, trigger the vibrator or by a signal transmitted through the ordinary 110-volt outlet. Transmission of signals through the power line is relatively simple and is the basis of common, inexpensive remote light control systems sold in many department and electronic stores for home use. So-called "wireless" intercoms operate on the same principal.

4.29 DETECTABLE WARNINGS.

4.29.1 General. Detectable warnings required by 4.1 and 4.7 shall comply with 4.29.

4.29.2* Detectable Warnings on Walking Surfaces. Detectable warnings shall consist of raised truncated domes with a diameter of nominal 0.9 in (23 mm), a height of nominal 0.2 in (5 mm) and a center-to-center spacing of nominal 2.35 in (60 mm) and shall contrast visually with adjoining surfaces, either light-on-dark, or dark-on-light. The material used to provide contrast shall be an integral part of the walking surface. Detectable warnings used on interior surfaces shall differ from adjoining walking surfaces in resiliency or sound-on-cane contact.

A4.29.2 Detectable Warnings on Walking Surfaces. The material used to provide contrast should contrast by at least 70%. Contrast in percent is determined by:

Contrast = [(B1 - B2)/B1] x 100
where B1 = light reflectance value (LRV) of the lighter area and B2 = light reflectance value (LRV) of the darker area.

Note that in any application both white and black are never absolute; thus, B1 never equals 100 and B2 is always greater than 0.

4.29.3 Detectable Warnings on Doors To Hazardous Areas. (Reserved).

4.29.4 Detectable Warnings at Stairs. (Reserved).

4.29.5 Detectable Warnings at Hazardous Vehicular Areas. [Provision suspended until July 26, 2001] If a walk crosses or adjoins a vehicular way, and the walking surfaces are not separated by curbs, railings, or other elements between the pedestrian areas and vehicular areas, the boundary between the areas shall be defined by a continuous detectable warning which is 36 in (915 mm) wide, complying with 4.29.2.

4.29.6 Detectable Warnings at Reflecting Pools. [Provision suspended until July 26, 2001] The edges of reflecting pools shall be protected by railings, walls, curbs, or detectable warnings complying with 4.29.2.

4.29.7 Standardization. (Reserved).

4.30 SIGNAGE.

4.30.1* General. Signage required to be accessible by 4.1 shall comply with the applicable provisions of 4.30.

A4.30.1 General. In building complexes where finding locations independently on a routine basis may be a necessity (for example, college campuses), tactile maps or pre-recorded instructions can be very helpful to visually impaired people. Several maps and auditory instructions have been developed and tested for specific applications. The type of map or instructions used must be based on the information to be communicated, which depends highly on the type of buildings or users.

Landmarks that can easily be distinguished by visually impaired individuals are useful as orientation cues. Such cues include changes in illumination level, bright colors, unique patterns, wall murals, location of special equipment or other architectural features.

Many people with disabilities have limitations in movement of their heads and reduced peripheral vision. Thus, signage positioned perpendicular to the path of travel is easiest for them to notice. People can generally distinguish signage within an angle of 30 degrees to either side of the centerlines of their faces without moving their heads.

4.30.2* Character Proportion. Letters and numbers on signs shall have a width-to-height ratio between 3:5 and 1:1 and a stroke-width-to-height ratio between 1:5 and 1:10.

A4.30.2 Character Proportion. The legibility of printed characters is a function of the viewing distance, character height, the ratio of the stroke width to the height of the character, the contrast of color between character and background, and print font. The size of characters must be based upon the intended viewing distance. A severely nearsighted person may have to be much closer to recognize a character of a given size than a person with normal visual acuity.

4.30.3 Character Height. Characters and numbers on signs shall be sized according to the viewing distance from which they are to be read. The minimum height is measured using an upper case X. Lower case characters are permitted.

Height Above Finished Floor	Minimum Character Height
Suspended or Projected Overhead in compliance with 4.4.2	3 in (75 mm) minimum

4.30.4 Raised and Brailled Characters and Pictorial Symbol Signs (Pictograms). Letters and numerals shall be raised 1/32 in (0.79 mm) minimum, upper case, sans serif or simple serif type and shall be accompanied with Grade 2 Braille. Raised characters shall be at least 5/8 in (16 mm) high, but no higher than 2 in (50 mm). Pictograms shall be accompanied by the equivalent verbal description placed directly below the pictogram. The border dimension of the pictogram shall be 6 in (152 mm) minimum in height.

A4.30.4 Raised and Brailled Characters and Pictorial Symbol Signs (Pictograms). The standard dimensions for literary Braille are as follows:

Dot diameter: .059 in.
Inter-dot spacing: .090 in.
Horizontal separation between cells: .241 in.
Vertical separation between cells: .395 in.

Raised borders around signs containing raised characters may make them confusing to read unless the border is set far away from the characters. Accessible signage with descriptive materials about public buildings, monuments, and objects of cultural interest may not provide sufficiently detailed and meaningful information. Interpretive guides, audio tape devices, or other methods may be more effective in presenting such information.

4.30.5* Finish and Contrast. The characters and background of signs shall be eggshell, matte, or other non-glare finish. Characters and symbols shall contrast with their background—either light characters on a dark background or dark characters on a light background.

A4.30.5 Finish and Contrast. An eggshell finish (11 to 19 degree gloss on 60 degree glossimeter) is recommended. Research indicates that signs are more legible for persons with low vision when characters contrast with their background by at least 70 percent. Contrast in percent shall be determined by:

$$Contrast = [(B1 - B2)/B1] \times 100$$

where B1 = light reflectance value (LRV) of the lighter area and B2 = light reflectance value (LRV) of the darker area.

Note that in any application both white and black are never absolute; thus, B1 never equals 100 and B2 is always greater than 0.

The greatest readability is usually achieved through the use of light-colored characters or symbols on a dark background.

4.30.6 Mounting Location and Height. Where permanent identification is provided for rooms and spaces, signs shall be installed on the wall adjacent to the latch side of the door. Where there is no wall space to the latch side of the door, including at double leaf doors, signs shall be placed on the nearest adjacent wall. Mounting height shall be 60 in (1525 mm) above the finish floor to the centerline of the sign. Mounting location for such signage shall be so that a person may approach within 3 in (76 mm) of signage without encountering protruding objects or standing within the swing of a door.

4.30.7* Symbols of Accessibility.

(1) Facilities and elements required to be identified as accessible by 4.1 shall use the international symbol of accessibility.

(2) Volume Control Telephones. Telephones required to have a volume control by 4.1.3(17)(b) shall be identified by a sign containing a depiction of a telephone handset with radiating sound waves.

(3) Text Telephones (TTYs). Text telephones (TTYs) required by 4.1.3(17)(c) shall be identified by the international TTY symbol. In addition, if a facility has a public text telephone (TTY), directional signage indicating the location of the nearest text telephone (TTY) shall be placed adjacent to all banks of telephones which do not contain a text telephone (TTY). Such directional signage shall include the international TTY symbol. If a facility has no banks of telephones, the directional signage shall be provided at the entrance (e.g., in a building directory).

(4) Assistive Listening Systems. In assembly areas where permanently installed assistive listening systems are required by 4.1.3(19)(b) the availability of such systems shall be identified with signage that includes the international symbol of access for hearing loss.

A4.30.7 Symbols of Accessibility for Different Types of Listening Systems. Paragraph 4 of this section requires signage indicating the availability of an assistive listening system. An appropriate message should be displayed with the international symbol of access for hearing loss since this symbol conveys general accessibility for people with hearing loss. Some suggestions are:

INFRARED
ASSISTIVE LISTENING SYSTEM AVAILABLE
——PLEASE ASK——

AUDIO LOOP IN USE
TURN T-SWITCH FOR BETTER HEARING
——OR ASK FOR HELP——

FM ASSISTIVE LISTENING SYSTEM AVAILABLE
——PLEASE ASK——

The symbol may be used to notify persons of the availability of other auxiliary aids and services such as: real time captioning, captioned note taking, sign language interpreters, and oral interpreters.

4.30.8* Illumination Levels. (Reserved).

A4.30.8 Illumination Levels. Illumination levels on the sign surface shall be in the 100 to 300 lux range (10 to 30 footcandles) and shall be uniform over the sign surface. Signs shall be located such that the illumination level on the surface of the sign is not significantly exceeded by the ambient light or visible bright lighting source behind or in front of the sign.

4.31 TELEPHONES.

4.31.1 General. Public telephones required to be accessible by 4.1 shall comply with 4.31.

4.31.2 Clear Floor or Ground Space. A clear floor or ground space at least 30 in by 48 in (760 mm by 1220 mm) that allows either a forward or parallel approach by a person using a wheelchair shall be provided at telephones. The clear floor or ground space shall comply with 4.2.4. Bases, enclosures, and fixed seats shall not impede approaches to telephones by people who use wheelchairs.

4.31.3* Mounting Height. The highest operable part of the telephone shall be within the reach ranges specified in 4.2.5 or 4.2.6.

4.31.4 Protruding Objects. Telephones shall comply with 4.4.

4.31.5 Hearing Aid Compatible and Volume Control Telephones Required by 4.1.

(1) Telephones shall be hearing aid compatible.

(2) Volume controls, capable of a minimum of 12 dbA and a maximum of 18 dbA above normal, shall be provided in accordance with 4.1.3. If an automatic reset is provided then 18 dbA may be exceeded.

4.31.6 Controls. Telephones shall have pushbutton controls where service for such equipment is available.

4.31.7 Telephone Books. Telephone books, if provided, shall be located in a position that complies with the reach ranges specified in 4.2.5 and 4.2.6.

4.31.8 Cord Length. The cord from the telephone to the handset shall be at least 29 in (735 mm) long.

4.31.9* Text Telephones (TTYs) Required by 4.1.

(1) Text telephones (TTYs) used with a pay telephone shall be permanently affixed within, or adjacent to, the telephone enclosure. If an acoustic coupler is used, the telephone cord shall be sufficiently long to allow connection of the text telephone (TTY) and the telephone receiver.

(2) Pay telephones designed to accommodate a portable text telephone (TTY) shall be equipped with a shelf and an electrical outlet within or adjacent to the telephone enclosure. The telephone handset shall be capable of being placed flush on the surface of the shelf. The shelf shall be capable of accommodating a text telephone (TTY) and shall have 6 in (152 mm) minimum vertical clearance in the area where the text telephone (TTY) is to be placed.

(3) Equivalent facilitation may be provided. For example, a portable text telephone (TTY) may be made available in a hotel at the registration desk if it is available on a 24-hour basis for use with nearby public pay telephones. In this instance, at least one pay telephone shall comply with paragraph 2 of this section. In addition, if an acoustic coupler is used, the telephone handset cord shall be sufficiently long so as to allow connection of the text telephone (TTY) and the telephone receiver. Directional signage shall be provided and shall comply with 4.30.7.

A4.31.9(1) A public text telephone (TTY) may be an integrated text telephone (TTY) pay telephone unit or a conventional portable text telephone (TTY) that is permanently affixed within, or adjacent to, the telephone enclosure. In order to be usable with a pay telephone, a text telephone (TTY) which is not a single integrated text telephone (TTY) pay telephone unit will require a shelf large enough (10 in (255 mm) wide by 10 in (255 mm) deep with a 6 in (150 mm) vertical clearance minimum) to accommodate the device, an electrical outlet, and a power cord.

A4.31.9(3) Movable or portable text telephones (TTYs) may be used to provide equivalent facilitation. A text telephone (TTY) should be readily available so that a person using it may access the text telephone (TTY) easily and conveniently. As currently designed, pocket-type text telphones (TTYs) for personal use do not accommodate a wide range of users. Such devices would not be considered substantially equivalent to conventional text telephones (TTYs). However, in the future as technology develops this could change.

4.34 AUTOMATED TELLER MACHINES.

4.34.1 General. Each machine required to be accessible by 4.1.3 shall be on an accessible route and shall comply with 4.34.

4.34.2 Clear Floor Space. The automated teller machine shall be located so that clear floor space complying with 4.2.4 is provided to allow a person using a wheelchair to make a forward approach, a parallel approach, or both, to the machine.

4.34.3 Reach Ranges.

(1) Forward Approach Only. If only a forward approach is possible, operable parts of all controls shall be placed within the forward reach range specified in 4.2.5.

(2) Parallel Approach Only. If only a parallel approach is possible, operable parts of controls shall be placed as follows:

(a) Reach Depth Not More Than 10 In (255 Mm). Where the reach depth to the operable parts of all controls as measured from the vertical plane perpendicular to the edge of the unobstructed clear floor space at the farthest protrusion of the automated teller machine or surround is not more than 10 in (255 mm), the maximum height above the finished floor or grade shall be 54 in (1370 mm).

(b) Reach Depth More Than 10 In (255 Mm). Where the reach depth to the operable parts of any control as measured from the vertical plane perpendicular to the edge of the unobstructed clear floor space at the farthest protrusion of the automated teller machine or surround is more than 10 in (255 mm), the maximum height above the finished floor or grade shall be as follows:

Reach inches	Depth millimeters	Maximum inches	Height millimeters
10	255	54	1370
11	280	53½	1360
12	305	53	1345
13	330	52½	1335
14	355	51½	1310
15	380	51	1295
16	405	50½	1285
17	430	50	1270
18	455	49½	1255
19	485	49	1245
20	510	48½	1230
21	535	47½	1205
22	560	47	1195
23	585	46½	1180
24	610	46	1170

(3) Forward and Parallel Approach. If both a forward and parallel approach are possible, operable parts of controls shall be placed within at least one of the reach ranges in paragraphs (1) or (2) of this section.

(4) Bins. Where bins are provided for envelopes, waste paper, or other purposes, at least one of each type provided shall comply with the applicable reach ranges in paragraph (1), (2), or (3) of this section.

EXCEPTION: Where a function can be performed in a substantially equivalent manner by using an alternate control, only one of the controls needed to perform that func-

tion is required to comply with this section. If the controls are identified by tactile markings, such markings shall be provided on both controls.

4.34.4 Controls. Controls for user activation shall comply with 4.27.4.

4.34.5 Equipment for Persons with Vision Impairments. Instructions and all information for use shall be made accessible to and independently usable by persons with vision impairments.

5. RESTAURANTS AND CAFETERIAS.
5.1* GENERAL.

Except as specified or modified in this section, restaurants and cafeterias shall comply with the requirements of section 4. Where fixed tables (or dining counters where food is consumed but there is no service) are provided, at least 5 percent, but not less than one, of the fixed tables (or a portion of the dining counter) shall be accessible and shall comply with 4.32 as required in 4.1.3(18). In establishments where separate areas are designated for smoking and non-smoking patrons, the required number of accessible fixed tables (or counters) shall be proportionally distributed between the smoking and non-smoking areas. In new construction, and where practicable in alterations, accessible fixed tables (or counters) shall be distributed throughout the space or facility.

6. MEDICAL CARE FACILITIES.
6.1 GENERAL.

Medical care facilities included in this section are those in which people receive physical or medical treatment or care and where persons may need assistance in responding to an emergency and where the period of stay may exceed twenty-four hours. In addition to the requirements of section 4, medical care facilities and buildings shall comply with 6.

(1) Hospitals—general purpose hospitals, psychiatric facilities, detoxification facilities—At least 10 percent of patient bedrooms and toilets, and all public use and common use areas are required to be designed and constructed to be accessible.

(2) Hospitals and rehabilitation facilities that specialize in treating conditions that affect mobility, or units within either that specialize in treating conditions that affect mobility—All patient bedrooms and toilets, and all public use and common use areas are required to be designed and constructed to be accessible.

(3) Long term care facilities, nursing homes—At least 50 percent of patient bedrooms and toilets, and all public use and common use areas are required to be designed and constructed to be accessible.

(4) Alterations to patient bedrooms.

(a) When patient bedrooms are being added or altered as part of a planned renovation of an entire wing, a department, or other discrete area of an existing medical facility, a percentage of the patient bedrooms that are being added or altered shall comply with 6.3. The percentage of accessible rooms provided shall be consistent with the percentage of rooms required to be accessible by the applicable requirements of 6.1(1), 6.1(2), or 6.1(3), until the number of accessible patient bedrooms in the facility equals the overall number that would be required if the facility were newly constructed. (For example, if 20 patient bedrooms are being altered in the obstetrics department of a hospital, 2 of the altered rooms must be made accessible. If, within the same hospital, 20 patient bedrooms are being altered in a unit that specializes in treating mobility impairments, all of the altered rooms must be made accessible.) Where toilet/bathrooms are part of patient bedrooms which are added or altered and required to be accessible, each such patient toilet/bathroom shall comply with 6.4.

(b) When patient bedrooms are being added or altered individually, and not as part of an alteration of the entire area, the altered patient bedrooms shall comply with 6.3, unless either: a) the number of accessible rooms provided in the department or area containing the altered patient bedroom equals the number of accessible patient bedrooms that would be required if the percentage requirements of 6.1(1), 6.1(2), or 6.1(3) were applied to that department or area; or b) the number of accessible patient bedrooms in the facility equals the overall number that would be required if the facility were newly constructed. Where toilet/bathrooms are part of patient bedrooms which are added or altered and required to be accessible, each such toilet/bathroom shall comply with 6.4.

7. BUSINESS, MERCANTILE AND CIVIC.
7.1 GENERAL.

In addition to the requirements of section 4, the design of all areas used for business transactions with the public shall comply with 7.

8. LIBRARIES.
8.1 GENERAL.

In addition to the requirements of section 4, the design of all public areas of a library shall comply with 8, including reading and study areas, stacks, reference rooms, reserve areas, and special facilities or collections.

9. ACCESSIBLE TRANSIENT LODGING.

(1) Except as specified in the special technical provisions of this section, accessible transient lodging shall comply with the applicable requirements of section 4. Transient lodging includes facilities or portions thereof used for sleeping accommodations, when not classed as a medical care facility.

9.1 HOTELS, MOTELS, INNS, BOARDING HOUSES, DORMITORIES, RESORTS AND OTHER SIMILAR PLACES OF TRANSIENT LODGING.

9.1.1 General. All public use and common use areas are required to be designed and constructed to comply with section 4 (Accessible Elements and Spaces: Scope and Technical Requirements).

EXCEPTION: Sections 9.1 through 9.4 do not apply to an establishment located within a building that contains not more than five rooms for rent or hire and that is actually occupied by the proprietor of such establishment as the residence of such proprietor.

Excerpts from ICC/ANSI Standards A117.1, *Accessible and Usable Buildings and Facilities,* revised 1998 ANSI Standards on Signage and Automatic Teller Machines (ATMs)

The following are excerpts from the revised accessibility standards adopted by the American National Standards Institute in 1998 that pertain to the ADA and particularly to accessible signage. Please note that the figures referred to in these sections are not included in these excerpts.

703 SIGNS

703.1 General. Accessible signs shall comply with Section 703.

703.2 Characters That Are Both Tactile and Visual. Characters required to be tactile shall comply with Sections 703.2.1 through 703.2.8.

EXCEPTION: Tactile characters complying with Section 703.3, where separate visual characters complying with Section 703.4 provide the same information.

703.2.1 Braille. Tactile characters shall be duplicated in braille complying with Section 703.5.

703.2.2 Finish and Contrast. Characters and their background shall have a non-glare finish. Characters shall contrast with their background, with either light characters on a dark background, or dark characters on a light background.

703.2.3 Tactile Character Depth. Tactile characters shall be raised 1/32 inch (0.8 mm) minimum above their background. Raised borders and elements that are not required shall be 3/8 inch (9.5 mm) minimum from tactile characters.

703.2.4 Character Forms. Fonts shall have characters complying with Sections 703.2.4.1 through 703.2.4.5.

703.2.4.1 Case. Characters shall be uppercase.

703.2.4.2 Style. Characters shall be sans serif. Characters shall not be italic, oblique, script, highly decorative, or of other unusual forms.

703.2.4.3 Width. Character width shall be 55 percent minimum and 110 percent maximum of the height of the character, with the width based on the uppercase letter *O* and the height based on the uppercase letter *I*.

703.2.4.4 Height. Character height, measured vertically from the baseline of the character, shall be 5/8 inch (16 mm) minimum, and 2 inches (51 mm) maximum, based on the uppercase letter *I*.

703.2.4.5 Stroke Thickness. Characters with rectangular cross sections shall have a stroke thickness which is 10 percent minimum, and 15 percent maximum, of the height of the character, based on the uppercase letter *I*. Characters with other cross sections shall have a stroke thickness at the base of the cross sections which is 10 percent minimum, and 30 percent maximum, of the height of the character, and a stroke thickness at the top of the cross sections which is 15 percent maximum of the height of the character, based on the uppercase letter *I*.

703.2.5 Character Spacing. Spacing shall be measured between the two closest points of adjacent characters within a message, excluding word spaces. Where characters have rectangular cross sections, spacing between individual characters shall be 1/8 inch (3 mm) minimum and 3/8 inch (10 mm) maximum. Where characters have other cross sections, spacing between individual characters shall be 1/16 inch (2 mm) minimum and 3/8 inch (10 mm) maximum at the base of the cross sections, and 1/8 inch (3 mm) minimum and 3/8 inch (10 mm) maximum at the top of the cross sections.

703.2.6 Line Spacing. Spacing between the baselines of separate lines of characters shall be 135 percent minimum to 170 percent maximum of the character height.

703.2.7 Mounting Height. Characters shall be 48 inches (1220 mm) minimum and 60 inches (1525 mm) maximum above the adjacent floor or ground surface, measured from the baseline of the characters.

EXCEPTION: Elevator car controls.

703.2.8 Mounting Location. Where a sign containing tactile characters is provided at a door, the sign shall be alongside the door on the latch side. Where a tactile sign is provided at double doors, the sign shall be to the right of the right-hand door. Where there is no wall space on the latch side of a single door, or to the right side of double doors, signs shall be on the nearest adjacent wall. Signs containing tactile characters shall have an 18-inch (455 mm) minimum by 18-inch (455 mm) minimum space on the floor or ground, centered on the sign, beyond the arc of any door swing between the closed position and 45 degree open position.

EXCEPTION: Door-mounted signs shall be permitted on the push side of doors with closers and without hold-open devices.

703.3 Tactile Characters. Where tactile characters are required, and separate tactile and visual characters with the same information are provided, tactile characters shall comply with Sections 703.3.1 through 703.3.7 and visual characters shall comply with Section 703.4.

703.3.1 Braille. Tactile characters shall be duplicated in braille complying with Section 703.5.

703.3.2 Tactile Character Depth. Tactile characters shall be raised 1/32 inch (0.8 mm) minimum above their background. Raised borders and elements that are not required shall be 3/8 inch (9.5 mm) minimum from tactile characters.

703.3.3 Character Forms. Fonts shall have characters complying with Sections 703.3.3.1 through 703.3.3.5.

703.3.3.1 Case. Characters shall be uppercase.

703.3.3.2 Style. Characters shall be sans serif. Characters shall not be italic, oblique, script, highly decorative, or of other unusual forms.

703.3.3.3 Width. Character width shall be 55 percent minimum and 110 percent maximum the height of the character, with the width based on the uppercase letter *O,* and the height based on the uppercase letter *I.*

703.3.3.4 Height. Character height, measured vertically from the baseline of the character, shall be 1/2 inch (13 mm) minimum, and 3/4 inch (19 mm) maximum, based on the height of the uppercase letter *I.*

703.3.3.5 Stroke Thickness. Characters shall have a stroke thickness which is 15 percent maximum of the height of the character, based on the uppercase letter *I.*

703.3.4 Character Spacing. Spacing shall be measured between the two closest points of adjacent characters within a message, excluding word spaces. Spacing between individual characters shall be 1/8 inch (3 mm) minimum to 1/4 inch (6 mm) maximum.

703.3.5 Line Spacing. Spacing between the baseline of separate lines of characters within a message shall be 135 percent minimum and 170 percent maximum of the character height.

703.3.6 Mounting Height. Characters shall be 48 inches (1220 mm) minimum and 60 inches (1515 mm) maximum above the adjacent floor or ground surface, measured from the baseline of the characters.

EXCEPTION: Elevator car controls.

703.3.7 Mounting Location. Where a tactile sign is provided at a door, the sign shall be alongside the door on the latch side. Where a tactile sign is provided at double doors, the sign shall be to the right of the right-hand door. Where there is no wall space on the latch side of a single door, or to the right side of double doors, signs shall be on the nearest adjacent wall. Signs containing tactile characters shall have an 18-inch (455 mm) minimum by 18-inch (455 mm) minimum space on the floor or ground, centered on the sign, beyond the arc of any door swing between the closed position and 45 degree open position.

EXCEPTION: Door-mounted signs shall be permitted on the push side of doors with closers and without hold-open devices.

703.4 Visual Characters. Accessible visual characters shall comply with Sections 703.4.1 through 703.4.5.

703.4.1 Finish and Contrast. Characters and their background shall have a non-glare finish. Characters shall contrast with their background, with either light characters on a dark background, or dark characters on a light background.

703.4.2 Character Forms. Fonts shall have characters complying with Sections 703.4.2.1 through 703.4.2.5.

703.4.2.1 Case. Characters shall be uppercase, lowercase, or a combination of both.

703.4.2.2 Style. Characters shall be conventional in form. Characters shall not be italic, oblique, script, highly decorative, or of other unusual forms.

703.4.2.3 Width. Character width shall be 55 percent minimum and 110 percent maximum the height of the character, with the width based on the uppercase letter *O,* and the height based on the uppercase *I.*

703.4.2.4 Height. Minimum character height, measured from the baseline of the character, shall comply with Table 703.4.2.4, based on the height of the characters above the floor or ground of the viewing location and the minimum viewing distance. Character height shall be based on the uppercase letter *I.* Minimum viewing distance shall be measured as the horizontal distance where an obstruction prevents further approach toward the sign.

703.4.2.5 Stroke Thickness. Characters shall have a stroke thickness which is 10 percent minimum, and 30 percent maximum, the height of the character, based on the uppercase letter *I.*

703.4.3 Character Spacing. Spacing shall be the two closest points of adjacent characters within a message, excluding word spaces. Spacing between individual characters shall be 10 percent minimum and 35 percent maximum of character height.

703.4.4 Line Spacing. Spacing between the baselines of separate lines of characters within a message shall be 135 percent minimum to 170 percent maximum of character height.

703.4.5 Mounting Height. Visual characters shall be 40 inches (1015 mm) minimum above the floor or ground of the viewing position. Mounting heights shall comply with Table 703.4.2.4, based on the size of the characters on the sign.

703.5 Braille. Tactile characters shall be accompanied by grade II braille complying with Sections 703.5.1 through 703.5.4 and Table 703.5. Braille dots shall have a domed or rounded shape.

Table 703.4.2.4—Minimum Character Heights for Visual Signs

Height above floor or ground to top of character	Minimum viewing distance	Minimum character height	Notes
40 inches–≤70 inches (1015 mm–1780 mm)	≤6 feet (1830 mm)	⅝ inch (16 mm)	Except elevators
40 inches–≤70 inches (1015 mm–1780 mm)	>6 feet (1830 mm)	⅝ inch (16 mm), plus ⅛ inch per foot (3.2 mm per 305 mm) of viewing distance beyond 6 feet (1830 mm)	Except elevators
>70 inches–≤120 inches (1780 mm–3050 mm)	≤15 feet (4570 mm)	2 inches (51 mm)	
>70 inches–≤120 inches (1780 mm–3050 mm)	>15 feet (4570 mm)	2 inches (51 mm), plus ⅛ inch per foot (3.2 mm per 305 mm) of viewing distance beyond 15 feet (4570 mm)	
>120 inches (3050 mm)	≤21 feet (6400 mm)	3 inches (75 mm)	
120 inches (3050 mm)	>21 feet (6400 mm)	3 inches (75 mm), plus ⅛ inch per foot (3.2 mm per 305 mm) of viewing distance beyond 21 feet (6400 mm)	

Table 703.5—Measurement Range for Standard Sign Braille

Measurement range for:	Minimum	Maximum
Dot base diameter	0.059 inch (1.5 mm)	0.063 inch (1.6 mm)
Distance between two dots in same cell, center to center	0.090 inch (2.3 mm)	0.100 inch (2.5 mm)
Distance between corresponding dots in adjacent cells, center to center	0.241 inch (6.1 mm)	0.300 inch (7.6 mm)
Dot height	0.025 inch (0.6 mm)	0.037 inch (0.9 mm)
Distance between corresponding dots from one cell to the cell directly below, center to center	0.395 inch (10.0 mm)	0.400 inch (10.1 mm)

703.5.1 Location. Braille shall be below the corresponding text. If text is multilined, braille shall be placed below entire text. Braille shall be separated 3/8 inch (9.5 mm) minimum from any other tactile characters.

EXCEPTION: Braille provided on elevator car controls shall be separated 3/16 inch (4.8 mm) minimum either directly below or adjacent to the corresponding raised characters or symbols.

703.5.2 Raised Elements and Borders. Raised borders and elements that are not required shall be 3/8 inch (10 mm) minimum from tactile characters.

703.5.3 Height. Braille shall be 40 inches (1015 mm) minimum, and 60 inches (1525 mm) maximum, above the floor or ground, measured from the baseline of the braille cells.

EXCEPTION: Elevator car controls.

703.5.4 Braille Standard. Braille shall comply with literary braille.

EXCEPTION: The indication of an uppercase letter or letters shall only be used before the first word of sentences, proper nouns and names, individual letters of the alphabet, initials, or acronyms.

703.6 Pictograms. Pictograms shall comply with Sections 703.6.1 through 703.6.3.

703.6.1 Pictogram Field. Pictograms shall have a field with a height of 6 inches (150 mm) minimum. Characters or braille shall not be in the pictogram field.

703.6.2 Finish and Contrast. Pictograms and their fields shall have a non-glare finish. Pictograms shall contrast with their fields, with either a light pictogram on a dark field or a dark pictogram on a light field.

703.6.3 Text Descriptors. Where text descriptors for pictograms are required, they shall be directly below or adjacent to the pictogram and shall comply with Section 703.2.

703.7 Symbols of Accessibility. Symbols of accessibility shall comply with Sections 703.7.1 through 703.7.2.

703.7.1 Finish and Contrast. Symbols of accessibility and their backgrounds shall have a non-glare finish. Symbols of accessibility shall contrast with their backgrounds, with either a light symbol on a dark background or a dark symbol on a light background.

703.7.2 Symbols.

703.7.2.1 International Symbol of Accessibility. Where the International Symbol of Accessibility is required, it shall be proportioned complying with Figure 703.7.2.1.

703.7.2.2 International Symbol of TTY. Where the International Symbol of TTY is required, it shall comply with Figure 703.7.2.2.

703.7.2.3 Volume-Controlled Telephones. Where telephones with volume controls are required to be identified, the identification symbol shall be a telephone handset with radiating sound waves, such as shown in Figure 703.7.2.3.

703.7.2.4 Assistive Listening Systems. Where assistive listening systems are required to be identified by the International Symbol of Access for Hearing Loss, it shall comply with Figure 703.7.2.4.

707 AUTOMATIC TELLER MACHINES (ATMS) AND FARE MACHINES

707.1 General. Automatic teller machines and fare machines that are required to be accessible shall comply with Section 707.

707.2 Clear Floor or Ground Space. A clear floor or ground space complying with Section 305 shall be provided.

EXCEPTION: Clear floor or ground space is not required at drive-up only machines.

707.3 Operable Parts. Operable parts shall comply with Section 309. Each operable part shall be able to be differentiated by sound or touch, without activation.

EXCEPTION: Drive-up-only machines shall not be required to comply with Section 309.2 or 309.3.

707.4 Input. Input devices shall comply with Sections 707.4.1 through 707.4.5.

707.4.1 Privacy. The opportunity for the same degree of privacy of input shall be available to all individuals utilizing the equipment.

707.4.2 Key Surfaces. All keys used to operate a machine shall be tactually discernible. Key surfaces shall be offset from the surrounding surface by 1/25 inch (1 mm) minimum. The outer edge of key surfaces shall have a radius of 1/50 inch (0.5 mm) maximum.

EXCEPTION: The touch areas of video display screens.

707.4.3 Separation Between Keys. Any key surface shall be separated from other key surfaces by 1/8 inch (3.2 mm) minimum. Function keys shall be separated from the keypad equal to a distance that is not less than three times greater than the actual distance between the numeric keys.

707.4.4 Numeric Keys. Where provided, numeric keys shall comply with Sections 707.4.4.1 and 707.4.4.2.

707.4.4.1 Arrangement. Numeric keys shall be arranged in a 12-key telephone keypad layout with the number one key in the upper-left-hand corner.

707.4.4.2 Marking. The number five key shall have a single raised dot.

707.4.5 Function Keys. Where provided, function keys shall comply with Sections 707.4.5.1 through 707.4.5.3.

707.4.5.1 Arrangement. Function keys shall be in the order of *enter, clear, cancel, add value,* and *decrease value* horizontally from left to right or vertically from top to bottom. Where provided, add value and decrease value shall be grouped with other function keys.

707.4.5.2 Marking. Function keys shall be marked with tactile characters as follows:

- Enter or proceed key: raised circle;
- Clear or correct key: raised vertical line or bar;
- Cancel key: raised letter *x*;
- Add value key: raised plus sign;
- Decrease value key: raised minus sign.

707.4.5.3 Color Coding. Where function keys are color coded, they shall be colored as follows:

- Enter or proceed key: green;
- Clear or correct key: black;
- Cancel key: red;
- Add value key: blue;
- Decrease value key: yellow.

707.5 Output. Output devices shall comply with Sections 707.5.1 through 707.5.6.

707.5.1 Privacy. The opportunity for the same degree of privacy of output shall be available to all individuals utilizing the equipment.

707.5.2 Operating Instructions. Machines shall provide visual and audible instruction for operation. Visual and audible instruction shall include all information required by Sections 707.5.2.1 through 707.5.2.5.

707.5.2.1 Initiation. Instruction shall be initiated by the user of the machine.

707.5.2.2 Expedited Process. After initiation, instructions shall be available to the experienced user to expedite the transaction.

707.5.2.3 Orientation. Orientation and assistance for unfamiliar users to the physical features of the machine, operational options, and details for each function shall be provided.

707.5.2.4 Transaction Prompts. All transaction prompts within each operation shall be provided.

707.5.2.5 Input Verification. Verification of all user inputs shall be provided.

707.5.3 Audible Instruction. Audible instruction shall be provided through a standard audio minijack, a telephone handset, a wireless transmission system, or another mechanism that is readily available to all customers.

707.5.4 Video Display Screen. The video display screen shall comply with Sections 707.5.4.1 and 707.5.4.2.

707.5.4.1 Visibility. The video display screen shall be visible from a point 40 inches (1015 mm) above the center of the clear floor or ground space in front of the machine.

EXCEPTION: This requirement shall not apply to drive-up-only machines.

707.5.4.2 Characters. Characters displayed on the screen shall be in a sans serif font. Characters shall be 3/16 inch (4.8 mm) high minimum, based on the uppercase letter *I*. Characters shall contrast with the background with either light characters on a dark background, or dark characters on a light background.

707.5.5 Dispensing of Bills. Machines that dispense paper currency shall dispense the currency so that bills are dispensed in descending order with the lowest denomination on top.

707.5.6 Receipts and Verification. Where a receipt is available and is requested, the following options shall be provided: a printed receipt, audible presentation of the transaction information provided on the receipt, or both.

Checklist for Communication with People Who Are Blind or Visually Impaired

GENERAL GUIDELINES

☐ Introduce yourself using your name and/or position, especially if you are wearing a name badge containing this information.

☐ Speak directly to persons who are blind or visually impaired, not through a companion, guide, or other individual.

☐ Use a natural conversational tone and speed when speaking. Do not speak loudly and slowly unless the person also has a hearing impairment.

☐ Address people who are blind or visually impaired by name when possible. This is especially important in crowded areas.

☐ Greet people who are blind immediately when they enter a room or a service area to let them know you are present and ready to assist. Initiating conversation right away also eliminates uncomfortable silences.

☐ Indicate the end of a conversation or encounter to avoid the embarrassing situation of leaving a person speaking when no one is actually there.

☐ Feel free to use words that refer to vision during the course of conversation. Vision-oriented words such as "look," "see," and "watching TV" are a part of everyday verbal communication. The words "blind" and "visually impaired" are also acceptable words in conversation.

☐ Be precise and thorough when you describe people, places, or things. Don't leave items out or change a description because you think it is unimportant or unpleasant.

☐ Feel free to use visually descriptive language. Making reference to colors, patterns, designs, and shapes is perfectly acceptable.

☐ When referring to a person who is disabled, refer to the person first and then to the disability. For example, say "people who are blind" rather than "blind people."

ORIENTATION AND MOBILITY

☐ Do not leave a person who is totally blind or visually impaired standing alone in "free space" when you serve as a guide. Always be sure that the person you are guiding has a firm grasp on your arm, or is leaning against a chair or a wall if you have to be separated momentarily.

☐ Be calm and clear about what to do if you see a person who is blind or visually impaired about to encounter a dangerous situation. For example, if a person who is blind is about to bump into a stanchion in a hotel lobby, calmly and firmly call out, "Wait there for a moment. There is a pole in front of you."

☐ Use the sighted guide mobility technique to escort those individuals who request it.

☐ Review business policy regarding dog guides. The ADA regulations require places of public accommodation to permit the use of dog guides or other service animals, unless doing so would fundamentally alter the nature of the services provided or jeopardize the safe operations of the facility.

☐ Designate and orient customers, patients, or guests to dog guide relief areas.

GIVING DIRECTIONS

☐ When giving directions to a person who is blind or visually impaired, refer to right and left as they apply to the other person. What is on your right is on the left of a person facing you.

☐ Indicate the approximate distance to a requested location and provide information about landmarks along the way. For example: "When you hear the escalator, walk several feet down the corridor and look for the next open doorway on your left."

☐ Be specific about the location of people, places, or things. Avoid vague terms such as "over there" when telling a person who is blind how to find a destination.

☐ Avoid pointing unless you are sure the gesture can be seen and understood.

Checklist of Required Elements for Accessibility under the ADA Relating to Communication Barrier Removal

Note: *This checklist includes references to the most recent ADAAG specifications as of January 1998, as well as to the appendix to the ADAAG. Specifications from the ADAAG are indicated by a numeric reference to the corresponding section or sections in the ADAAG. References to items from the ADAAG appendix are indicated with the letter A ahead of the number. Items from Section 4.1 of the ADAAG refer the reader to the scoping, or technical application requirements, of the specifications. Some items in this checklist are AFB recommendations that are not from the ADAAG and are so indicated.*

EXTERIOR AND INTERIOR ACCESSIBLE ROUTES

☐ At least one accessible route from public transportation stops, accessible parking spaces, passenger loading zones, and public streets and sidewalks to one accessible building entrance. [4.1.2(1),(2); 4.3.2; A4.3]

☐ Protruding objects protected at ground, mid-, and head level and complying with other ADAAG specifications. [4.1.2(3); 4.4, A4.4.1]

☐ Detectable warnings complying with the ADAAG at the edge of boarding platforms in transit facilities. [4.29.2; A4.29.2; 10.3.1(8); 10.3.2(2); 10.3.3]

☐ Surface textures that are firm, stable, and slip resistant. [4.1.2(4); 4.1.3(3); 4.1.5; 4.1.6(a), (b); 4.5.1; A4.5.1]

☐ Curb cuts, curb ramps, elevators, or platform lifts provided where an accessible route has a vertical change in level greater than 1/2 inch [4.1.3; 4.1.5; 4.1.6; 4.3.8]

STAIRS

☐ Stairs that have uniform riser heights and tread widths complying with the ADAAG. [4.1.3(4); 4.1.5; 4.1.6(d); 4.9.2; A4.9.1]

☐ Stairs that do not have open risers. [4.1.3(4); 4.1.5; 4.1.6(d); 4.9.2; A4.9.1]

☐ Stair treads that are not less than 11 inches wide. [4.1.3(4); 4.1.5; 4.1.6(d); 4.9.2; A4.9.1]

☐ Stair nosings (the part of the step where the tread and the vertical riser meet) that are curved and not abrupt. [4.1.3(4); 4.1.5; 4.1.6(d); 4.9.3]

☐ Handrails that are continuous on both sides of all stairs, do not rotate within their fittings, and are mounted according to ADAAG specifications. [4.1.3(4); 4.1.5; 4.1.6(d); 4.9.4(1), (7); A4.9.1; 4.26; A4.26.1; A4.26.2]

☐ Handrails that extend beyond the top and bottom risers according to ADAAG specifications. [4.1.3(4); 4.1.5; 4.1.6(d); 4.9.4(2); 4.2.6; A4.26.1; A4.26.2]

☐ Handrails that have a clear space between the rail and the wall that meets ADAAG specifications. [4.1.3(4); 4.1.5; 4.1.6(d); 4.9.4(3); A4.9.1; 4.26; A4.26.1]

☐ Handrail gripping surfaces that are uninterrupted by obstructions. [4.1.3(4); 4.1.5; 4.1.6(d); 4.9.4(4); A4.9.1; 4.26; A4.26.1; A4.26.2]

☐ Handrail endings that are rounded or returned smoothly to the floor, wall, or a post. [4.1.3(4); 4.1.5; 4.1.6(d); 4.9.4(b); A4.9.1; 4.26; A4.26.1; A4.26.2]

☐ Handrails that contrast visibly with the background to which they are mounted or are clearly visible to persons who are visually impaired. *(Note: This is not required by the ADAAG, but it is recommended by AFB.)*

ELEVATORS

☐ Call buttons in elevator lobbies that meet ADAAG specifications for design and installation. [4.1.3(5); 4.1.6(1){k}(i); 4.10.3]

☐ Visible and audible signals, sounding once for the "up" direction and twice for the "down" direction at each hoistway (elevator shaft) entrance to indicate which elevator car is answering a call. [4.1.3(5); 4.1.6(1){k}(i); 4.10.4]

☐ Raised and braille floor designations on both elevator door jambs that meet ADAAG specifications. [4.1.3(5); 4.1.6(K{i}); 4.10.5]

☐ Illumination at car controls, platforms, and car thresholds that meet ADAAG specifications. [4.1.3(5); 4.1.6(K{i}); 4.10.11]

☐ Elevator control panels with raised and braille markings that meet ADAAG specifications. [4.1.3(5); 4.1.6(K{i}); 4.10.12; A4.10.12]

☐ Visual car position indicators above the car control panel or above the elevator doors with a visible display or one that emits an audible signal. [4.1.3(5); 4.1.6(K{i}); 4.10.13; A4.10.13]

SIGNAGE

☐ Signs in raised letters and grade 2 braille that meet ADAAG specifications for design and installation at permanent rooms and spaces. [4.1.2(7); 4.1.6(1){b}; 4.30.1; 4.30.4; A4.30.4; 4.30.5; 4.30.6]

☐ Informational and directional signs that meet ADAAG specifications for design and installation. [4.1.2(7); 4.30.1; 4.30.2; 4.30.3; 4.30.5]

☐ Pictogram signs that include a clear verbal description of the pictogram graphic. [4.1.2(7); 4.30.4; A4.30.4]

☐ Pictogram signs at permanent rooms and spaces (e.g., restrooms) that include raised letters and braille; the pictogram graphic itself need not be raised. [4.1.2(7); 4.30.4; A4.30.4]

☐ Signs for the International Symbol of Accessibility located at accessible entrances when not all entrances are accessible. [4.1; 4.30.7; A4.30.7]

☐ Signs that display the International Symbol of Accessibility at inaccessible entrances that provide information about the location of the closest accessible entrance. [4.1.2(7){c}; 4.30.7; A4.30.7]

☐ Signs that display the International Symbol of Accessibility at toilet and bathing facilities when all are not accessible. [4.1.2(7){d}]

☐ Suspended signs that are at least 80 inches above the finished floor or protected with a barrier detectable by people who are blind or visually impaired. [4.4.2]

AUTOMATED TELLER MACHINES

☐ Automated teller machines (ATMs) that provide independent access to all instructions and displayed information in a manner usable by persons with visual impairments. [4.1.3(20); 4.34] Examples of specific accommodations can include voice output devices, refreshable braille displays, electronic voice mail access (using a telephone and keypad to listen to and access the menu choices), tactile marking for operation controls, and braille or speech instructions for ATM use.

Checklist for Providing Accessible Food Services to People Who Are Blind or Visually Impaired

FORMAL DINING SERVICE

☐ Provide priority seating for customers who are blind or visually impaired, if requested to do so, in an area that has adequate lighting or is away from the glare of large picture windows. Note that if dim ambient lighting is an essential part of the dining atmosphere you offer, the ADA does not require you to fundamentally alter the nature of your business by turning up the lights for a person who is visually impaired.

☐ Instruct table service personnel to identify themselves by name and function to customers who are blind or visually impaired. For example, a waiter might say, "Good evening, I'm Walter. I'll be your waiter for the evening. How may I help you?"

☐ Instruct table service personnel to describe the placement of tableware, flowers, ashtrays, candles, or other items on the table.

☐ Offer customers braille or large-print menus if they are available. Be sure to tell guests about any selections that have been added since the menu was prepared. Also, describe daily specials that do not appear on the menu.

☐ Offer to read menus to customers who are totally blind when braille menus are not available or if your customer does not read braille. Likewise, offer to read menus to customers who are visually impaired.

☐ Inform customers when servers are about to place food or items on the dining table. Describe where all food and beverage items are placed as they are served.

☐ Identify the location of food on a plate if requested to do so, using the face of a clock as a reference. For example, say "Your meat is at 12 o'clock, your vegetables are at 3 o'clock, the rice is at 9 o'clock."

☐ Provide assistance in cutting food items or mixing beverages, if requested to do so. Cutting food items in the kitchen prior to serving or returning a plate to the kitchen is a discreet way of handling a request to cut a customer's food.

BUFFET SERVICE

☐ Identify and briefly describe the food and beverage items available.

☐ Assist with locating tableware and utensils.

☐ Assist in serving food items from the buffet and escorting customers to a seat.

☐ Inform customers about how to obtain assistance for return visits to the buffet.

FOOD SERVICE LINES AND CAFETERIA SERVICE

☐ Be alert for aging customers or others whose visual impairment may not be readily recognized so you may assist them. These customers may not appear to be blind because they do not carry long white canes or use dog guides, but they may have difficulty reading menus posted above the food service counter or identifying food selections available at steam tables.

☐ Provide sighted guide assistance to customers who are totally blind so they can make their way through food service lines, select food, and locate condiments, napkins, and utensils. Guide them to a seat and offer assistance for later disposal of trays and refuse.

☐ Provide customers with clear verbal information about visually displayed menus, advertised specials, and promotional services.

☐ Have braille or large-print menus available for standard items in a fixed location; for example, at both ends of the service counter. Although braille and large-print menus are not required by the ADA, providing them is a thoughtful service that makes a positive statement about your interest in customers' comfort and convenience.

VENDING MACHINES

☐ Install vending machines in areas that are well illuminated and protected from glare or deep shadows.

☐ Provide vending machines with raised keypads similar to those on a push-button telephone. Avoid membrane or touch-screen operation controls, which are inaccessible to customers who are severely visually impaired. Characters on keypads should contrast visibly with the background.

☐ Provide operation controls (coin and bill slots, change returns, and the like) that contrast clearly with the background of the machine. Label all controls in clear, contrasting large print using a sans serif or a simple serif typeface.

☐ Provide braille labels for selection keys and operation controls wherever possible. A commercially available braille label maker and assistance from a local blindness service organization can be very helpful for this.

☐ Consider installing vending machines that "talk."

Checklist for Employers of People Who Are Blind or Visually Impaired

RECRUITMENT

☐ Make information about job openings that is posted in print on public bulletin boards in your organization available upon request in an accessible format, such as audiotape, braille, or large print.

☐ State in job notice announcements that applicants who need accommodations for an interview should request them in advance.

☐ Place help wanted advertisements in newspapers and publications that are available on the Internet.

☐ Carry out recruitment activities in locations that are or have been made accessible.

☐ Include information about only the essential functions of a job in position announcements, help wanted advertisements, and other recruitment notices.

☐ Provide clear and specific directions to the location where recruitment activities take place.

PREEMPLOYMENT ACTIVITIES, INTERVIEWING, AND TESTING

☐ Schedule medical examinations for persons who are blind or visually impaired only if these examinations are required for all potential employees.

☐ Request medical information or a medical examination only after an applicant has received a conditional job offer.

☐ Use medical and eye exams only to determine the applicant's ability to perform the essential functions of the job.

☐ Provide forms used for drug screening and medical examinations in accessible format, such as large print, recorded formats, or braille, or through a reader.

☐ Accept a nondriver's license as a form of identification.

☐ Refrain from asking a job applicant about his or her ability to get to work.

☐ Pose interview questions that probe the applicant's ability to perform a job, rather than the nature or extent of the applicant's visual impairment.

☐ Ask applicants to describe how specific job functions will be carried out only when it reasonably appears that a visual impairment might interfere with job performance.

☐ Provide a suitable location or opportunity for applicants to demonstrate how job functions are performed using adaptive methods or technology.

☐ Administer preemployment tests in an effective alternative format, such as in braille, on audiotape, by a reader, or on a computer.

☐ Provide sufficient time to complete tests when an applicant requires testing accommodations.

☐ When it is not possible to test an individual with a visual impairment in an alternative format, use another means, such as an interview, license or certification, education credentials, prior work experience, or a trial job period, to determine his or her job qualifications.

MANAGEMENT AND SUPERVISION

- [ ] Provide job descriptions that are based on job functions and not on individual attributes.
- [ ] Provide the same job orientation and on-the-job training to a new employee who is blind or visually impaired that is provided to all new employees, using effective accommodations as appropriate.
- [ ] Provide employee orientation material, organizational policy and procedures manuals, salary and benefits information, and the like in accessible formats.
- [ ] Provide reasonable accommodations for completing required employment, benefits, and tax documents.
- [ ] Provide orientation to the physical layout of an organization's buildings and facilities.
- [ ] Provide official organizational policy notices, notices of internal job postings, and other essential documents in accessible formats and in a timely manner.
- [ ] Carry out a site survey to eliminate barriers to access in the organization's buildings and facilities.
- [ ] Develop a system for emergency exits with the employee.
- [ ] Work with the employee to establish which equipment and services may be necessary to obtain reasonable accommodations.
- [ ] Provide reader services and document accessibility as appropriate. E-mail transmission of routine office correspondence can be a useful approach for employees who use assistive technology.
- [ ] Create a work space in which adaptive equipment can be installed and operated and that has suitable illumination for the employee's needs. Provide adaptive equipment and work space modifications in a timely manner.
- [ ] Establish work schedules for employees who use dog guides to allow proper toileting for the dog guide.
- [ ] Provide the same nature and quality of supervision or discipline, as well as opportunities for advancement, for employees who are blind or visually impaired that is provided for all employees.
- [ ] Determine that all on-the-job training (on-site or off-site) is carried out with adequate accommodations for information and document accessibility.
- [ ] Identify nonessential functions of a job that a visually impaired person may not be able to perform, and reassign those functions to another employee.

Checklist for Accommodating Patients Who Are Blind or Visually Impaired

INPATIENT CARE

Admitting and Financial Services

- ☐ Verbally identify all health care personnel by name and position.
- ☐ Read aloud and assist in completing admission forms and consents.
- ☐ Communicate the contents of important documents, such as patient information brochures, the Patients' Bill of Rights, admission and discharge procedures, health care proxies, and the like.
- ☐ Review bills verbally prior to discharge.
- ☐ Identify and count currency used for all transactions.
- ☐ Ensure that a policy regarding the admittance of dog guides is in place.

Medical Treatment Services and In-Room Patient Care

- ☐ Verbally identify all health care personnel by name and position.
- ☐ Orient patients to the layout of patient rooms, restroom facilities, the nurses' station, patient lounges and waiting areas, and emergency evacuation areas.
- ☐ Orient patients to emergency call buttons located at the bedside and in restrooms, to controls for televisions and radios, and to controls that raise and lower bed positions.
- ☐ Understand and respond to patients' degree of visual functioning. Ask the patient to describe his or her visual impairment and the manner in which it may affect participation in treatment, for example, creating difficulty in measuring fluids to be taken in advance of a medical procedure.
- ☐ Provide treatment consent forms and related patient-care documents in accessible formats.
- ☐ Use basic sighted guide mobility techniques to escort patients to and from treatment areas; provide verbal orientation information to patients who are being transported in wheelchairs or on gurneys.
- ☐ Orient patients to treatment or examining rooms and supplies; for example, the location and use of such items as gowns and specimen containers.
- ☐ Explain medical procedures verbally, using language that is precise, or demonstrate them before they are performed.
- ☐ Identify and label medications that are self-administered in a manner patients understand and can use.

Dietary Services

- ☐ Communicate verbally information on written diets or menu plans.
- ☐ Assist patients with filling out forms to indicate menu choices for future meals.
- ☐ Inform patients when food has been delivered.
- ☐ Identify the location of the food tray and where plates, cups, utensils, and other items are placed on the tray.

☐ Assist with preparation or cutting of some food items, if requested by patients.

☐ Assist with feeding only if it is required by patients' medical conditions and if such assistance is also provided to patients without disabilities.

☐ Specify a location for food trays to be left for removal from the room.

Discharge Services

☐ Communicate written discharge information (e.g., home care instructions, medication names and dosages, follow-up appointments, etc.) in accessible formats.

☐ Provide a signature guide or template for official documents.

☐ In cooperation with patients, customize discharge plans to patients' lifestyles as persons who are blind, deaf-blind, or visually impaired.

☐ Identify and label medications prescribed at discharge in a manner patients understand and can use.

☐ Identify and make referrals when necessary to appropriate community-based programs, such as rehabilitation agencies, local agencies for blind persons, and public school districts.

☐ Provide training in self-care (including the operation of any necessary medical equipment), utilizing strategies and equipment that are effective for patients with visual impairments.

AMBULATORY CARE

Admitting, Financial, and Discharge Services

☐ Verbally identify all health care personnel by name and position.

☐ Read aloud and assist in completion of admission, discharge, and consent forms.

☐ Communicate contents of important documents, such as patient information brochures, the Patients' Bill of Rights, and follow-up procedures and instructions.

☐ Review bills and charges verbally prior to discharge.

☐ Identify and count currency used for all transactions.

☐ Ensure that a policy regarding the admittance of dog guides is in place.

Medical Treatment Services

☐ Verbally identify all health care personnel by name and position.

☐ Understand and respond to patients' degree of visual functioning.

☐ Provide treatment consent forms and related patient-care documents in accessible formats.

☐ Orient patients to the layout of waiting areas and restroom facilities.

☐ Use basic sighted guide mobility techniques to escort patients to and from treatment areas; provide verbal orientation information to patients who are being transported in wheelchairs or on gurneys.

☐ Orient patients to treatment or examining rooms and supplies; for example, to the location and use of such items as gowns and specimen containers.

☐ Explain medical procedures verbally, using language that is precise, or demonstrate them before they are performed.

☐ Identify and label medications that are self-administered in a manner patients understand and can use.

Cafeteria and Vending Services

☐ Communicate verbally the contents of cafeteria menus or provide braille or large-print menus.

☐ Provide assistance in making menu selections, using self-serve amenities (such as coffee urns and juice bars), carrying food trays, selecting silverware, and locating tables in the cafeteria.

☐ Provide assistance in locating tray disposal areas and in disposing of self-service trays.

☐ Place vending machines in well-lit areas.

☐ Install vending machines with raised key pads, rather than those with membrane pads. Consider installing "talking vending machines" that have voice output for the menu of choices and for confirmation of selection made, cost, amount tendered, and change returned.

☐ Mark vending machines and microwave ovens with braille labels.

PROFESSIONAL CARE IN THE PRIVATE OFFICE OF A HEALTH CARE PROVIDER

General Office Procedures

☐ Verbally identify all health care personnel by name and position.

☐ Assist with sign-in procedures.

☐ Assist with reading and completing insurance and consent forms.

☐ Assist in completing initial history and intake forms.

☐ Use basic sighted guide mobility techniques to escort patients, when necessary.

☐ Provide clear and specific directions to patients about the location of waiting rooms, examination and treatment rooms, restrooms, and offices.

☐ Orient patients to examination or treatment rooms and supplies; for example, to the location and use of such items as gowns and specimen containers.

☐ Identify medication bottles, containers, or specimen cups in a manner that is useful to patients.

☐ Communicate clearly information about home care instructions, medication names and dosages, and follow-up appointments.

☐ Review billing information and procedures for making follow-up appointments.

☐ Communicate other pertinent information; for example, that a telephone-access system is located at the entry to the building, that a taxi stand is located right outside the door, or that there is an ongoing construction project in a common area of the building or parking lot.

☐ Ensure that a policy regarding the admittance of dog guides is in place.

Medical Treatment Services

☐ Verbally identify all health care personnel by name and position.

☐ Understand and respond to patients' degree of visual functioning.

☐ Provide treatment consent forms and related patient-care documents in accessible formats.

☐ Orient patients to the layout of waiting areas and restroom facilities.

☐ Use basic sighted guide mobility techniques to escort patients to and from treatment areas; provide verbal orientation information to patients who are being transported in wheelchairs or on gurneys.

☐ Orient patients to treatment or examination rooms and supplies; for example, to the location and use of such items as gowns and specimen cups.

☐ Explain medical procedures verbally, using language that is precise, or demonstrate them before they are performed.

☐ Identify and label medications that are self-administered in a manner patients understand and can use.

Checklist for Accommodating Customers Who Are Blind or Visually Impaired

COURTESY AND INFORMATION SERVICES

- ☐ Assist with completion of printed service request forms, order forms, and sales documents.
- ☐ Review or read aloud fee schedules, and credit, loan, or layaway agreements.
- ☐ Use basic sighted guide and mobility techniques to escort customers who request assistance.
- ☐ Provide clear information and directions when customers ask for assistance locating store facilities or departments.

RETAIL SALES AREAS

- ☐ Inform customers of the location of merchandise.
- ☐ Provide clear information and directions to destinations such as dressing rooms and lounges.
- ☐ Read aloud size, price, and other product information.
- ☐ Assist customers in retrieving items from shelves or displays.
- ☐ Describe the colors, patterns, and other features of clothing and other items.
- ☐ Read aloud a customer's itemized bill, if requested.
- ☐ Count and identify currency during financial transactions.
- ☐ Place all cash, credit cards, and receipts directly in the customer's hand.
- ☐ Hand credit cards back to customers after they are imprinted.
- ☐ Make signature guides or templates, felt-tipped pens, or high-intensity lighting available at sales desks.
- ☐ Use basic sighted guide and mobility techniques to escort customers, if requested.
- ☐ Ensure that a policy allowing the admittance of dog guides is in place, unless doing so would fundamentally alter the nature of the services provided or jeopardize the safe operations of the facility.

FACILITIES AND ENVIRONMENTAL ACCESS

- ☐ Provide clear aisle space between displays.
- ☐ Provide display racks, water fountains, ice machines, telephones, signage, and other elements that do not protrude dangerously into the path of travel.
- ☐ Provide braille, large-print, or voice access to customer-operated equipment, such as vending or other point-of-sale machines.
- ☐ Provide posted information regarding sale notices and return policies using large, clear signs printed on nonglare material.
- ☐ Provide price tags that use large, clear lettering and numbers.
- ☐ Train staff to orient customers to common-use areas and elements, including restrooms, lounges, elevators, stairs, and escalators.
- ☐ Install raised-character and braille signs that meet ADAAG requirements in elevators, at restrooms, and at exits.

☐ Install or modify stairs, escalators, and elevators to meet ADAAG standards.

☐ Control environmental background noise created by fountains, ventilators, or music that may mask environmental sound clues used for orientation by customers who are blind or visually impaired.

☐ Provide adequate lighting, controlling glare and shadows in public-access areas.

☐ Highlight contrast on stair handrails, stair nosings, door frames, and store aisles.

Checklist for Accommodating Hotel and Motel Guests Who Are Blind or Visually Impaired

FRONT DESK OR RECEPTION SERVICES

☐ Train staff to orient guests to common-use areas, including the lobby, restaurants, meeting rooms, exhibit areas, and business center.

☐ Assist with completion of any registration documents.

☐ Assist with completion of other required forms.

☐ Review or read aloud all consents, service guides, and the final bill.

☐ Provide clear information and directions about the layout and any special features of buildings and rooms.

☐ Provide clear information and directions about the location of stairs, elevators, and emergency exits.

☐ If plastic card keys are used for hotel rooms, mark them for orientation and demonstrate how they are used, and provide room numbers and clear descriptions of rooms.

FACILITIES AND ENVIRONMENTAL ACCESS

☐ Provide guests with essential safety information for evacuation and rescue in accessible formats (braille, large print, or audiocassette).

☐ When providing water fountains, ice machines, telephones, and other amenities, make sure that they do not protrude dangerously into the path of travel.

☐ Provide access to guest-operated equipment such as laundry, vending, or other point-of-sale machines in braille, large print, or voice output.

☐ Install raised-character and braille signs that comply with ADAAG requirements in elevators, at rooms, and at exits.

☐ Install or modify stairs, escalators, and elevators to meet the ADAAG standards.

☐ Have on hand equipment such as talking or large-print clocks and BrailleTalk alphabet for persons who are deaf-blind (BrailleTalk is a small plastic board with both raised print and braille characters that a deaf-blind person can use to spell out words).

☐ Control environmental background noise, such as that created by fountains, ventilators, or music, that may mask environmental sound clues used for orientation by people who are blind or visually impaired.

☐ Provide adequate lighting that controls glare and shadows in common-use areas.

☐ Highlight contrast on stair handrails, stair nosings, door frames, and baseboards.

IN-ROOM SERVICES

☐ Communicate contents of in-room documents, such as menus and information brochures. Consider having these available in braille, in large print, or on audiotape.

☐ Use basic sighted guide mobility techniques and clear, descriptive language to orient guests to their rooms.

☐ Orient guests to the location of fire alarms, emergency exits, and other equipment in their rooms and in corridors.